THE GOSPEL OF JOY

Shannon Marie

www.ShannonofJoy.com

The Gospel of Joy
Solstice Edition, published December 21, 2020
ShannonofJoy.com

And he that sat on the throne, said: Behold, I make all things new. And he said to me: Write, for these words are most faithful and true.

REVELATION 21:5 (DOUAY-RHEIMS, 1899)

CONTENTS

INTRODUCTION

Greetings! Joy and peace of Christ be with you! By way of introduction, I am Shannon. I was born in the Los Angeles area of California on Sunday, the 17th of the 7th month in the year 1977 at 5:47 PM. When I was 7 years old, my family relocated to the city of Concord, located in the San Francisco East Bay area where the BART transit line used to end before it was extended further east. Most of my growing up years were in Concord, and I went to school in adjacent Walnut Creek near the north gate to the slopes of Mount Diablo.

These days home in my heart is nestled in the Adirondack Mountains at Lake Placid in New York because the village is known for its miracles. Although, over the years my heart did grow quite fond of New Jersey's sandy shores, especially family trips to Wildwood; riding the Great Nor'easter and Sea Serpent roller coasters and stepping to the side on the boardwalk every time we heard, "Watch the tram car please." Pieces of my heart are no longer stranded in memories of California like they were in the summer of 2009 when my world shattered. This is important for you to know upfront to better understand that the person who I was then is not who I am today.

You are about to embark into the story direct from my journals of what led to the completion of this book and the announcement Christians have been waiting for nearly two millennia to hear, "Christ Jesus is returning to the world in a blaze of glory among the people!" Yet, from my heart in Christ, I know this is not the way anyone may have expected it to come, and because of that, there may be shaking and tribulation before all is said and done.

There is no sugarcoating the truth of our current situation. It is the year 2020 and the Earth is engulfed in flames. Humanity, and all living beings right along with us, are in the lake of fire. All of which is particularly evident here in America. Our nation is ablaze and if you are familiar with the book of Revelation in the Bible, you will know the moment of which has come (Revelation 20/21). Yes, it is here, and it is now.

Temperatures on Earth reflect the human-induced changes in our climate that are transforming our way of life. Wildfires blazed through Australia earlier in the year and more than 2.2 million acres burned across the western states in the United States in less than a month. A global virus pandemic is still flaring, and systemic racism continues to rear its unrighteous wicked head. If we turn to the scriptures for evidence of what was expected when Christ would return, we find additional indicators, including the terrible times prophesied in 2 Timothy 3:

People will be lovers of themselves, lovers of money, boastful, proud, abusive, disobedient to their parents, ungrateful, unholy, without love, unforgiving, slanderous, without self-control, brutal, not lovers of the good, treacherous, rash, conceited, lovers of pleasure rather than lovers of God—having a form of godliness but denying its power… They are the kind who worm their way into homes and gain control over gullible women, who are loaded down with sins and are swayed by all kinds of evil desires, always learning but never able to come to a knowledge of the truth (NIV).

Further, it was written in 1 John 2:18 they were already living in the last hour and many antichrists had come. Since scholars believe this epistle originated between 95 and 110 AD/CE this means our generation has lived nearly 2000 years in the end times waiting for Christ's return. Whether looking to the scriptures, the science, or both, no one has to look far to see our world is breaking apart in chaos, division, fear, hate, sickness, corruption of systems and politics, and multiple cataclysmic losses.

The good news is the time has come to stop waiting for a savior. We are entering the hour of healing, miracles, and dreams coming true as love and peace begin their reign on Earth. As prophesied in Revelation 21, the City of the Holy One established from the heavenly Kingdom of God. But the temple is not made of stone, mortar, or wood, it is built within our hearts through the light of our souls where Christ shines like the sun (Revelation 21:22).

Yet, until more hearts are open to discern the light and the Good and receive the grace of wisdom and understanding through love, we the people— including the established churches of the Christian religion—will remain part of the colossal problem that is preventing Christ from reigning in full power and glory in our world. This goes especially for the Christians and churches who have been evangelizing the name of Jesus for nearly 2000 years without pure love and the faith that moves mountains in their hearts.

This may be difficult to hear, but please consider if the hearts and minds of Christians and the spirit/energy/life force within the churches were shining bright with the joy of Jesus and with the fruits of the Holy Spirit today, this world would already be a much better place. Imagine if all 2 billion professing Christians actually lived virtuous lives of love, nonjudgment, and peace just like Jesus did; not to mention more than 200 million Christians in the United States alone (data: Pew Research Center and census.gov). A world where joy and rejoicing reign instead of conflicts, sickness, and death. With the rivers clapping their hands as the mountains sing out together and all the Earth bursts into jubilant song for the power of Christ that will come forth into the world through the hearts of all God's children.

Right now this vision does not seem likely to come to fruition even with our greatest intentions. "Thoughts and prayers" offered in times of crisis and suffering are not moving the needle enough. Unless we put more effort into truly living as saints in Christ we will continue to fall short. This in itself—even before we go any farther into the fray together—is where this gospel will go off the rails for some people. No one wants to hear they are part of the problem. It is certainly not the apocalyptic rapture or an all-powerful King and Lord dashing in like Prince Charming to sweep us all off our feet and carry us on his snowy white steed into Heaven. The truth of the matter is: suffering may get worse before it gets better. We must remember this is what perseverance of the saints was all about.

The entire world, and particularly here in America, is in dire need of the faith that rouses the waters of the deep and makes the mountains move. A worldwide remedy of goodness and peace from the Holy Spirit through the light of love that is pure. Faith the size of a mustard seed that is guaranteed to usher in Christ through the hearts of his true disciples. But here is the next hurdle and a spoiler of what is to come: it does not look like most of Christianity does in our world today.

This is also where some egos may get upset, and I understand, I honestly do. I used to stand in the very same beliefs that judge, divide, and destroy in puffed-up knowledge and pride instead of building up in charity and love (1 Corinthians 8:1). The truth, as you will see through this gospel, is the inner pilgrimage to restoring the light of the Holy Spirit and joy in the soul does not end in the "saving us all from our sins" moment in the crucifixion of the Son of God and man, Jesus.

The cross is only the halfway point in establishing what is Holy, Love, and Good; it is not the completion of the inner work of a Christian or the mark of a saint. It leaves the progressing—but not yet mature—disciple in a crossroads, battling the storms of good versus evil and right versus wrong. Freedom is ours; joy is ours, yes, even here on this Earth as it is already in Heaven. We are all children of the same One God/Source/Universe/Life force and are made of the same light as the stars. Joy is our birthright, and we were meant to experience life and the beauty of every single one of our heart's dreams come true, within or outside of the doctrine of the Christian Churches.

It is as if in a Divine dose of irony, God is directly answering the call of His Holiness Pope Francis as written in his Apostolic Exhortation from 2013, The Joy of the Gospel, in a prayer to the Virgin Mother Mary, *"Obtain for us now a new ardor born of the resurrection, that we may bring to all the Gospel of life which triumphs over death. Give us a Holy courage to seek new paths, that the gift of unfading beauty may reach every man and woman... that the joy of the Gospel may reach to the ends of the earth, illuminating even the fringes of our world."*

Although the Pope made the call for a new ardor born of the resurrection, the announcement of Christ's return is not coming through the leadership of the Catholic Church, nor through a leader of any one of the more than 33,000 denominations (World Christian Encyclopedia by Barrett, Kurian, Johnson; Oxford Univ Press, 2nd ed, 2001). For how could Jesus choose between some of God's children and not others? When contemplated with a heart filled with wisdom, this truth becomes as clear as the sky on a sunny day for the fullness of God's glory and love to prevail for all people.

Neither does the One church exist in 2020, so God's apostle pronouncing the return of Christ could not return through the church. When Mary Magdalene announced the resurrection to the other disciples (John 20:18), telling them she had seen the Lord and relayed what he said to her as his messenger and the designated Apostle of the Apostles, they were one group of believers. But now the church body is broken into thousands of pieces with Christians scattered everywhere; many of them pointing fingers at each other.

In Biblical alignment of how Jesus' resurrection from the crucifixion was reported, this gospel ("good news") includes a personal testimony of Christ's work in real life on earth through one who stands on the rock of Christ with the peace that surpasses understanding and love for all in her heart, with the light and power of the Holy Spirit, who traveled the path of Christianity through multiple denominations and was courageous enough to let go of the cross into the imageless Father God into the grace that is found in faith, beyond where images, symbols, creeds, and doctrines have a foothold in minds and hearts. Even beyond the edges of God's promises and beliefs into the great unknown where light and darkness exist together in harmony within creation.

And thus, one who has compassion in her heart for the light of righteousness found in the faithful, both within and outside the church. This is the calling of the light of Christ, the way to the promised land of miracles and the American Dream come true for every one of us. Where joy reigns and the sun shines within the soul in service to Good in the world every single day. It is here for all who stand in the truth of the infinite glory of God, just like Jesus did before us.

This brings us to a timely moment for a cautionary note before I share my testimony of Christ and reveal the establishment of the Messianic Age as described in the New Testament (the living Christ within us), with a special message to my fellow Americans in the United States in this time of suffering and patriotic unrest.

Whether you are a professing Christian, ex-Christian, a believer in another spiritual/religious tradition, "spiritual but not religious," agnostic, atheist, or "other," wherever this gospel finds you, please may I forewarn unless you have a completely open mind and heart there is a great likelihood that at least one of these chapters will spark judgment or dissent within you. That is, of course, unless you are already living as a saint, sage, bodhisattva, and/or guru. (If this is you, namaste with love.)

For everyone else, when you recognize opposition within your mind, body, or heart, that is good. It means you are alive inside. (Whatever you do, don't go back to sleep.) I implore you to explore the deeper meaning found beneath the surface of any inner discord and lean on the guidance and support of mental and emotional health and spiritual ministry professionals for the greatest good.

Having said that, if you are inspired and encouraged by this gospel with hope for the future, even better. Your heart is already prepared to spread the good news of joy by being the Good you want to see in the world. (Let your inner light shine in all you do.)

This book is a roller coaster of inner transformation, and you are in the front row for the entire ride. Please prepare your heart and mind to be presented with the entire spectrum of beliefs about Jesus of Nazareth crucified on the cross, horizon to horizon, from my first-person narrative as a fundamentalist Christian, through the deconstruction of my beliefs, and to the idea that Jesus was a hoax and myth created for mass deception, power, and control, or simply a founding myth written as celestial metaphor to guide all of us into the next stage of humanity's development on Earth into the Age of Aquarius. All of these beliefs existed inside me at one time or another, even if I only tried them on temporarily to receive understanding through wisdom in fullness from the Holy Spirit.

As we begin, it is important to establish the context of what my life was like when the first chapter commences. Desires of the world reigned within me. As a sinner, adulteress, and worse, I believed I was going to Heaven because I was baptized as a baby. I believed everything I'd learned at church growing up, Jesus loved me, and I was saved from my sins. I had no need for active participation with spirituality, no need for Jesus, or even God. My beliefs were static, and as a baptized Christian, in my mind, I could do no wrong. That was, until my world shattered into a multitude of pieces.

In my own words, and not embellished or exaggerated, these pages are as my life actually transpired, extracted from writings in my journals over 30 years, with a focus on the last 11 years, from the breaking open of my heart through renewal and transfiguration; shared so your joy can manifest, just like the joy within my soul, for Christ is in me.

In the moments when you may wonder if all of this was true, if it seems impossible that the events really happened, and if you start down a cynical path of skepticism of believing it was too fantastical, crazy, or amazing to be anything more than fiction—I get it. I understand, I really, truly do. If I had not lived every single moment of this, I may have had a difficult time believing it, too. That's where faith will come in for you.

I am living proof of what Christ Jesus can do in the hearts and minds of his disciples who persevere in the work of the saints, all the way through healing to miracles and dreams come true, and this is my gospel of joy.

Author's Notes:

· These writings were journal entries from my life between the ages of 13-43 and thus, in many instances, references and citations were not included. Translations of scriptures, sacred texts, and historical records and "facts" reflected upon in these pages were true to the best of my knowledge through research gathered at the time of writing. Please forgive typos and grammatical errors as due to the nature of this living book, the edition is unedited.

· Unless otherwise specified, Bible verses are from the New International Version (NIV).

· Names with an asterisk (*) at first appearance are mirrors.

PROLOGUE

I let go of all preconceived ideas about the world,
and I am open to receive the truth of my soul's greatest joy.
I welcome the highest Good to flow with ease into my heart as wisdom
and into my mind as understanding.
I may be required to trust and have faith in a power I cannot see,
and leaping may be required
before I feel ground beneath my feet.
By the fruits within, I will know the Holy light
and I shall believe in the light within me.

(ODE TO THE REBIRTH OF THE SOUL, SEPT 5, 2020, AGE 43)

THE BREAKING

…WHEN THE WORLD SHATTERED, AND I
CRIED OUT FOR HELP FROM ABOVE.

Tuesday, June 30, 2009

Condensation streaked the window as the airplane landed on the runway and taxied to the arrival gate, blurring my vision of Newark Liberty International Airport. I was returning home from California, where I grew up and where I'd just left my heart.

The trip was more than catching up with family and friends. I took the time to think about what I wanted in life. At the age of 31, I was already divorced and remarried once. Career-wise, after graduating with my bachelor's degree five years ago, last year I landed a job at one of the top global pharmaceutical companies. Although I was steadily climbing the corporate ladder, I was not happy. Something was missing.

So, what did I discover during my soul searching in California? True love, as in the one. The man of my dreams who I had given up on finding years ago. Oh, where do I begin…

Jeremie* and I met in person and then traveled to a lake area for a few days. We'd known each other online from playing one of the popular multiplayer roleplaying games. In the game, large groups of players got together and ran dungeons to defeat super powerful bosses. Yes, I admit I was a geek gamer girl in my free time when I was not out driving in my Jeep Wrangler and singing to music with my St. Bernard dog, Sadie, by my side, or snuggling with my rescued cats at home.

Jeremie and I started talking in the game and when I first heard his voice while running dungeon raids, I felt a connection in my heart. We developed a secret affair over online chats and phone conversations. Well, what semblance of one we could have with both of us in separate unhappy relationships and the fact he lived across the country from New Jersey.

The moment we met in person was electrifying. It was as perfect as I could have ever imagined perfect to be. I knew that I felt a connection with him I'd never, ever experienced before with anyone else. Without a doubt in my mind, he was the man I was meant to be with.

On the last morning when we were getting ready to leave in opposite directions, we promised each other we would reduce complications in our lives to be together in the future. We committed to being together within five years or so down the road, maybe less, maybe more. He handed me a folded note he'd written on the hotel's stationary and told me to read it after we parted. After he drove away, I opened it and read,

> *"I love you more and more every second of every day.*
> *This time I have spent with you has been some of the best days of my life.*
> *I ache for the day when you and I will be together forever.*
> *You make my heart soar."*

Questions flooded my mind as I settled back into the routine of life at home in New Jersey. I had to figure out how I was going to do this, how I would perfectly balance continuing the affair while in parallel plan an exit to my marriage. But it was not merely the logistical decisions to make, deeper questions arose in my heart. How does one know when perfect love was experienced? Was I wrong in giving up on the idea there was a man out there who would be "the one"? My soulmate? Was I wrong in pushing aside my childhood dreams of true love and a knight in shining armor, my Prince Charming sweeping me off my feet?

All I could think about was how much I missed California. And how much I did not want to be back in this life I was living—not in my house or with my husband, Paul.

At a crossroads? Without a doubt. What was I going to do and how was I going to unravel the complicated mess I'd created? I had no clue.

If I was being honest, the idea of starting all over again was not appealing. But I was uncertain whether I was resisting it because of being afraid of what people would think of me if I was a twice-divorced woman or because I'd have to admit I made the wrong decision in marriage again. Was it because I was "happy enough" and didn't want to deal with the heartache of another break-up? Was I too afraid of the chance of being alone if it didn't end up working out? Mostly it was because I didn't know how to explain this to my family, my friends, or... to myself.

Years ago, I gave up on the idea that there was one man for me. Paul did not believe in soulmates. I decided he must be right. "The one" didn't exist, and as he put it, there were many people with whom anyone can be happy and make a good life. No man of my dreams, no soulmate. Thinking back, I recalled feeling upset each time I thought about the fact that my own husband did not believe in "the one," because it meant I was one of many mates who in his mind, he'd be willing to marry. Even on the first day of our relationship, I lost all sense of being special or loved.

The reality though, was that in my heart it was not ever more than friendship, even after we took the next step:

"This morning (the morning of our wedding) I was becoming a little worried. I did not feel anxious about getting married: no cold feet, no second thoughts. In fact, I felt nothing at all. I so wanted to, but there was nothing."
(August 2003, age 26)

Were my ideals of a fairy tale happy ending and true love with the man of my dreams just a fantasy I was right to give up on? Was this as close as I would ever get to finding a "good enough" marriage—and was this all I should ask for? I didn't know.

Maybe I'd found my soulmate in Jeremie but how could I try it out to see if it was perfect without losing what I already had? Even as I wrote this, I realized how unfair it was for everyone but me, so selfish for me to consider leading a dual life.

Just a seven-year-itch? I did not think so, and that would complicate whichever path I took forward. I had no idea what the future held, and the unknown terrified me.

Friday, July 17, 2009

My heart tore with indecision when I talked with Jeremie and he revealed that he was moving out of his home. He broke up with his girlfriend today. We'd missed each other more and more in the last couple of weeks and what started as a five-year plan now turned into him willing to move out on his own and wait for me.

Although we'd talked about being afraid of the same thing, leaving the status quo in our lives for the unknown, he made his decision. Neither of us knew whether what felt as perfect as what we shared was possible to sustain. He bravely took the step to leave and move in with family to begin a new life and to wait for me; it would take me longer to extricate myself from my marriage.

Sunday, July 26, 2009

Once again I tried to hold onto my dreams.
they've fallen through my hand like an hourglass of sand.
Don't tell me I shouldn't give up.

I know enough that shows me loud and clear.
I am standing all alone in love.
I never should have let my hopes get this high. The memories scolded me.
Once again I turn the pages of life.
Once again they're burned before I can live them...
(September 1992, age 15)

* * *

Nine days later and the step forward was already undone. Tomorrow Jeremie was moving back home to his girlfriend. Part of me did not blame him. When he said he was renting a moving truck, I got a deep pit of fear in my stomach, a realization of, "Oh my God, this is really happening." I knew that since he made a decision and took action that meant I needed to figure out how I was going to unravel obstacles on my end. Now, suddenly everything changed.

During our last telephone call, he told me that he made his decision of who he needed to be with. He was going home to his girlfriend to work on their relationship. It didn't sit quite right, after all, his family and friends knew how unhappy he'd been with her even before I was in the picture. Yet, reeling from shock and heartbreak in the moment, rational thoughts eluded me. In the same sentence, he acknowledged how special I was to him and that he'd never before felt how he did when we were together. He said it was perfect, and he still thought so. He talked about timing and told me that I'd be the first to know when they ever broke up.

Fear held me. Hoping we weren't just an affair, and so scared that I would never feel that complete and perfect ever again in my life. To lose my dream of spending the rest of my life with the one for me and worse, to lose it now when I believed I'd found him.

Tuesday, July 28, 2009

I was the walking dead, a shell of myself. My heart was wrenched out of my chest and a gaping incomplete hole remained. Nothing was real, everything was a shade of gray, and emotions consumed me. I lost count of how many times at work I had to hide in the restroom to cry.

On the way home I started sobbing, deep cries convulsed through my entire being. I could not breathe; I could not stop the pain. It ripped through the hole in my heart. A summer thunderstorm crashed down around me in a downpour of rain flooding the road as I drove alongside the Raritan Canal. Water splashed up over the hood as the road pooled with the torrent.

Thunder boomed all around, rolling and crashing as the storm churned. My uncontrollable crying deepened until I could not stand the pain in my heart any longer.

I cried out from the depths, "God help me! I can't keep going on like this. Help me, please!" I began pleading to God in Jesus' name.

My chaotic thoughts swirled with confusion as I begged God to answer, "What am I supposed to do now? Who am I supposed to be with?" Jeremie was perfect, if there was anyone who I thought would have been my soulmate —he was it. And now, he has left my life.

"Help me, God!"

Trying to steady the wheel in the storm, thunder boomed from the skies as my body shook in deep sobs. I could not go on like this. What was I going to do now?

❋ ❋ ❋

How can the sun shine into my life if my world has stopped revolving…
will I forever be kept back in the darkness?
Only time will tell.
(April 1992, age 14)

Thursday, July 30, 2009

Hopeless and lost in a sea of heartache, I was without direction. With every breath I took tears flowed and I needed answers. For the first time in my life, I did not know what to do. The goal-driven, determined, strong, bright, organized girl who had always found a way to get what I wanted in life was completely lost.

I decided to do something I'd never considered before in my life. I called psychics. I wasn't sure what I wanted to get out of it, but I was in such a state of confusion I could not think of anything else to do. I didn't know if I should work on my marriage or wait for Jeremie, especially now that he'd left my life.

It was easy to find psychic phone numbers; they even advertised on television. The first phone reading seemed on target but because I believed psychics used scripts and were scammers, I decided to call a few different psychic hotlines and compare notes between them. The advice was all over the place. One psychic said he would contact me in mid-August. Another psychic told me that I should go see him in September. A third psychic said he would be relocating soon. The last one advised she saw him walking away from me. Uhm, yes, thanks for that insight, I knew that much already.

Not having any resolution and since I'd already taken the step, I decided to go to a psychic in person. Part of me could not believe I was going to do this. It was wrong. It was evil. It was not of God. It was everything from my upbringing in the Lutheran church I was taught not to do.

Friday, July 31, 2009

My heart was racing, and I was unable to focus all morning. I called the first phone number from a page of local psychics I'd printed out last night. The first psychic I spoke with did not leave me with a good impression. It was difficult to hear her because she had The Price-Is-Right game show blaring on her television in the background. She could not even turn it down to answer a call? I still set up an appointment for later in the day but after I hung up I asked myself, "This was the person I'm going to for wisdom and advice?" It seemed so unprofessional. I shook my head in disbelief and to keep my options open, I moved to the next psychic on my list.

The next psychic sounded much more together on the phone, so I scheduled a session. Later in the day, I found the location, a cottage off of a main highway with attractive landscaping and flowers. An assistant answered the door when I knocked and directed me into the darkened reading room. Upon entering, I did not feel major heebeegeebees. It was different than I expected though, similar to what I would expect a séance room to feel like, not that I'd ever been in one before.

The air was still but heavy, cool but not eerie chill. In the middle of the room were two high-backed upholstered chairs with a low table set between them. On the table, I saw tarot cards and other astrological items. On a table in the back of the room, I saw a bundle of dried sage and some bottles. The walls held angel-themed artwork and framed Bible verses. Across the back shelves, I noticed more angels, a nativity set, and what struck me as oddest, an open Bible.

I sat in one of the chairs and took it all in, hands folded in my lap and heart racing, I waited. After a few minutes, the psychic entered the room. She did not smile or shake my hand. In a monotone voice, she said hello and then seated herself across from me. The psychic then asked for my full name and date of birth and instructed me to focus on the question I came to have answered as she took both of my hands in hers.

With as much concentration and focus as I could muster, I projected my thoughts on the sole question burning deep within my mind, "Who was I supposed to be with? Paul or Jeremie?"

Silence held the room until the psychic asked, "Did you concentrate on the question?"

"Yes," I answered, and she let go of my hands and sat back in her chair.

Remaining still without emotion on her countenance, the psychic advised, "If you continue on your current path, you will destroy everything you have worked so hard for."

She went on to say that she saw I did not have control over my emotions. She described that although I had a smile on my face, there was not a smile in my heart. She stated she could sense I was kind and caring to the point of being taken advantage of by others and I'd been wounded by love twice in my life. She reiterated that neither of the two men in my energy was a part of my future if I continued on this path.

The psychic kept speaking, but I did not hear it. My mind was reeling with shock. The future was nothing but destruction. No future with Jeremie. No future with Paul. Numbness consumed me and a sense of doom filled my being. When she offered to do my astrological charts for life, love, and destiny for more money I shook my head no in a daze and despondently thanked her for her time and found my way back down the cottage steps.

Was this my future? Despair and ruin? This was not the answer I hoped to receive. I noticed there was still time before my late evening session with The Price-Is-Right psychic, so I looked down at my list for another phone number. Maybe if I went to three psychics then I could compare what was similar between their advice and that would hopefully provide a clearer view of the path forward.

A Wiccan psychic named Sofie* was next on my list. She seemed pleasant on the phone and told me she could fit me in, so I headed over to her location. A big "Psychic Readings & Advice" sign on the sidewalk of the downtown area welcomed me upon arrival. As I opened the door to her shop and walked in some bells chimed and I noticed light and bright colors filling the walls. The space invoked a much different feeling than my experience earlier in the day. I noticed a sectional couch filling the front area, shelves with dolls and angels, and a more secluded area with a table and two chairs in the back.

Sofie greeted me with a smile and introduced herself, confirming my name as she shook my hand. She motioned for me to follow her to the chairs in the back and to have a seat. Glancing at the table, I noticed some crystals, an incense burner, and what surprised me most again, an open Bible.

She asked me to state my full name and date of birth while she held my hands in hers. This sounded just like the previous reading, but she did not ask me to focus on a question. A few moments of silence passed. Still holding my hands in hers, Sofie began to speak. She advised I was kind and generous to the point that I was at times taken advantage of by others. She gazed into my eyes and squeezed my hands gently, "There is always a smile on your face, but your heart is not smiling." So far, what Sofie relayed was exactly what the other psychic said.

Sofie continued by saying that she saw I was searching because of the void that I felt in my soul and that I was hurt by love twice. The two readings diverged at this point though because Sofie went on to advise the negative thoughts and feelings surrounding me were destroying my life. She described that an entity formed from negativity was trying to prevent me from regaining hope and happiness. She said she could see I had psychic abilities, but they were blocked by this current state. Further, she explained this was why I was unable to depend on my intuition to know what to do.

"One of the two men in your life loves you more than you love him, and you've been unhappy for quite a long time," she said, and I knew this meant Paul. "The other man," she paused before continuing, "is confused like you, but he does love you."

With that, she let go of my hands and smiled as she offered to help. She explained that the work of cleansing and healing needed to be done before I could start to think about who I was supposed to be with in the future. She described a first step of eliminating negativity and confusion so we could find out if Jeremie was my soulmate.

Startled, I looked at Sofie. Questions raced in my mind. My what? My soulmate? There was such a thing? I shouldn't have given up? I shook myself back to the discussion and explained to her I was uncomfortable with any sort of cleansing, "I was raised Christian, in the Lutheran tradition, and…"

Sofie interrupted me, "I am a born-again Christian."

Disbelief filled my head. No that's not possible, she was a Wiccan psychic. Psychics weren't Christian. Sofie must have noticed the face I made because she pointed to the Bible on the table. Remembering the open Bible at the other psychic's cottage, I was still skeptical.

"How do you justify it? How does what you do fit into God's word?" I asked.

Sofie reminded me that there were prophets in the Bible, including the three wise men who followed the Star of Bethlehem in the sky. She went on to give examples of healing with herbs, prayer, and laying on hands.

"Furthermore," she concluded, "most of the healing work will be done on your own through prayer and working with crystals."

I wasn't convinced. I still did not believe it was okay. Part of me thought it was a scam, but I found myself saying, yes, I would give it a try. I mean, honestly, what more did I have to lose?

With a smile, she had me write down my full name and date of birth and asked for photos of everyone involved so she could "open the case" and "go to work" to find out more about what was going on.

After telling me to spend time praying over the weekend, Sofie hugged me goodbye saying, "God bless you."

As I left her shop, nervousness gripped my stomach. She told me I could not tell anyone, or their energies might impede her work with me and my healing process. My mind was screaming, "Scam!" But for some reason, I felt like I needed to see where this led. I canceled the appointment with The Price-is-Right psychic. This work with Sofie was the next step forward that I could see.

Later in the evening, I took my written journal pages from the last couple of weeks and burned them in the backyard. All the hopelessness, despair, what-ifs, scenarios, responses to scenarios, plans, secondary plans, and generally confused gibberish, were destroyed to ashes. I felt a little better inside.

❈ ❈ ❈

I can't go on being the way I am—
would it be such a change they would realize something was wrong?
Would I find myself having what I've always longed for?
Is it worth the pain to be triumphant?
Can't they see what's happening to me?

I'll do it, not for those who never found any good in me,
but for myself,
because then I'd know that I reached to make my dreams into reality,
and the impossible became possible because I believed in myself,
and I made the decision.
And I did something right.
(August 1992, age 15)

Monday, August 3, 2009

The confusion was clearing in my mind. I remembered who held my heart —and it was not my husband. In good conscience, my marriage could not continue. Admitting to Paul all I hadn't already, I told him that he deserved to be with someone who loved him as much as he loved. We talked about how we should have dealt with these issues and baggage from previous relationships years ago. In hindsight, I recognized jumping into a relationship with Paul a few months after exiting a nearly six-year relationship with my first husband, Tony, was not a wise decision at the time.

Then it was time to head over to Sofie's for a second session. I was a ball of nerves going in. Over the weekend I prayed like she told me to do and struggled to hear God's voice above the constant negativity that was running rampant in my head. Not to mention, I still wasn't convinced that going to sessions with her was okay to be doing.

As I sat down in the chair at the back of her shop, I told Sofie how I'd burned all the pages of my negative thoughts and decided who I wanted to be with. She gazed at me with a small smile and asked, "Who?"

"Jeremie."

Smiling, she pulled out the photos that I'd dropped off to her last week. Laying them out on the table, she pointed at them as she relayed her findings. She said Jeremie was confused and although he moved back home to work on his relationship with his girlfriend he did not understand why. He knew that damage was done when he burned the bridge with me but knew I still loved him.

Sofie continued, "And he does want to be with you too." This part was key as she'd mentioned in my first session that she did not work to help get people back together if it was not what they both wanted.

"The reason he is so confused," Sofie conveyed, "is because his girlfriend went to some sort of malevolent, black magic Wiccan and had spells cast so he'd return to her, to bind him with her for the rest of their lives."

I blinked in surprise and tipped my head to the side, not expecting to hear this. I'd never known anyone who cast spells or was affected by them. At least not that I was aware of anyway, but somehow, I believed it could be possible. It made sense. Jeremie was a strong enough person that if he'd decided to move out, to stick with it, instead of going back to a relationship where he was unhappy.

Sofie mentioned there were more complications and negativity to deal with than she first anticipated, and it would cost me more money, but she did not know how much yet.

"I know you are having a hard time trusting me," she reassured, "You need to place your trust in God." Sofie went on to say that she was a tool God placed on the path to help me through this and on the road to healing. "Then," she reminded me, "you'll be ready for the man you are meant to be with."

She explained that this was going to be a war and one that wouldn't be won overnight. There might need to be fasting, lots of praying, and most important of all, Sofie emphasized, "You must stop planning. From this point onward, be spontaneous with God."

Nodding my head in agreement, nervousness struck within me again. I didn't quite believe it was of God, of MY God. I decided to test her. As I was leaving, I turned back and with a casual tone in my voice, asked Sofie, "I was thinking I may want to start going to church again. Is that okay or do I need to wait until we're done with all this?" I waved my hand around in the air indicating all the metaphysical paraphernalia in her shop.

Sofie inhaled. Her eyes looked sharp and wide at me. Then she exhaled dramatically as she admonished me, "Shannon, you SHOULD be going to church during all this!" She went on to say she attended church on Sundays with her family and explained how she could see the differences in the weeks they did not make it to church, because her children were more disobedient and impatient.

Hmm, not the response I expected. I pondered it while walking out her door, bells chiming behind me. I was still skeptical but saw no other path ahead.

Later during the night, I was lying on my bed reading a book I'd picked up at the local bookstore. It was on the highs and lows of true love and how infatuation matured into unconditional love. Out of nowhere, I felt a sense of pressing tiredness in my mind. Not a falling asleep feeling, but I felt like I needed to relax and zone out. Jeremie was very heavy on my thoughts.

I said in my mind, "I love you."

"I love you too, Shannon," he responded.

We conversed for a few minutes although it was a blur, and as I felt his presence fading, strangely I felt Sofie's presence. I asked her in my thoughts, "Is he coming out of it now?"

"Yes, he is," the presence of Sofie answered.

"We needed this, didn't we?" I asked her.

"Yes, you did."

Anxiousness rose in my heart, and I questioned, "Will I be ready for him?"

"Yes, you will be ready."

And I faded into sleep…

Tuesday, August 4, 2009

This morning I woke up after a night filled with dreams about Jeremie. I felt a bit like I was crazy. Did I dream that I had a conversation with him and Sofie in my head last night? It felt so real. Even though I knew it might sound nutty, I called Sofie and left a voicemail. I asked her if I had a conversation with him last night and if she facilitated it because I could have sworn I talked with her too.

Although I missed her call back, she left a voicemail later in the day confirming I was right. She said I must have picked up on the energies when she was working on my case and we'd put it all together at the next session.

My jaw dropped in astonishment. We communicated telepathically? Oh my gosh! How amazing!

Wednesday, August 5, 2009

Sofie and I chatted about the telepathic experience at my session today. She asked me to relay what I remembered and then smiled and said I had pinned the conversation.

"Is that normal?" I asked, still a bit incredulous that telepathy was real.

She said it meant she and I were connected in spirit with a strong bond. She seemed pleased and announced, "There will be a meeting between you and Jeremie."

A small gasp emitted my mouth in surprised delight, "When?"

"Definitely by your trip to California," she responded with a smile. Sofie knew I was planning another trip to visit family in November. Wondering seized me. A meeting? When would it be? Would he come here? When would I see him?

I'd thought quite a bit lately about how I did not want to hold onto something that wasn't meant to be in the future. I asked Sofie, "Are you able to tell yet if we are soulmates?"

She advised negativity was still blocking it. But I impatiently persisted with my question, emphasizing that if Jeremie and I weren't meant to be together I wanted to know, so I could let go and move on.

Sofie listened and waved away my words. Raising an eyebrow in her direction, I gazed at her. She stopped and sighed, "You're going to keep asking me until I tell you, aren't you, Shannon." Grinning, I nodded.

"Shannon, know there are some things that cannot be revealed to you yet," Sofie said as I scowled. She continued, "Right now you need to focus on healing and learning to love yourself before you can think about loving anyone else." But the wide smile on her face all but told me the answer. He was! She in-so-much-as confirmed without saying it!

Saturday, August 8, 2009

Today I took time for myself. With the top off of the Jeep, I drove out to the beach. The ocean was one of my happiest places and I knew sitting out on the sand for a while would help re-energize and balance my heart. The roar of ocean waves and crashing surf rising to meet the shore was one of the places I felt most alive and connected with God.

Slipping into inner thoughts with the ocean nearby, I thought a little about Jeremie but then reminded myself that this was for me—my healing—not him. As I pulled out my journal, one question remained in my heart. I do love myself... don't I?

What was I missing here? My mind flitted back to a conversation I had with my father recently. He'd mentioned after he and my mom divorced, one of the things he did was write down all the qualities that he was looking for in a future wife. At first, I rolled my eyes thinking that it was a silly exercise, but then I realized he may have had a point.

Not once in the last fifteen years since my first boyfriend at the age of 16, did I ever stop to think about what I wanted in a relationship. I was more concerned with the idea of being with someone. When I had a boyfriend or was dating someone, I felt better about myself. Back in junior high and high school, I was the 5'2" fat girl with plain brown hair and blue-green eyes, who was sweet but shy. I believed no guy would ever be interested in me and I constantly compared myself to the cheerleaders at school and celebrities on television and in teen magazines.

Imagine my surprise when I discovered at least one man was interested in me "more than a friend." It filled the void inside my heart temporarily and when I was not in a relationship, I found the next most available man nearby. It was not until these new flings fell apart that I realized how unhappy I was and sought another safety net. Too scared to be on my own and trapped in my own creation of a constant cycle of bouncing from one relationship to another over the last 16 years. I realized that's what Jeremie was in the beginning. A new safety net.

But now I understood I must be willing to be on my own—without a safety net—before I could go into the relationship I wanted to be in. As Sofie had said, before I could go into the marriage that God had for me. It was an interesting concept to consider how what used to scare me was now what I was embracing as if it must happen this way for me to finally be happy inside. No matter what happened next, I would get divorced and be on my own. I couldn't continue life as it was.

Faith and trust were appearing in my heart. I believed the future was opening in the way it was meant to be and remembered there was a reason why this was happening. Life reminded me of what I'd always wanted. My Prince Charming. My soulmate. The one man who would love me with his whole heart and whom I would love equally in return. I couldn't take the easy way out anymore. I remembered years ago when I wrote:

> *"I've wished on countless stars growing up that I would someday find my Prince.*
> *A man who rode into my life on his snowy white steed and swept me off my feet,*
> *who embraced me with love and affection,*
> *and who spoke with me with support and understanding,*
> *who protected me and held me safe from any harm,*
> *who was loving, kind, and gentle."*
> (May 1998, age 20)

Feeling the breeze sweep across my face and hearing the roar of the waves reaching the surf and breaking onto the sands of the shore. I inhaled the salty ocean air... and as I exhaled, I let go. I felt peaceful. I felt stronger. By letting go of who I was, I was beginning to find myself after all these years.

Tuesday, August 11, 2009

During the next session with Sofie, she revealed the total cost for the spiritual work and healing over the next few months. It was a lot more money than the hundreds I'd already paid her, a lot more money, so much that I about fell out of the chair in her shop. Part of me was willing to continue but if I was getting divorced the money should go to paying off debt, not knowing how long I would be on my own.

Shocked and numb, I walked out of the session. I thought this was the path forward. Now, what was I supposed to do? If I went to a church, sure they would help me with healing, but they wouldn't help with removing whatever was binding Jeremie to his girlfriend. The downward spiral in my heart commenced as I fell into despair. Feeling so lost and hopeless, my plan slipping through my fingers and crashing on the floor in pieces again.

ATONEMENT

...BECOMING A LEGITIMATE DAUGHTER OF THE LIGHT.

Wednesday, August 12, 2009

This morning I left a voicemail for Sofie telling her I would not be continuing sessions. The cost was too expensive. It was time to go in another direction; I needed to find a church.

When I had asked Sofie if it was okay to go to church, I did not actually intend on going to one. While I was growing up, my family went to a traditional Lutheran Church. I went, but not by choice. I'd much rather have slept in on Sundays. My parents forced me to go, every weekend without fail. I completed all the initiations and rituals for first communion and confirmation and even taught Sunday school for the little kids throughout my high school years to avoid going to youth group.

Most of my adversity towards religion did not stem from the church itself but was due to my parents' increased differing beliefs about religion. It blew up in our household in the years leading up to their divorce. Constant tension created turmoil within me, and I pushed away from what I perceived was the root cause. The day after graduating from high school, at the age of 17, I moved out and stopped going to church.

Whenever anyone asked about my beliefs, I'd share that I still believed in everything I did growing up in the church. That part was true. I believed in Jesus and knew I was going to Heaven because he died on the cross for my sins. Since baptism as a baby and confirmation in eighth grade, I'd done what I needed to do, and the ingrained beliefs stayed with me. I did not feel the need to practice religion.

I still wouldn't have gone back to a church, but life twisted unexpectedly. My mind traveled back in memories: while playing one of the early text-based multiplayer roleplaying games when I was 19, during the time of my parents' divorce, I met a man named Tony from Washington State. He moved down to California to be closer to me, but with the chaos of my family breaking apart, I wanted to move away from home. We decided to move together to the

Pacific Northwest. This way Tony would be closer to his friends and family, and I could get farther away from mine.

We planned out all the steps and put them into action. I gave notice at my job, dropped classes at the community college, and packed up everything I owned. A week before we were set to move north, Tony broke up with me. He said he could not live in sin and was going to make the move on his own instead. My heart broke into pieces. Religion struck again. First in my parents' divorce and now as the reason that Tony was giving for leaving me behind in the aftermath.

For four months after Tony moved to the Seattle area, I pleaded with him to let me move into his apartment. I even suggested that I could be just a roommate until I could get on my own two feet. He relented, and I moved north in May 1998. Whatever issue Tony had about us living in sin disappeared shortly thereafter, and everything was as it was before.

But my heart did not trust him. At any moment, he could turn around again and demand I move out. A year later, he landed a new job in the Portland, Oregon area. Having nowhere else to go, I followed him to Oregon and put off returning to college for another year.

In late 2000, Tony met a new friend at work and connected in conversations about spirituality. At some point, he began going to his friend's church—and kept it a secret from me. He knew I did not want anything to do with any church. When I found out, my world crashed in on itself. No, no, no! Religion and church caused chaos! Instability! Tension! Turmoil! Relationships break up! My mind stormed with fear, but I calmed down enough to tell him that as long as he did not force me to go, I was okay with him going.

A few months later, we moved into a larger rental house and had a house-warming party. Tony invited his friends from church. I could not have prepared for what would happen after the party.

Cold spots.

Tony's church friends called him after leaving the party and warned that they felt multiple cold spots in our home. They wanted to come back with more people from the church to pray throughout the house and cleanse the rooms of the unholy spirits and evil that were present.

Spirits? Ghosts? Evil? In the house? I panicked and told Tony they could come rid the house of whatever was in it, but I did not want to be there while it was done. Each day over three days, a group of people spent hours praying in each room of the house.

My head spun when Tony and his church friends shared the stories after completing the spiritual warfare. There were angels, demons, visions, and revelations. There was even a march of the entire group around the property seven times like in the Bible story about the Jericho walls in the Old Testament.

The final room they prayed over was the coat closet in the living room, the location of where the crawlspace was for under the house. The vision that came upon one of the elders was there was a huge-headed snake through the crawlspace and underneath the home. In the vision, he saw God as the Lion of Judah slay the huge-headed snake and was victorious. When the elder received this vision, they agreed the house was clean.

Reeling from all I heard, I was incredulous. How was it even possible? It could not be real. I did not see any of it, did not feel any of it. After they'd all left on the third day, Tony and I walked out of the house, and he stopped and smiled. While gazing towards the end of the driveway, his smile turned into a large grin, and he exclaimed, "That's too cool. Look!"

Squinting towards the end of the driveway, I did not see anything. I raised my eyebrow and turned to him, asking, "What?"

"The Lion of Judah," Tony pointed, "He's sitting there at the end of the driveway protecting our house now." I gazed at the end of the driveway again. I blinked, then blinked again. Nope, still did not see anything as inner apprehension and turmoil grew. Was this real? Was this the God that I'd believed in since I was a little girl?

Later that day, troubled with everything they'd "seen" and told me about, I cried out to God in prayer—for the first time I could ever remember in my life, I begged God to show me that this was real and He was still the God I'd always believed in.

A few days later the cable company technicians arrived at the rental house to do an installation and asked where the access to under the house was located. I showed him to the coat closet. Starting to work, one of the men went around to the outside of the house and the other came inside and opened the access cover and went down into the crawlspace to run the cable.

Moments later, he scrambled back up into the living room and shut the access cover. I looked over at him from where I was sitting and noticed that his face looked drained of all color. His voice shaking, he asked me, "Have you guys ever had an exterminator out here?"

I told him no, that we had just recently moved in. He nodded and continued, "There's... there's a really big snake head down there and... and lots of snakeskin." He did not wait for an answer, turned, and rushed out the front door. I heard him meet up with his partner out front where he relayed the story again, "Dude, I'm not going back down there. There's a HUGE dead snake down there."

As soon as I heard him say it a second time the dots connected in my mind. In amazement, I put everything together. A huge-headed snake? Under the house? That was what Tony and the group from the church said! The Lion of Judah was victorious and slay a huge-headed snake just a few days ago!

Tony came back home later in the day. In excitement, I shared the story, and he grabbed a flashlight and went under the house to see what he could find. There was not anything under the house, no snakeskin, no snake head, nothing. Whatever the cable guy saw was supernatural.

God answered my prayer, God was real, and I believed:

> *"The events reminded me of who created the world*
> *and whose Word I should place my trust in.*
> *It was a turning point for me.*
> *As a child, Christianity was drilled into me,*
> *and as an adult, I had not yet been able to decide for myself what I believed in."*
> (March 2001, age 23)

During that time, Tony became even more involved in the church and sprinted on a zealous path towards God. His church friends told him that he could no longer "play house," and if he wanted to get his life right with God he had to stop living in sin. This meant either marry me or kick me out.

So, we discussed marriage. Honestly, by this time, it wasn't even on my mind anymore. I knew he was not "the one." The one would have wanted to marry me in the beginning, not break up with me but then change his mind. Yet, in the moment of decision with an ultimatum on the line, I took the easy route. I needed stability, I needed financial support. And above all else, I needed to finish college if I was ever going to get on my own two feet with a career in medicine. I planned our wedding in a matter of weeks.

Over the first year of marriage, I tried going to the church. But it was uncomfortable: all the spiritual warfare, praying in tongues, and prophesying over people. Even though I thought I'd grow more accustomed to it in time, the reality was the exact opposite. As fanatical as my husband was running towards God, he lost sight of me behind him. The chasm between us grew.

When I stopped going to the church, things spun out of control. Two women came over to our home to talk with me. They scolded me that if I did not go to the church or stay in my marriage there would never again be happiness in my life, and I would go to hell.

I couldn't understand this? No happiness? Going to hell for not going to church? This didn't sound like the God I knew. It was everything I had been so afraid of for years. Religion forced upon me again.

My world was crashing down on itself. I was not ready for that church or its charismatic services. Not ready for prophetic events where people were overcome by the Spirit falling down, like Holy Rollers, when prayed over by one of the whistle-stop tour prophets. I just couldn't do it anymore. Within a month later, I fled...

"Always believed someday my Prince Charming would
ride into my life on his snowy steed,
and ride off with me into the sunset to our castle.
Life did not seem to bring him to me
—and I committed myself for the wrong reasons."
(March 2002, age 24)

After I left Tony, I entered a platonic relationship with Paul, a friend who was a safe agnostic, who eventually ended up becoming my second husband. I hadn't stepped foot in a church in seven years, and now here I was trying to pick one.

I knew I needed to get over my fear and scars from what happened in the past. Discarding the Lutheran churches, I focused on the more charismatic denominations I found in the local listings: Baptist, Assemblies of God, and other Pentecostal churches. I wanted to talk with a pastor and find out if it was true that negativity was consuming me and if what Sofie was saying was real.

After calling at least a dozen churches from my list and getting nowhere, one pastor answered and was available and we set up an appointment for later in the afternoon. When my phone rang a few minutes later, I answered with surprise. It was Sofie. She said that she would be willing to reduce the total cost for the work—it was still a lot—too much, but I agreed. Part of me still felt it was my path. Yet, I planned on meeting with the pastor at the church I'd found. I wanted to confirm a few things and thought if I should be going to church right now during this healing, then perhaps I did need to go.

Later in the afternoon, I took a deep breath to steady myself as I reached out to open the door to the church office. Stepping inside was one of the biggest single steps in my life. Part of me could not believe I was walking into a church of my own free will. The pastor welcomed me into his office, and I was at ease and comfortable.

After giving him a short synopsis of my religious background, the pastor spent almost an entire hour talking with me. He described his church; it was a Pentecostal church that offered both traditional and contemporary services. He suggested I may want to attend the more traditional service given what I'd shared with him. Grinning, I shook my head and said that if I planned on getting over my fear, I needed to challenge myself. I'd go to the contemporary service first.

He smiled and then asked if I had a Bible. I thought about it and realized I didn't know where mine was that I'd been given in confirmation classes in middle school. Was it packed in boxes? Did I donate it accidentally? From the look on my face, he gathered I did not, so he pulled a new one from his bookshelf and handed it to me. As he did, the pastor advised for me to read the Bible daily.

He said it did not matter how much or how little I read, as long as it was every day. He suggested keeping a notebook to write down all the verses that struck a chord as I was reading and explained these were verses God was speaking directly into my life. I giggled as he wouldn't have known I've journaled anything and everything since I was 13 years old. I walked out of the church office with a smile on my face and joy in my heart. I needed to do this.

When I got home, I logged into the online multiplayer game for the first time in weeks. I'd stayed clear, not only because of my focus on healing, but I was adamant about not wanting any of my online friends to feel put in the middle. I did not want to instigate more drama than I'd already created. It was easier to stay away from the game.

A mutual friend sent me a message as soon as she saw me come online. She was worried because I hadn't been around. Then she shared how upset she was about the situation that was going on with Jeremie. She told me his girlfriend was watching over his shoulder and controlling his communications so much that he couldn't talk to anyone anymore. She confided that because she and Jeremie had been friends for so long she knew he was miserable. She wanted to support and be there for him, but it was impossible.

She went on to say she believed he was trying to find out how I was through her. He kept asking her, "How are things?" and hinting at it again and again. She told him she didn't know. No one knew because I hadn't been around in weeks. In the case she had an opportunity, I let her know she could pass along the update that I was about to start the process for a divorce.

Sunday, August 16, 2009

Before going to church this morning, I struggled with doubts and fear again. Thoughts that I should not spend the money on sessions with Sofie and I should not be going to her for wisdom and help. I worried it may very well be leading me down the wrong path and away from God. I prayed as I had in previous days asking God to show me if I should still be doing the work with her. I needed to know if it was okay. Was I on the path He wanted me to be on?

I went to the church for their more contemporary service. Three words described my experience, it was perfect. I should have known God placed me at this church for a reason. My most pressing prayer was answered in the pastor's sermon. The message was on James 3:13-18, which discussed Holy wisdom from God versus the wisdom of the world. The pastor described each type of wisdom. Wisdom from God's Heavenly well has the qualities of purity, peace, love, consideration, mercy, impartiality, and sincerity; that is, it bears bear good fruit.

Whereas, the wisdom of the world, which is not of God, is the opposite. It is strife-filled, uncaring, rude, rebellious, judgmental, biased, hypocritical, contentious, and uncaring. The fruits of worldly wisdom are negative, such as bitterness, envy, and self-ambition. He explained they cause confusion, chaos, and disorder in life and the world.

The pastor went on to preach that wisdom from God and the wisdom of the world were like oil and water, "You can shake them, but they cannot mix together. One will always end up on top and the other on the bottom." He explained there was no hiding the true nature and type of wisdom. Eventually, it would show itself.

In amazement, it answered my prayers about whether I should continue the work with Sofie. I'd begun feeling a bit better about my life, and as of now, the fruit was good. If in the future it revealed itself to be unholy, I would stop going.

Tuesday, August 18, 2009

I called Sofie to check-in and to see if she wanted me to come in for an appointment. She said she wanted to wait until Friday, but then she asked a question, "Did you go to church last Sunday?"

Questioning her motives, I paused. Doubts flooded my mind even though I'd felt so much better about everything since the sermon. How did she know? She must feel it in my energy. Maybe she was asking because she was not God's tool and was going to tell me that I should not have gone. I shoved all these thoughts back as I responded, "Yes, I did."

"Which church did you go to?"

I paused again, why does she want to know? But, I replied, telling her the name of the church.

"The one off of route 22?" She asked.

"Yes, that one," I wondered where this was leading.

"I thought I saw you!" Sofie gushed, "I was sitting a few rows behind you. We came in late. That's my church."

My mind raced. No, she was lying. She was trying to prove she was a Christian, so I'd keep coming to sessions. We wrapped up the conversation and set my next appointment for Friday. I was still feeling a bit off about the conversation. It could not be her church because she was not really a Christian. She couldn't be, a Wiccan Psychic who believed in Jesus and a born-again Christian? Nope, no way, it was not her church.

Sunday, August 23, 2009

Today I attended the church for the second time. Heading in to find a pew, I decided I would sit in the very back. This way, I had a view of the main entry doors. If this were Sofie's church and if she walked in, I'd have a clear view. But I still thought she was lying.

I stood and sang along with the congregation during the worship music. Then, I sat with my head bowed, hands folded, during the brief prayer before the offering. Right before the sermon, I saw a family walk in from the entry doors to my left. My entire being melted into shame.

Sofie came walking in with her children and waved, smiling at me as she crossed in front to another row. I felt so bad. All this time I kept coming up with every reason I could think of not to continue working with her and had not trusted her. Sofie was telling me the truth, she did go to this church. I felt awe in how God was putting all of this together.

As the pastor began preaching, the awe inside dissipated and my gut seized with a sense of unease and fear. He discussed how the war on the outside of our lives was often caused by the war on the inside. Conflict in our hearts spills over into the world and starts affecting our relationships and our entire life. The cause of the inner war, he said in a direct, blunt voice, was often because we did not get what we expected or wanted in our lives.

He had the congregation speak out loud, repeating after him, "I may be the problem." He continued and described how people become dissatisfied in life and particularly with God because they begin to feel that God was not coming through for them. The pastor stated, "You have not because you've asked not, or you are praying for the wrong things or with the wrong motives."

The pastor said, "There are some things in life only God can give you... and there are some things in life God may never give to you." Fear struck me. I may not get what I wanted? My heart began to sink. God may never give me? Oh, no, no, no, no, no.

After the service ended, I walked out to the Jeep, a bit numb, not quite knowing the meaning of the message I should take away from the sermon. Knowing in my heart there was something I was missing and so afraid the one thing I wanted most for God to bring into my life, was the one thing that might never be. That perhaps, Jeremie was not the one God had for me after all.

Wednesday, August 26, 2009

I really, really wanted to chicken out. Looming in front of me was the building where I had an appointment for a counseling session. It was the first of a series of six sessions that were free, paid through a benefit from my work. My boss suggested it since she knew I was about to go through a divorce and I reluctantly agreed. And here I was. The counselor invited me into her office, which was pleasant, as I was sure most counseling offices were... I already mentioned I wanted to chicken out, didn't I?

My hands were clenched together in my lap as I sat on the edge of the couch. The therapist noticed my apprehension and before she could question me about it, I chuckled with nervousness telling her this was my first session as an adult. My other experience with counseling was when I was in 5th grade, and my sister, who was a year younger than me, was in 4th grade. We argued and competed much of the time, so much so, our parents had us go to therapy to resolve the issues.

My sister and I loathed going. We came up with an idea a few sessions in and made a sisterly pact. Neither of us would speak. If we did not speak, then our mom wouldn't make us go anymore. She and I walked into the counselor's office that day, and neither of us spoke a single word. Tears streamed down both our faces, but we kept our pact so we would not have to ever go back.

The therapist asked me why I was there for a session, and I shared the story of my history in love relationships. Then, I went on to share how I believed my parents' divorce may have contributed to the decisions I'd made over the years. I told her that I needed to figure out how not to make all the same mistakes again, considering I was now 32 and about to get divorced for the second time.

A few insights came out of the initial session. One, my entire history in love and relationships was based on making concessions for the relationship itself, and I was never truly happy. She confirmed a contributing factor in all this was seeing my parents' unhappy marriage and asked if I could remember back to when I was young. She asked what I dreamed about and wanted in love and marriage.

"That's easy," I answered, "Prince Charming." She raised her eyebrow, but I continued. "I loved the story of Cinderella. The idea that my Prince Charming would ride into my life and think I was beautiful despite my flaws. He'd want to marry me and sweep me off my feet and then we'd live happily ever after."

Seeing the look on her face, I acknowledged, "But I know Prince Charming does not exist in the real world, and I've grown up now and know that's not possible."

She then disagreed as she said, "No, you've had two Prince Charmings."

Now it was my turn to raise my eyebrows. The therapist reminded me of my own story: my first husband rescued me from the chaos and pain of my parents' divorce and then my second husband rescued me when I fled from my first marriage.

I'd never thought about it that way before. Walking out of the first session, I had a smile on my face and felt gratitude warming my heart. It appeared as though God placed another guide on my path to help me figure out how to work through this life's baggage. As Sofie said, I was on the way to learning how to love myself, and then love the man of my dreams.

Friday, August 28, 2009

Today we filed the divorce paperwork. We did not go through attorneys because they cost money to retain, and we didn't have much. We split up the work to get it done. Paul went to the county law library and copied the forms and I filled them all in and attached everything else that needed to be filed.

While signing the documents my mind drifted to wondering what it was that I needed to change or do differently to love myself like Sofie said I needed to do. I must be missing something, somewhere. I sat down and began to journal, and ideas poured onto the pages:

Believe in myself: I am beautiful and deserve to have the love and happiness in my life that I want and not compromise for less; I can make the best choices and decisions for my life on my own. I should not feel guilt, pressure, stress, anxiety, sadness, depression, or otherwise upset about the comments and opinions of others (especially from family members). Their disappointment, expectations, views, and opinions are theirs. While they have a right to feel and express them, I do not have to internalize or accept them; I should not spend so much energy trying to make others happy. This is the energy I can use towards making myself happy.

I still felt like I was missing something big. Hopefully, I'd figure out what that was soon.

Tuesday, September 8, 2009

You will call out to me for help.
And I will answer you.
You will cry out. And I will say, "Here I am."
(Isaiah 58:9)

The last few nights during my prayers, the peace I normally felt when I heard the gentle voice of God dissipated. I did not know if it was God's voice I heard or something else. I felt like I heard someone in my thoughts tell me that Jeremie would contact me on Saturday. Then a more comforting voice told me if he did contact me Saturday, then I'd know I was hearing God's voice.

Saturday passed, and I did not hear anything at all. I was struggling—lots of crying, sobbing, and despair. I had an overwhelming need and desire to give up. I didn't think I'd ever been this close to giving up.

Every time I tried to pray, the turmoil rose again, and I sobbed. What did Saturday mean? Why did I hear it in my head? Did this mean it was not God's voice I heard? Then whose was it? What could I trust? Was God there with me? What if this was all a lie?

The thoughts swirled around, and I began to feel like a fool. It was getting harder to keep believing in this path and I doubted I could handle much more of this inner torment. I'd done everything asked of me. I'd come to God every day and listened to His voice and trusted His confirmations. Up until now, I'd believed God was with me. But now when I asked God to remove this from my mind and my heart and He did not, I questioned His presence. Where was God?

This was way beyond anything I could handle. The pain, the hurt, "Why God, why aren't You here now?"

"I am."

I wanted to give up and go back to the easy road. There was no answer. Nothing. No matter how many times I cried out to God.

It was as if everything I'd worked towards disappeared. I stood alone, divorce filed, no sign of Jeremie on the horizon, and God was not answering me. I couldn't do this!

I wanted the pain to go away, the floods were drowning me again. "God, please answer my prayers and confirm it's Your voice I hear. I can't do this alone. I can't…" I cried, "…God, please!" Did I make a huge mistake going down this path? Did God desert me although I was continuing to cry out to

Him?

In desperation, I asked Paul if he'd consider trying to work on things with me. He scoffed and said there was no going back, and that he knew deep down it was not what I wanted either.

I wept, crumpled on the floor, sobbing. Where was God?

Later in the day, I called Sofie. She heard the desperation in my voice and worked me into her schedule. When I went in, tears fell as I explained what led up to the state of despair I was in. She was peeved at me, to say the least. Especially when I told her that I wanted to give up and I believed God deserted me.

"God will never desert you!"

Thinking it over now as the anguish and confusion were clearing from my head, I replayed the sequence of what happened in my mind, and knew she was right. The one voice in my mind had said, "He'll contact you Saturday." In response, I'd prayed, "God, how do I know this is really you?" And God comforted me with, **"if it comes true it was me, if not, then you know it was not of me."** In the moment of it all happening I was too caught up in the desperation of wanting to hear from Jeremie, that I did not stop to realize the fact it did not come true meant it was not God. He did not desert me after all, and this was my first lesson in discernment.

❈ ❈ ❈

Finally, let the Lord make you strong.
Depend on his mighty power. Put on all of God's armor.
Then you can stand firm against the devil's evil plans.
So put on all of God's armor. Evil days will come.
But you will be able to stand up to anything.
And after you have done everything you can,
you will still be standing. So stand firm.
Put the belt of truth around your waist.
Put the armor of godliness on your chest.
Wear on your feet what will prepare you to tell the good news of peace.
Also, pick up the shield of faith.
With it, you can put out all of the flaming arrows of the evil one.
Put on the helmet of salvation. And take the sword of the Holy Spirit.
The sword is God's word.
At all times, pray by the power of the Spirit.
Pray all kinds of prayers.
Be watchful, so you can pray.

Always keep praying for all of God's people.
(Ephesians 6:10-11; 13-18)

Wednesday, September 9, 2009

I called the courthouse to check on the status of the divorce and found out the judge signed it as final, literally eight days after filing. From what I understood, going from filing to final divorce so quickly was a miracle in itself.

The evening's counseling session focused on the reasons why I withdrew from relationships. Why was it I didn't love fully with my entire heart or allow someone else to love me? Why had I chosen long-term relationships with men with whom I did not feel a spark?

My response to all the "why's" was easy. I was afraid if I gave my heart fully and loved someone with everything that I was, I'd eventually be rejected. Why though? It was simple. I was afraid I did not deserve love because... I was not perfect.

The more I tried to be perfect for my parents, friends, and significant others, the more I stumbled and fell because I wasn't being true to myself. Over the years, I'd blamed myself each time I made mistakes, and shamed myself for not taking a traditional road.

I'd never fit into the "mold," always walked, skipped, and forced my way with determination to get what I wanted in life differently than everyone else. Even as a woman, I did not fit in any mold. One of my friends joked that I was the epitome of an identity crisis because I was not a city girl, not a suburban girl, not a country girl, and not a corporate woman. I was kind of all of them but none of them. I was me, and I was not perfect.

But as the counselor explained, I could very well be perfect for someone else. Further, I knew God loved me even though I was not perfect. Maybe I was getting a little closer to this whole loving myself thing now.

Friday, September 11, 2009

During my appointment with Sofie today, God answered many of my recent prayers, although it happened in an unexpected way. We were chatting, and in the middle of sharing what had been going on, her countenance froze. She suddenly held out her hand, waving at me to stop talking.

"I'm getting a message for you." She stated as she looked off somewhere in the distance past my left shoulder.

Sofie's expression changed. She sat still in her chair; eyes transfixed on something in the distance. She remained motionless and then opened her mouth and began to channel a message, "Stop worrying about your friend, he is okay. He is becoming a changed being."

I nodded and thought to myself, "Okay, so I need to stop praying for God to show me that he is okay right now."

"Do not ever say you are weak," she conveyed.

I cringed and nodded, I needed to stop crying out to God, stating I was too weak to get through this.

"Now is not the time for your husband to move out. Treat him as if he were a roommate. Ignore him."

That answered my recent prayer asking whether I should try to get him to move out.

"You will receive a financial gift if you believe." I nodded again, okay, that answered another prayer.

"God knows what you want, and He is bringing him to you. He will cross your path when the time is right."

The messages continued, although I don't remember what the rest of them were. At the end, Sofie's countenance returned to normal. She said, "Thank you," to the spirit messenger and then looked at me.

A little in awe, I thanked Sofie and acknowledged it answered all my recent prayers. She pointed upwards as she said, "Don't thank me."

Held in the rapture of astonishment, I beamed. Never in my life had I experienced anything like that before. It was not made up; she literally channeled a messenger right in front of me. Answering all my recent questions and requests in prayers. God knows what I want? He would cross my path when the time was right? God was bringing him to me? Yes!

Friday, September 18, 2009

The emerald leaves cling tightly onto the lush trees.
Buried sprouts claw their way to the surface.
Petals allow hovering sunlight to penetrate and breach into their beauty.
Docile clouds roam the eternal skies at leisure.
Wings of the wild flap hurriedly, traveling home once again.
They dodge through the puffs,
restrained only by their weariness after a prolonged journey.

Tangled weeds hidden away by the sweet, fresh scents of honeysuckle and heather
guard their fields with pleasure.
Dandelions wave to the world, wishing all many memorable days.
Breezes twirl around, waltzing with exuberance and joy.
Wise trees, solid against the trembling weeds of ignorance.
the clouds chasing away the frightening schemes of the darkened hours.

Soon the image of creation breaks,
and winter remains strong.
She stands on the hilltop, drenched with the controlling forces of destiny.
Alone she stands, trying to fit pieces of the springtime long ago in her mind.
To no avail,
all that remains is a mound covered with mud and a fading memory,
taking her back through time.
(January 1992, age 14)

❋ ❋ ❋

Another stage of healing was beginning. Sofie began the session today with a new type of item in her hand. It was a wand that had crystals on both ends and some stones and crystals along the length. She'd mentioned this a while back, when the time was right we would pray together over my past, present, and future. I did not think it would be so soon and it was nice to know things were moving along.

Sofie rolled the wand into my hands and told me to hold onto it with both hands. She said to allow my arms to relax into my lap and advised she would be praying and may have to lay hands on me depending on what happened. I was supposed to sit and feel tingles from the energy in the wand. Before we were about to begin, she looked at me and got a serious look on her face, "Shannon, I have something I need to tell you."

Ugh, I thought to myself. Here it comes... Here it comes... Yep, okay now you're going to tell me that Jeremie was not the one God had for me and he was not going to be at the end of all this healing and work we were doing, but I didn't say a word out loud.

Sofie paused, and after a few short moments said, "Your greatest fear is you will not end up with Jeremie." I looked at her and pursed my lips in a slight scowl. She went on to say I must believe, I must have faith, and I must stay positive. She then sat back in her chair and watched my aura change. Whatever we were removing was draining into the wand. If it was possible to feel the energy flowing between my hands and the wand, I think I felt it in slight tingles that ran up my arms from my hands.

She then prayed over me and my past. At first, I thought she was praying over the last part of my life, but I quickly realized she was praying to remove all oaths, curses, bindings, and anything else remnant to past lives. At one point, she mentioned one of my past lives "chose" what had happened in this lifetime. It was similar to what I would pray to God in Jesus' name, and she prayed against evil and all the same types of things I would have, so I was comfortable.

Sunday, September 27, 2009

The morning was drippy drizzle and gray skies as far as I could see, but I did not feel that way inside—I felt anticipation. Something was about to happen. God placed on my heart recently during prayer, "**Sooner than you realize all your dreams will come true.**"

The focus of the sermon at church reminded us to pray at all times whether we were in trouble or troubled in mind and heart. The pastor preached for us to change "why's" to "what's," such as, "What do You want me to learn from this? What are You trying to tell me? What do You want me to do?"

I remained seated as some members of the congregation went to the altar to pray at the end of the service. I had never had more faith in anything in my entire life. I felt Jeremie coming back into my life was imminent. I mean, after all, God placed on my heart, "**Sooner than I think all my dreams were coming true,**" right? That was what that had to mean. He was my dream come true.

Sofie was sitting beside me and saw me getting emotional. She nodded and said, "You're good." I nodded back and said I knew it was close and I was not sad. She smiled and said she could see "it" in my aura energy.

This was where I messed up. I thought she meant Jeremie. I assumed she saw him arriving back in my life. I'd already convinced myself he was going to arrive without contacting me first. It was my constant daydream. One day I'd come home from work, get out of my car and see him walking up the driveway.

Now I was even more excited because she saw "it" around me. I hugged her and gushed, "I have a feeling I'll have good news to share with you when I see you on Tuesday. I think I'll hear from him." I beamed.

Sofie looked a little startled at me, but I did not think anything else of it as I waved goodbye and walked out to the Jeep. As I drove home, I was convinced that I was going to hear from or see him imminently. I recounted all my evidence. One, there would be a meeting with him "by" my trip to California. Two, he would cross MY path when the time is right. Three, sooner than I realize all my dreams were coming true. Now, to top it all off, four, Sofie saw "it" around me.

Monday, September 28, 2009

When will I learn? I saw Sofie for a session, a day earlier than planned. My thoughts had carried me away again and I drew false conclusions based on my assumptions and theories. I convinced myself I knew exactly what was happening when I didn't have a clue.

Sofie spoke at length, reprimanding me. What she saw around me was my healing—being healed and ready, not Jeremie back in my life. I misinterpreted pretty much everything and ran off with my wild ideas.

She said I needed to listen slowly and be slower to speak, that storms were coming, and I needed to spread my wings like an eagle and soar through them. Sofie emphasized I needed to cry out to God and go to Him in prayer and act in faith with patience. She reminded me to forget the past and give up my future completely in trust to God.

"Most important of all of these," Sofie stressed, "You need to humble yourself and respect God."

Respect God? I did... didn't I?

Didn't I?

Tuesday, September 29, 2009

Doubt consumed me more and more. It had always been in the back of my mind, the little nagging voice that said, "You won't be with him at the end of all this." I was struggling. How did I know what God was doing and what His plans were? If I was supposed to "believe" He was doing it for me, how could I not then be disappointed when it didn't happen? Ugh, I confused myself even more.

How long do I not pursue other potential mates if Jeremie didn't come around? At what point do I realize we may not be meant to be together at all? I was supposed to hold fast and believe—soar with my faith through the storms—but how long should I continue before moving on?

I felt like I was a rat in a maze who was repeatedly beating my head into a wall. I'd tried going down so many corridors already that at this point, I just wanted to bust open a wall to get to the end. I was so frustrated and could not figure my way out! I was confused and doubting, afraid I would get to the end and realize that there was nothing. All the while I'd had faith in what God was doing, for nothing.

God was with me. I knew He'd never desert me (that was a previous lesson), but I felt like I was not doing anything right. I kept stumbling and falling and every time I got up, I'd fall again.

The Bible said God wouldn't give me anything I could not handle. I was trying to spread my wings and soar, but I still needed help. I needed God to lift me up and help me learn how to spread my wings. If Jeremie was not coming back into my life soon, then what did it mean when I felt God tell me sooner than I realized my dreams would be coming true?

❀　❀　❀

When you cry out to the Lord for help he will show you his favor.
As soon as he hears you, he'll answer you...
You will hear your Teacher's voice behind you.
You will hear it whether you turn to the right or the left.
It will say, "Here is the path I want you to take. So walk on it."
(Isaiah 30:19-21)

Wednesday, September 30, 2009

The lesson from God cumulated in a powerful love pat while reading the Bible tonight. I finished the last book I was reading and felt in my heart to turn to the book of Job. I remembered the pastor at church mentioning something about it being a story about patience. I could not remember much about Job or his story, so when I felt it on my heart to turn to the pages I figured it would speak about being patient. Wow was I ever wrong about what God wanted me to hear. These were the verses I felt God leading me to journal in contemplation. They summed up where I'd gone completely wrong...

Aren't God's words of comfort enough for you?
He speaks them to you gently.
Why have you let your wild ideas carry you away?
(Job 15:11-12)

The Lord spoke to Job out of a storm.
He said, "Who do you think you are to disagree with my plans?
You do not know what you are talking about."
(Job 38:1-2)

I had myself convinced Jeremie was going to be back in my life "any day now." In this, I was... not respecting God. As the realizations poured over me, I cringed in shame. Even though I'd tried not to analyze, I continued to concoct scenarios based on the little I knew about what was going on. I thought I'd given it all over to God and believed that I respected God's will and greater plan, but I guess I hadn't.

Continuing to read, I finished all of Job and started in Isaiah. The lessons were unrelenting. More about respect (Isaiah 5:12-13) and patience (Isaiah 5:19). Ugh, I cringed again. I'd been disrespectful and I did not realize it. Not a good feeling, especially when all this was so important in my life.

Bowing my head, I prayed, "Dear God, in Jesus' name, I thank you for speaking to me and training through your Word. I do release all plans to you. I believe you are beginning to pour out wonderful blessings. I will surely stumble again, but your Word helps guide me." Then I asked God what more I needed to do before Jeremie came back into my life and on my heart was,

"Do what you can while you're patiently waiting for the Lord to act."

More patience. This was perhaps going to be the biggest lesson of them all.

Thursday, October 8, 2009

During my session with Sofie today she had quite a bit to say to me. She advised I'd been in the "being pruned stage" so that soon my life would bear the fruit of God and Jeremie was taken away because I was going to use him as a crutch, but he would be brought back, and it would be even better. She reminded me again that I needed to praise and thank God even if I had not received it yet and pray as though I've already received, such as saying, "my husband."

She acknowledged how evil would continue to try to trap and knock me from God's path and reiterated that I must stay strong in my faith and turn to God's Word. It was recurring in her messages to live God's Word and turn to it frequently. Towards the end of the session, she smiled and said, "God has big plans for your future."

Sofie's messages were confirmations of what I was already doing until she gave me an example of how Satan might try to trap me. Like, if I left for California and still had not heard from Jeremie yet. I froze. This was the first time in months I'd even considered that as a possibility. It had not occurred to me there'd be any chance he wouldn't have already contacted me before my planned trip because Sofie told me that he would cross my path by then and I believed her.

I tried to explain this, to which Sofie replied, "Then why are you letting it trap you?" Yeah, she put me in my place again. I should have known.

Sofie acknowledged she had worked on communication between us but Jeremie's girlfriend was binding him to her more strongly with other spells. Then she affirmed that she intended to find out what was going on, who was casting them, and why they hadn't come off for good.

Sunday, November 8, 2009

The church worship band and singers led the congregation as the service started and I sang along. Reflecting sunlight off something outside shone through the outer church door and across a hallway, and through a little window on the inner church door at the front of the church. The light suddenly flashed directly in my face, causing me to squint.

I traced the light with my eyes to see where it was coming from and amazement held me. Here I was standing on the far opposite end of the sanctuary in one of the back pews and not one person's body or head blocked the light from shining on me. Awe coursed through my body and I felt God's presence embrace me,

"My Glory."

Remembering that I'd asked God in prayer yesterday to show me His glory, my astonishment deepened in the realization my prayer was being answered miraculously.

In the presence of God's warmth around me, I felt like a betrothed daughter being groomed for her wedding. God placed within my heart that a new life was about to begin, and I should prepare to receive the happiness that was coming. It felt as though God was telling me that my life was changing forever.

Tuesday, November 10, 2009

The day I planned to leave for my trip cross-country, Friday, November 13th, crept closer on the calendar and I'd held out hope I might hear from Jeremie before then. But today I canceled my trip because of what happened. I was supposed to call Sofie and kept putting it off until leaving work. I still almost did not call her, but something inside me kept nagging while I was walking out to the Jeep in the parking lot. She said she needed to see me; it sounded urgent and I really did not want to go.

As I sat in the chair in her shop, Sofie told me what I didn't want to hear. I would not hear from Jeremie by Friday, and furthermore, I should not by any means go to California right now, period.

The reason?

She explained that she saw one of my friends reconnected her friendship with Jeremie's girlfriend. As she said this, I immediately knew who she was referring to, and everything started falling into place.

That friend had recently unfriended me on Facebook, and I reached out to ask why. She said she felt so in the middle between the girlfriend and me that she could not do it anymore. It was confusing at the time because the last I had heard she loathed his girlfriend, and they were no longer friends.

Then I recalled all that I'd shared with her about my walk with God and how I believed God was bringing him back into my life. All of that may have gone right back to his girlfriend. UGH! Sofie was right, I shouldn't have told anyone.

Sofie also mentioned there were still too many connections and ties and it was time to get Paul moved out of the house. I nodded with numbness in my heart. I was not sure of how I would make it on my salary alone, but I believed what she said about needing to break all connections.

Even though it was hard to see, this might be part of the happiness that God had for my future. Finance-wise it would be tough, but I knew God was with me and would bless me. I needed to keep walking in faith.

INTO THE FIRE

…A TEST OF FAITH IN THE CRUCIBLE LIKE DANIEL (3:1-30).

Friday, November 20, 2009

Paul moved out about a week ago and I was feeling in my heart that I should still go to California. It was getting stronger each day. My heart sensed that God had a new life for me on the horizon and it had something to do with me driving cross-country. I prayed for confirmations of whether God wanted me to go and I realized maybe… just maybe… I was receiving them.

Last night I got up to let Sadie out into the backyard. As I walked back in my ears caught part of a commercial, "Come to California!" It was a California tourism commercial on television. I paused and spoke to God, "Okay, but that could be a coincidence." If I was supposed to go, I needed another confirmation.

Then during lunch at work today I went out to run an errand and saw a car with a California license plate pass me on Route 1 and paused in wonderment again. The third confirmation came when I was shopping and I heard someone from across the store say the words, "cross county."

As with other miraculous signs and confirmations, I was not convinced these weren't just my imagination. Maybe they meant something different than what I thought they meant, especially since my conversation with Sofie was not to drive to California at all. Not feeling like I could decide on my own, I called and left her a voicemail asking if she thought it would be okay to go now.

Faith was harder to hold onto as the days kept progressing onward. I'd done everything I believed God wanted me to do. He had to have something great prepared for me, right? Something that would bring me so much more happiness than I could ever dream of, so I asked God again, "Where is it?"

"Wait for the Lord"

"No, seriously, where is it, God?"

"**Coming.**"

I was afraid my hope wouldn't hold out long enough. This was one of the hardest experiences I'd gone through in my entire life and even though I was stronger in faith, I still felt like crawling into a hole and waving a white flag. But I did not. Just like I did not go to California when I first planned to go. I trusted in God. I'd given everything to Him and must believe He was making all my dreams come true. I must continue holding on until that happens.

Tuesday, November 24, 2009

I really might go to California. I got a voicemail back from Sofie this morning. She said, by all means, go to see my family, to enjoy it, and that I deserved to take the trip. She relayed that nothing had changed yet as far as Jeremie was concerned, but it didn't mean it would not. It was a much different response than the last time I saw her when she told me not to go at all.

My mind doubted again, questioning whether it was or was not God's will for me to go. "But maybe," I thought, "he was supposed to 'cross my path' in California—not in New Jersey." Maybe the three confirmations, "Come to California, driving, and cross-country," were not just coincidences.

Not trusting myself, I cried out to God again asking for a crystal-clear confirmation either way. I told God that if I was to go, I'd prepare and head out on the road as soon as I got the final confirmation. Then, I waited for an answer. I could not make this decision on my own! This was up to God.

Wednesday, November 25, 2009

I decided to fast from eating until God answered my prayer. This meant everything, and I wanted to show God that I was humbling myself and surrendering to whatever His will was for me. During the day, I also did something I had never done before. I posted a spiritual-related status on Facebook asking my friends to pray that God would reveal His will and path because I had a decision to make.

Never did I imagine the answer to my prayer would come quickly. A few short moments later one of my friends from college responded to my post, he wrote, "Isn't that where faith comes in? Make the decision and have faith that you've already been given the wisdom to make the best choice. Even if it is not the most optimal decision… God has the power to make ANY decision work out right."

There was no possible way my friend could have known how perfect his comment fit and that it answered my prayer completely. It was time for me to walk the path laid in front of me in faith.

"Do you believe I can do this?"

"Yes, God, I do," I replied.

"Go."

So, guess what? I was heading to California. I have to admit, I was excited. No matter what happened, I knew in my heart I was obeying and I would continue to do exactly what God wanted me to do.

Later in the evening, the Jeep was packed, and Sadie was ecstatic and road-trip happy. I had no idea what the next two weeks held, but we were off.

Saturday, November 28, 2009

Around 6:00 in the morning, I crossed the state line into California. As I entered and saw the "Welcome to California" road sign tears sprung from the corners of my eyes as I thought again about how my full trust was in God. I had faith that all would go according to His plan. I believed God was giving all my dreams back to me—and that's why I was here. Even if I could not see it yet or figure out how it would happen.

With about an hour left to go until I reached Concord, I received a surprise phone call from Sofie asking where I was. I told her California and asked if she had any good news. She said yes, the binding ties within my household severed after Paul moved out of the house. I thanked her for that good news and then I asked if she could see whether or not I would cross paths with Jeremie. Sofie replied that it was something she was going to work on. I thanked her and hung up, taken aback.

Hold up. Wait. Why was I here? Why did I drive 3000 miles if this wasn't a given? Why did Sofie have to work on it? I didn't understand. I believed God was giving me a new life on this trip. Now there was a huge possibility he was not ready yet? Then what was the new life from God? Why was I here? My thoughts were troubled in the last hour towards Concord, I cried out as I drove over the Benicia Bridge, "God, why am I here?"

"Trust me."

The storm of questions inside persisted after I arrived in Concord. My mom thought I was upset because of a lack of sleep and driving 3000 miles on my own in less than three days but that was not it. I had this whole dream of a new life from God on this trip, and there was now the very real possibility nothing would happen. I was so almost completely done. I'd been patient, obeyed, listened, and prayed and still had not seen what God promised me.

I just wanted to go back home—where I had my own routine all by myself. Alone but at least it was not stepping out in faith 3000 miles cross country to then find out something still needed to be "worked" on. It was easier living with the delusion of my daydreams and not wasting vacation days and money drained to go on a wild faith chase.

"Give it time."

Fine, I'll give it a "little time" as I kept hearing God tell me in my head, but I didn't know how long I would be able to hold on.

Monday, November 30, 2009

If I questioned why I was here a few days ago, by today the feeling more than quadrupled. I came to California because I believed God wanted me to be here, not because I wanted to go. There was much more to lose by stepping in faith than staying at home and waiting. The biggest? My belief in Sophie's wisdom as "God's tool" as she called it. If Jeremie did not cross my path "by" my trip to California, then Sofie's prediction did not come true and she was not God's servant after all.

If this was the case, it would call into question all the work I'd done with her, and I made the decision not to continue sessions if her prediction did not come to pass the way she said it would. I could not in good faith continue because I trusted God's words from the Bible in Isaiah 44:26, *"I make the words of my servants the prophets come true. I carry out what my messengers say will happen."*

It would have been much easier to stay at home until I heard from Jeremie rather than put all the work I had done with Sofie on the line. But now, that I'd taken this step, I was teetering on a potentially ungodly path.

Beyond Sofie, I was also realizing trust in my walk with God over the last four months would crumble. I called out to God again and again for Him to reveal His will and show me the path or release me. God knew how much I could handle and so He knew I was at the breaking point. The brink of lost hope. At the point of giving up. Genuinely... giving up.

I came to California with one purpose: to follow God's path for me. Before I left, I told God to throw up blocks and close doors if He did not want me going and I left with ease. With renewed determination, I demanded in prayer, "God, it is time. I followed you to California. I obeyed. Show me Your will or release me!"

"I am not releasing you."

"Show me or release me!"

Later in the evening, I felt sleepy and went up to lie down. Sofie's presence entered my thoughts. I remember babbling at her for a bit but did not recall what I said. At one point, she stopped me and said, "Now let me get to work." And this part I remembered vividly; this was what followed...

I projected in my thoughts, "I love you, Jeremie."

There was surprise, kind of like a "Huh? What, is that you?" I repeated, "I love you, Jeremie."

"I love you too, Shannon."

"Call me, contact me, I'm here. I'm in California." I sensed surprise from him again. "I came to start our lives together."

"I want that." He replied.

"Contact me, I love you."

He responded in my thoughts, "I love you more than you will ever know."

"Contact me, I'm here. I'm ready for you."

He answered, "I'm ready too."

Sleep was restless overnight, why was he surprised to hear me say that I loved him? Did he think I gave up? Moved on? Maybe he gave up...? At least I knew we were a step further now... and something... maybe something was happening.

Friday, December 4, 2009

I have put my hope in your word.
My eyes grow tired looking for what you have promised.
I say, "When will you comfort me?"
I'm as useless as a wineskin that smoke has dried up.
But I don't forget to follow your orders.
How long do I have to wait?"
(Psalm 119:81-84)

❊ ❊ ❊

Seven days later and I was still waiting. I finally asked God in exasperation, "If I'm ready, and if he is ready, why hasn't anything happened yet? Why haven't

I heard from him?"

"You won't compromise, Shannon."

I gasped, "What?"

I went back to read through my journaling and smacked my forehead when I realized what I previously overlooked. Months ago I literally journaled, "*And no God, I won't compromise. He has to leave his girlfriend before contacting me.*" Furthermore, I won't even begin to recite all the dates where I wrote, "*He has to contact me first!*" Ughhhh, why do I do this to myself? It sure seemed like MY will blocking God's will.

Immediately I prayed and asked for forgiveness, affirming I only wanted God's will in my life. How could His glory shine unless I submit everything over to Him? And to think… for weeks I thought I'd already released it all to God.

Sunday, December 6, 2009

As I sat upstairs on the guest bed trying to pray, I felt an onslaught of attacks on my thoughts. The only I could describe the sensation was that every fear and doubt in my head over the last few days was mind-blasting me in a raging storm.

"You blew it, you blew it!" "I'm so mad at you!" "Give up, you already said you were giving up!" "You blew it, Shannon! You should go home!" "I'm so mad at you! I'm so mad at you!"

Among the voices, I heard someone who identified herself as Sofie, and she was the main voice scolding me although I heard more than one swirling in my thoughts: "You blew it, you blew it!" "Give up, you already said you were giving up!" "You blew it, Shannon! You should go home!"

The torment strengthened, "YOU BLEW IT!" GIVE UP!" again and again striking louder each time. I could not continue praying because the voices blasted through any concentration I was trying to maintain.

"I did not blow it!" I responded to the voices in my head while holding my head between my hands in agony, and continued, "To all spirits, including the evil and unholy spirits attacking my mind right now, I am not giving up. I did not blow it! I believe and have faith in God! You do not have any authority over me! I am putting on God's armor! The belt of Truth, the chest piece of godliness, the boots to share the good news of peace, the helmet of salvation, the sword of the Word. I am holding up the shield of faith against you to block all fiery darts you are attempting to torment me with. I am not giving up. DO YOU HEAR ME? I am not giving up! I AM NOT GIVING UP! The Lord rebuke all unholy spirits attacking me right now in Jesus' name!"

The storm dissipated into a single voice who said, "Good, good. You are ready."

I asked, "What am I ready for?"

"You've taken your stand in the spiritual realm. It is time for you to claim him as yours in the physical realm. It is time for you to go find him."

Then other voices came back in, one said, "A little over the top, but she took her stand."

Another crooned sarcastically, "Aww, did you hear her? How cute, she put on God's armor."

The voices faded, and I sat on the bed drained of energy. I called out to God to continue working His will. My sole reason for being in California was to follow His path and I needed God to make it clear what I was supposed to do next.

Monday, December 7, 2009

Today it was on my mind even more to act, I could not decide on my own. With reluctance in my heart, I called Sofie and explained bits and pieces of what happened and asked for guidance. Sofie told me Jeremie's girlfriend was still doing everything within her power to keep him bound to her. She described how it could be witchcraft, binding spells, brainwashing, or even seduction and advised me to find a way to reach out to him somehow and at least reaffirm that I loved him and was waiting.

She reminded me that even though we talked telepathically a week ago, his conscious mind did not know and at this point, the bindings were so strong I should not be disappointed if he was abrasive when I was able to get a hold of him. His spirit was ready, but his mind was still bound strongly to his girlfriend.

I explained my concerns to Sofie, I was waiting because I did not want to act and place my will in an outcome. Sofie repeated what my friend on Facebook had said, reminding me the outcome was still in God's hands and if I was operating in faith that this was what God wanted me to do, the results of my actions were still up to God's will.

Since I did not have a phone number other than their house landline my options were limited to try to reach out to him. When the idea of me driving to find him in his hometown came up in our discussion, firmly, Sofie said, "No, don't go."

During the evening, conflicting decisions struggled against each other in my thoughts. I was not certain where God was directing my path and was not sure where I would head when I left my mom's house the next day.

Part of me felt like I needed to head north to see if God had something for me there, but Sofie told me not to go. I knew I could not do this based on my own decision or on what I felt—because if went it might spark a whole chain of events such as Jeremie's girlfriend seeing me and all hell would break loose. But then again, I reminded myself, God was in control.

"Go."

It was the same soft, "Go" as I heard in my thoughts when I was praying in the final moments of deciding whether to drive cross country at all. "Go find him, God?"

"Go."

I continued praying, "God if I'm not supposed to go close the doors, shut every single one of them so I cannot head north. But shine a light on the path you want me on, I will go if it is Your will." I would leave the next day on I-80 and either take the split up to Northern California or continue east towards home. When I settled into sleep I had no clue which way the Jeep would be headed in the morning.

Tuesday, December 8, 2009

When I woke up I discovered the roads to the east on I-80 were closed due to a severe winter storm. I could not drive home, but the way north was clear. The road conditions and weather forecast determined it; God closed doors as I asked.

Sadie was road-trip happy again with her big head and front paws next to me on the middle console of the Jeep as I pulled out of my mom's driveway. I knew I was following where God wanted me to go in faith. There was no fear. No doubt. No dread. No joy. No excitement. No anticipation. I sensed only peace within. I was obeying God and no matter what happened or how events unfolded, I knew God was with me.

In the late morning, I felt someone in my thoughts, "It's Sofie, checking in with you, where are you?"

I replied I was on my way to Jeremie's hometown.

The voice in my thoughts responded that she did not think I was going to go, and I answered that I believed God was directing my path there and I was following His will. The voice replied she'd continue checking in with me during the day and dissipated from my thoughts.

There were times when I knew for sure it was Sofie speaking to me in my mind; times when I knew for sure God was speaking to me. This was one of the other times when I was not sure whether I was making up the entire conversation in my head.

I decided to call Sofie to talk with her in person to make sure she knew. I mean, after all, she previously told me decisively not to go. I called and left a voicemail, explaining in detail that I was already on the way north, and asked her to call back if she thought there was any reason why I should turn around.

Later in the day, I made it to Jeremie's hometown, and I found myself exactly where I didn't want to be and doing what I didn't want to do. I drove to his home and saw two cars parked in the driveway, so I parked on a nearby side street to observe the area.

The home was in a small residential area with a couple of narrow streets that appeared to lead in and loop around, and I saw industrial buildings lining the main highway. Sighing, I rolled my eyes at my current situation. Sadie (currently, Ms. Growly Pants) and I were oh-so-very conspicuous in my Jeep Wrangler with out of state license plates.

I prayed again, "God, am I supposed to be here?"

"Yes."

Oh, and the other answer was… **"Patience."**

I wondered what to do next because none of this was preplanned and decided that I would find a hotel to stay in overnight and then I'd come back over in the morning. I could only trust this was God's will, and there would be enough time for whatever was supposed to happen.

Around 9 PM I got checked into a hotel room in the local area and began to get organized for the night. As I was carrying Sadie's water bowl to fill it up in the sink I felt Sofie's voice on my thoughts, "Hello dear, checking in with you. Where are you?"

I responded, "Near their town, I went to his house, but it looks like they are in for the night. I'm going to go back in the morning although I'm not sure what I'm supposed to do."

"Oh, good, good," she replied in my thoughts.

"I am still giving this up to God's will, and I know Jeremie will cross my path if the timing is right."

"Good… good, well…" The voice paused, "…good luck!" And the presence left my thoughts.

I froze where I stood, paralyzed in terror. Sadie's water bowl shook in my hand that had started trembling. I inhaled sharply in realization, the spirit presence and the voice I heard were not Sofie! Sofie did not say good luck, she always said, "God bless you."

"No, it was not Sofie, but it is too late for them now. There's nothing they can do about it."

The comfort from God eased my alarm and my fear dissipated. The fact that someone was impersonating Sofie in my head faded out of my thoughts as I settled in for the night. I did not think further about what God's words meant or what may happen the next day. All I knew was that the morning would come soon enough, and God's will would be done. After praying, I opened my Bible, and this was the verse God gave to me from where I'd left the bookmarked page from yesterday...

> *Those who go out sobbing as they carry seeds to plant*
> *will come back singing with joy.*
> *They will bring the new crop back with them.*
> (Psalm 125:6)

Wednesday, December 9, 2009

After tossing and turning all night, I got up around 6 AM and wondered if I'd slept at all. I decided to head out and over to near Jeremie's home, although I was still unsure of what God wanted me to do. I yawned as I parked in the small lot in front of the industrial building I'd seen the night before. It was parallel to the main road and from what I could tell, at the only cross-street anyone coming from the residential area would use to turn onto the highway.

I had no idea what to expect and noticed some butterflies in my stomach although I still felt mostly peaceful inside and I petitioned, "Please God if it is Your will, let me see Jeremie."

"It is yours."

7:15 AM

His girlfriend saw me. Instead of staying in the small parking lot, I decided to drive a loop around their neighborhood streets. When I was passing their home, she was standing on the porch. I averted my eyes and looked straight forward, forcing my face to be expressionless. I knew she must have looked at the Jeep. Must have looked at the plates. I was pretty certain she even had enough time to look at me. Could I just say #%@!&. This was the one thing I was afraid would happen, that she would see me and know I was here.

"You have to trust me. He will cross your path."

Yeah. I guess that means I should not move, I should have stayed put. Ugh, I so screwed up.

"I am in control. I let it happen. Trust me. Shannon, you must trust me."

Okay, I planned to stay in the lot near the highway, out of view of their home and I would wait for God to have him cross my path if it was His will. It seriously felt surreal. Thinking back, I realized that as I started driving around the loop, I felt God tell me, **"You don't have to, he will cross your path."** But God did not stop me.

I did not feel a gut, "NO! STOP! Don't go that way," like I remembered when back a few months ago while driving up in the Niagara Falls area when I was going to make a left turn, hesitated with the feeling of "Stop!" but then continued forward and got hit in a minor car accident.

God let it happen... of that I was certain. Did she need to know I was here? Was this to create an opening or initiate a chain of events? Did I mention this was totally surreal? I now had no doubt he would cross my path.

8:30 AM

Sadie was asleep in the back as I surveyed the area around me again, I was about 20 feet off the cross-street and parallel about 50 feet from the main road. As I sat with the engine idling I realized the occupants of almost every vehicle passing were looking at the Jeep. So, when I thought that a woman and her St. Bernard, in a Wrangler with out of state plates would not be inconspicuous, I guess I was right.

A few minutes later out of my peripheral eyesight, I noticed a car approaching from the left. It was Jeremie's car! He was driving and his girlfriend was in the passenger seat. I noticed the look on Jeremie's face seemed pensive at first as he gazed at the license plate of the Jeep for a long time, and then glanced up at me with his jaw dropped before looking back to the road again.

As they neared the corner to turn onto the main road, I heard a voice in my mind say, "Follow," and I knew that was what I had to do. I noticed his girlfriend craning her neck around as they neared the turn.

They turned the corner, and I shifted into drive and turned to follow their car. With the jolt and turn, Sadie lifted her head from where she was peacefully sleeping in the back but then dozed off again as I got up to speed. I stayed back at a distance because honestly, I wasn't too sure why I was following or what would happen when we arrived at a destination.

I powerfully cried out to God in prayer, "God, in Jesus' name, let Your will be done! I am here because You led my path here. This is not my will this is Yours. No matter what happens, no matter what changes in my life. Let Your will be done. You are in control; You can do anything You want to do. Keep me in the place You want me. No matter what happens, I trust in You and Your plans. My entire life is in Your hands, my God!"

A light turned red ahead, and I pulled in behind them. I saw Jeremie look back through his rearview mirror, but when our eyes met, he just as quickly looked away. After a slight left turn onto another street, I heard the voice say, "Do not follow them. He will be where you see them pull in later today."

Nodding, I agreed with what I heard, and immediately I noticed Jeremie began slowing their car. He looked up at me through his rearview mirror and held my eyes in a locked gaze. His eyes were wide and intense, holding mine until the second he turned the car left onto the driveway. I got the feeling he was warning me.

Seeing a sign that it was a municipal center, I continued driving down the street beyond where they turned in. I was startled by the sudden intensity of his eyes and I did not know what he was trying to communicate. The voice spoke again, "She'll have to leave him alone because she needs to do selfish things."

"Well, I guess that's the opening I'm waiting for?"

The voice exclaimed, "We will be victorious!"

I shook my head and responded, "No, God, my Almighty Father. You are victorious! It is You who is all-powerful and in control. This isn't me, there is no we, it is You!"

Hmmm. What now? I wondered as a tapped my fingers against the steering wheel observing the suburban area around me, "What should I do now, should I go back to the driveway?" The voice said it did not matter they were gone, but he would be there later.

As I questioned what to do next, I realized now that she knew I was in town, she and her family were going to be looking for me. My memory recalled what Sofie mentioned when we were talking about whether there was anyone in his family I could contact to reach him. She'd said, "Word travels fast in families."

"Do not go back to their house."

Okay yeah, I wasn't going back there. But where am I going to go?

"Do not go back to the hotel; they will be looking for you there."

Okay, that left one possibility, north. I drove out of the town and continued farther north to the next town.

10:49 AM
I'm not sure where I was, somewhere north a few towns up in a shopping center parking lot.

"They are looking for you."

Yeah, I figured that much. I was not even going to try to figure out how the rest would turn out; I was still in awe at all that had happened so far. Sophie's prediction from a few months ago seemingly came true, he crossed my path. I wondered what would be next.

1:00 PM
My throat was a little scratchy and I found a coffee drive-through and ordered a green tea latte. I'd never tried one before and it sounded good. The barista held out the drink and I went to take it from her with one hand while trying to hold back a protective Sadie with my other hand. I squeezed the cup just a little too hard, and brightly-colored green tea latte splattered everywhere on my jeans. Ugh! I so don't want to see Jeremie with green splotches!

"It's okay, go back to your room and clean them. Feed Sadie. Get gas."

Really? I trusted God so I agreed and drove back south to the hotel, cleaned my jeans, fed Sadie, grabbed a couple of things, and headed back out into the Jeep. I had about a quarter of a tank of gas left and stopped at a gas station near the hotel to fill up.

3:30 PM
Later in the afternoon, I was leaning back in the driver's seat, singing along to songs on my iPod, and Sadie was asleep in the back. We were hanging out and waiting until I knew what to do next.

Suddenly, I heard the voice say, "Time to go! Time to go find him where you saw him pull in this morning!"

Sitting up in the driver's seat, I prayed, "Shut the door if this isn't what I am supposed to do. I will proceed but God shut this door if I'm not supposed to go there. Let Your will be done, my God."

"I am with you," spoke a soft voice.

As I pulled out onto the streets I questioned which way I should go. The highway would be faster but would put me closer to their house.

"It does not matter, they aren't there anyway," the voice replied in my thoughts then it spoke again, "Shannon, you are about to receive the happiness that I have for your future. This is what I have for you, your dreams, your new life."

Praising, I replied, "Thank you, God, You are so great my God, You are the one true God, the only One who could do this. Thank You so much. I've waited so long for this."

"No, thank you," the voice said.

Pausing, I shook my head. "No, my Almighty Father. It is You. This is what You have done. Thank You!"

"No, thank you, Shannon."

I paused again. "No, God, thank You."

"No, thank YOU, Shannon."

Pausing longer, I began to realize something was not right.

"Trust me. I am with you." A soft voice spoke to me again.

As I continued driving down the highway, the voice exclaimed with glee, "We are victorious!"

Immediately I cried out, "No, no my God. You are victorious. This is not me, there is no we. You are in control. You can do anything. This is Your will for my life, not mine. This is Your glory, this is Your power, this is not of me."

The voice responded, "No, Shannon, it IS you. You are obeying me."

I froze inside. Something definitely did not feel right.

"Trust me. I am with you. I will not let you fall." The soft voice spoke again.

Continuing on the highway, I was navigating back to the location by memory. Although I had not looked at street names on my way there in the morning, I was normally good at finding my way by photographic memory when I'd been somewhere once. I passed a downtown area and saw a campus that did not look familiar.

The voice exclaimed, "Hurry, Shannon, Hurry!"

"This does not look right," I responded, looking around at my surroundings with the realization I must have missed a turn-off somewhere.

Crawling along in the traffic with pedestrians all around, Sadie stood up in the back barking and growling at all the people around us. It was not the right street; we did not pass by this in the morning. My gut tensed as I realized I definitely must have overshot a turn and I became confused. How did I miss it? Where was it? Did I not remember how to get back there?

"Hurry, hurry he's going to leave!" The voice exclaimed over and over again in my thoughts.

"God, I'm trying, please show me where to go!" I cried out loud.

"It's okay, Shannon, trust me." Came the comforting reply.

The voice persisted again and again, "Hurry! Hurry! Hurry!"

"God, help me!" I looked at the buildings all around me and did not recognize where I was at all.

"It's okay, Shannon, trust me. I am with you."

After a few more minutes driving with the traffic through the congested streets, I turned right onto a side road and pulled over to the curb. As I did this, immediately, a single word permeated my entire senses and consciousness. **BLOCKED!**

My insides tensed again, "What? What did I do? What did I do wrong? What was blocked?"

"It's okay Shannon. They are gone now. Go back to where you saw them pull in this morning."

Still thinking I somehow screwed up and not understanding what happened, I pulled up the GPS on my iPhone and saw I'd missed a left turn by more than three miles.

I headed in the right direction and arrived, turning into the municipal center parking lot a few minutes before 4:30 PM. I chose a parking spot about three rows back from the street towards the entrance of a utility depot and noticed there was another parking lot off to the side behind a fence with parked police cars. There must be a police station somewhere nearby.

I was uncertain what I was waiting for at this point. I asked God, "Is this the place?"

"Yes, stay. Do not move from the spot you are parked in."

I must stay. Wow, I hadn't seen that coming either.

"Do not get discouraged. There will be time for everything. You will be at work on Monday."

The reassurance was good, but I had a feeling it was going to be a long evening in the Jeep and part of me still thought Jeremie was going to meet me there. For comfort I turned my Bible to Psalm 23 and read:

The Lord is my shepherd. He gives me everything I need.
He lets me lie down in fields of green grass.
He leads me beside quiet waters.
He gives me new strength.
He guides me in the right paths for the honor of his name.
Even though I walk through the darkest valley I will not be afraid you are with me.
Your shepherd's rod and staff comfort me.
You prepare a feast for me right in front of my enemies.
You pour oil on my head. My cup runs over.
I am sure that your goodness and love will follow me all the days of my life.
And I will live in the house of the Lord forever.
(Psalm 23:1-6)

The sun had set a long time ago, and the parking lot was now practically empty in the mid-hours of the evening. If I did not expect any of the other events thus far, this was right up there with them. There was a perfectly good hotel room paid for and awaiting my arrival but here I was in the Jeep.

"I am keeping you safe."

Hmm, I was not sure from what or who, and I needed to use a restroom. I hopped out and headed over to a nearby building to see if it was open and to see there were any public restrooms. I knew I was not supposed to leave this area or move from the parking spot. The nearby building was the only place I could think of to go.

As I walked through a covered walkway, two policemen walked towards me. They said hello and I smiled and asked if there was a public restroom nearby.

"There's one right inside the police station," one of them responded and turned to point back in the direction they were coming from. Smiling, I thanked them and continued walking straight into the building. I opened the door and sure enough, it was the reception area for the police station. It did not dawn on me until walking back outside, earlier in the morning I was being led to the police station.

Wait, and now God was keeping me safe here? The age-old story of Daniel in the lions' den washed over my thoughts when Daniel was protected and held safe from the ravenous lions by an angel sent from God. Curiously, it almost felt like I was like Daniel, trusting and faithful, protected, and truly safe.

The story fell from my mind just as fast as it had arrived as my thoughts raced forward and possibilities took hold. Maybe he would be coming back here because God would place on his mind that this was the last place we saw each other. It sounded reasonable, and God could do it since God could do anything. I asked upward into the night sky. "Maybe that's why I was waiting here after all?"

"I am keeping you safe, Shannon. Trust me."

I'd lost track of time and was leaning back in the driver's seat, listening to my music playlist, trying to be patient and not to think negatively, and felt God tell me, **"He is yours."**

I dismissed the thought, thinking I did not hear God right or that I made it up in my head. But then, seconds later, torturous voices struck and pelted my thoughts.

"Do not be discouraged. Do not be discouraged. Do not be discouraged." The voices persisted, unrelenting, over and over again. Then more voices joined in. The same experience of being mind-blasted came upon me quickly. Except it was worse this time, much, much worse. The voices taunted me, cursed me. Voices so angry with me and they were explicitly trying to destroy me with words. My head swirled with the torment…

"She is seething."

I nodded in pain holding my head in my hands as the thoughts blasted through my senses from all the voices. They swirled in attack louder in crescendos of rage. I squeezed my head tighter within both of my hands in agony. "Make it stop!" I burst, pleading to God, "God, my Almighty Father, in Jesus' name, I cry out to You for help. Please place Your protection all around Sadie and me. Please send down legions of angels to protect us. Please rebuke all unholy and evil spirits that are attacking me right now. Please make the voices stop my God, please…"

My prayer trailed off as I began to weep in suffering.

The gentle and comforting response from God spoke, **"Shannon, I am already protecting you. You are completely protected. I am protecting everywhere around you. I am holding you."**

"They are doing everything they can to harm you. But I will not let them. Not now. Not ever."

"Shannon, you are my child with whom I am pleased. You were patient, you obeyed, and you trusted me. Now you are receiving what I promised you. He is yours."

I exhaled between tears, "He is mine?"

The voices were gone, and peace had come back over me. I pulled the blanket across my body and nestled my head on another blanket scrunched between the headrest and the window. With the engine running to keep the heat on I fell asleep in the police station parking lot where God was keeping me safe, but from what and to what extent I did not fully understand.

Thursday, December 10, 2009

6:17 AM
The sun hadn't risen yet, but I was awake. Part of me still hoped I would see Jeremie again. The other part was not sure what to believe. I kept praying to God to release me if I was not supposed to be here anymore.

"I am not releasing you."

I continued to wait in the same parking spot. The engine had run all night long so I could keep the heater on because of the cold. I noticed that I'd already burned well over a quarter of a tank of gas and remembered God had told me to get gas yesterday. When I had stopped for gas, I only had a quarter tank. In a bit of awe, I realized the Jeep would have run out of gas in the parking lot overnight.

Over the hours, I saw police officers drive in and out of the nearby fenced-off parking lot. The lot where I was remained empty most of the night except for me. When I had to use the restroom, I went inside the police station. I let Sadie out a couple of times to walk around and do what she needed to do as well. I just didn't know how long I was supposed to stay.

9:00 AM
Another day began in full swing at the municipal center. Utility trucks deployed for the day, workers came and went. And here I was, still parked in the same spot as when they all had left yesterday. The feeling that I was not going to see Jeremie again became stronger but each time I asked if I could leave, God said no.

The hotel check-out was coming up at 11:00 AM. Frustration set upon me, I felt like I should extend the check-out time because I still was not released by God to leave. I called the hotel as a precaution and they gladly extended my check-out time to 1:00 in the afternoon.

10:00 AM
The bouts of frustration about waiting so long were increasing. "Why was I still here?"

"I am keeping you safe. Trust me."

Right, same answer. I sighed, "God if I am supposed to be here. If You still want me in this place, give me a miraculous sign. You've said in Your Word that I can ask for a miracle. Anything within the deepest graves or the highest heavens. Give me a miraculous sign and show me Your glory my God that this is Your will!"

"Shannon, there have been miracles happening everywhere around you, and you don't even know."

Sighing, I placed my head back down on the blanket wedged to my side. A few short minutes later, I felt I should look around. Raising my head and looking through the side-view mirror, I spied movement. Turning my head to look, three deer strolled across the parking lot, coming towards the Jeep.

"Miracle."

With one hand, I reached back to feel for Sadie's head and grabbed her collar to keep her head down, so she would not see them. She grunted softly in contentment when my hand touched her, but then fell back asleep. I exhaled in awe as the deer passed right next to the driver's side, "God, I've never seen deer up this close before!"

"I know, Shannon."

The deer continued across the parking lot in front of me and walked into the utility depot area. Wow, that was cool. Once they were out of view, I put my head back down on the makeshift pillow. Unexpectedly my sight was blinded as the sunlight reflecting through the side-view mirror shone directly into my face.

"Glory."

The sun was in the perfect position that I could see the entire circle of its light through the mirror and every bit of the light reflected directly into my face.

I sighed again. Okay, miracle and glory like I asked God to give me. God does want me here. I settled in to try to sleep. I mean, what else could I do besides journal, sleep, and pray?

12:00 PM

Emotions welled up again as it was nearing the hotel's late check-out time. I'd been in this parking spot for 20 hours and I needed time to get my belongings out of the hotel room to start the drive back east to home to be at work on Monday! Tears tugged at the corners of my eyes as I cried out, "God, can I please leave?"

"You are not released. Trust me. I am keeping you safe."

I wondered, "Should I call and reserve another night at the hotel just in case?"

"You can, but you don't have to call."

Pausing, I furrowed my brows in contemplation of what I'd heard from God. Then I dialed the number to the hotel. In my earlier conversation, I told the hotel clerk that I needed a delayed check-out time because I was stuck, and I could not make it back to the hotel to get my belongings out of the room. I began this conversation the same way.

The hotel clerk interrupted me, "Oh, Hon, don't worry about it! We had a water main break here this morning, so some of the rooms are in disarray. We're trying to dry them out." She went on to say whenever I was able to make it back to the hotel was fine. She even said I could shower before heading off on my way and offered that unless I really needed to stay another night, I did not need to pay for the extra time or reserve an additional night's stay.

My jaw was dropped as I thanked her and hung up the call. Another confirmation God still wanted me here. I resigned myself to more waiting.

1:30 PM

Frustration set in again, this time it was more intense. The drive home was about 3,000 miles and I needed to be at work on Monday morning. In my head, I calculated the hours for the drive and really (really) needed to get on my way to make it home on time.

Praying to God, I asked Him again to release me. This time, I did not receive a response. My agitation grew, what was I supposed to do? I started feeling like maybe I should call Sofie to ask her what she thought. I did not want to; I'd been following God in this all on my own.

Inner frustration and struggling intensified. Not knowing what else to do, I called Sofie. Tears of indecision ran from my eyes as I left a voicemail, "Sofie, it is Shannon. I'm at a police station near where Jeremie lives. I have been here in this same parking spot for almost 22 hours because God wanted me here. Now I don't know what to do. I need to drive home to be back for work on Monday. Please call me back."

About a half-hour later, Sofie called back. She was livid, "I told you not to go!"

"I know, but..." I tried to reply.

"No, Shannon, I told you not to go!"

"I know, but God wanted me here." I brokenly tried explaining what happened through tears. I also told her I'd left her two voicemails in the last days. One when I was heading to his hometown and another after he crossed my path to let her know that her prophecy may have come true.

Sofie told me she never received those two voicemails and admonished me soundly, "Shannon, I told you not to go!" She steadied her voice enough to continue, "It is time to come home, Shannon. Go to the hotel, get your things. It's time to come home."

She paused and then said more calmly in a matter-of-fact tone, "You are going to get arrested for stalking."

My little world crashed down on itself. Stalking? Me? Oh no! No, no! That was not possible! That's not why I was here! But…oh! My insides churned with fear. Realizations began punching me in the face of what I'd done. Two days in his hometown. Twenty-two hours in the same parking spot at the police station.

All of God's comforting words disappeared as I hung up the call with a singular focus, "I had to get out of here! They were going to try to arrest me for stalking!"

I threw the Jeep into reverse and backed out of the parking spot, shifted into drive, and sped out of the parking lot. Once on the main road, I drove as fast as I could; my entire body shaking with adrenaline and fear. I had to get out of this town as fast as I could. They were going to arrest me for stalking!

Arriving at the hotel, I ran to the lobby to get a new card key from the hotel clerk and then hurried to let Sadie and myself into the room. I took the fastest shower in my life and packed up all my bags with one hand while brushing my teeth with my other hand.

Still shaking and rushed, I prepared everything to leave while Sadie laid down on the hotel bed stretched out content to be on a comfy hotel bed. I lugged my bags out of the room, taking as much as possible with each trip out to the Jeep. When I came back for Sadie on the last trip, she didn't want to go as she was quite content to sleep for a while on a real bed. I finally got her 130-pound body back up and on her leash and hurried with her outside.

The hotel was near the highway, so it did not take me long to high tail it out of the parking lot and then onward towards the interstate. My body was still shaking with fear as I drove as fast as possible past all the exits and powered over the mountains. My mind screaming over and over, "I have to get out of here! They are going to arrest me for stalking!"

I remember trying to figure things out, trying to understand where I went wrong but my mind was a big mushy glob of swirling thoughts and exhaustion. After driving well into the night, I stopped at a motel, checked in at the front counter, and led Sadie into the room with me. We both collapsed on the bed in exhaustion. It was the deepest night's sleep for either of us on the entire trip.

A NEW LIFE

…WHEN JESUS CALLED MY NAME.

Sunday, December 13, 2009

I woke up after a 2-hour catnap among the big rigs at a rest area somewhere in Ohio and saw it was about 2:30 AM. I decided to grab a quick bite to eat and another coffee for the next hours on the road and then stopped for gas at a truck stop before easing back up onto the on-ramp for I-70 when Jesus came to me.

Now I know people describe it as coming "to" Jesus, but no, he most definitely came to me. I felt his presence surround me as I listened to the lyrics of a song talking about Jesus saving us, a song of the redeemed, of those made free. Tears streamed from my eyes in awe.

It was an incredible feeling in my heart because I was the same Shannon. I didn't change. I did not have to be like my father, or my ex-husband Tony, or a pastor, or a "revivalist," or a "Bible thumper." I was me, and that was enough to be kept safe from whoever the evil spirits were who attacked me.

He loved me for who I was inside and out, faults and all. I sobbed with the realization I never had to be someone I was not. That just being me, genuine to who I am, was all I ever needed to be.

Jesus talked with me throughout a series of songs that came up on shuffle mode on my playlist. Every song flowed in connection with our conversation. My favorite moment was when Jesus said,

"Now Shannon, you can say that you are born again. But I know you won't, and that is okay with me."

Laughing until the tears started falling again, I nodded. Jesus was right. I didn't want to call myself a "born again." It was something I was adamant about because of the connotation it had in the United States of America. I'd always believed in Jesus. It was not that I "accepted him in my life" as my savior; he always was my savior. I'd believed ever since I was a little girl reading Bible stories, going to Sunday school, and singing the song, "Jesus

Loves Me," whenever I was upset.

My mind recalled back to October while in prayer when God spoke, "**Jesus before Jeremie.**" I did not understand what it meant at the time, but now it made sense. As I drove down the road, I stared into the darkness in awe. Jesus was my Prince Charming! I surrendered what I wanted, the fairy tale of Jeremie coming back into my life in the way I wanted, to receive what God had for me, and it was Jesus.

It was then that I reiterated to Jesus what I'd already prayed earlier in the evening. For the rest of my life, I only wanted to walk on God's path. I hereby gave up my life for God's will for the rest of my days. If it was true that Jesus was my Prince Charming and rescued me out of whatever was happening in Jeremie's hometown for some greater purpose, my life was now God's for good.

We conversed through six songs, then Jesus told me the last one was next. As the notes began, I realized it was the song, "Bless the Broken Road." I broke into joyful tears again. Jesus told me I was now ready for my new life, and that also meant my new marriage. He described how God's path would unfold in front of me and I would be guided by him; everything would be placed on my path and I would no longer have to search for open doors.

Jesus said I would be leading for him and that my husband would be more so supporting me, but we would be doing this together. I was in such awe that I did not think to ask what exactly I was going to be leading and doing for Jesus.

Jesus went on to say these were big plans for my life and that the love my husband and I would share was as close to God's love as was possible on Earth. My husband would indeed be the "one," my soulmate, and Jesus confirmed that it was God's plan to bring us together in this manner, to love each other and serve God for the rest of our lives. Jesus told me everyone would know God's hand did this.

Even though I still did not know what it meant for my future, a memory flitted into my thoughts. A prophecy that was spoken over me at a charismatic event in 2001 I attended with Tony. The prophet was praying over others and saw me come in. Without hesitation, he came directly over to me and took my hands in his, saying, "You're beautiful." As he continued, the prophet spoke of a healing anointing and described how I would help the burdened of heart. How did I forget that for all these years? Did the prophecy have anything to do with what Jesus was now appointing me to do?

Shaking my head out of the reverie, I realized Jesus came to me and said my life was changing from this point onward and that I was born again, and he had big plans for my future. Did this mean he baptized me in the Holy Spirit?

Into service for Father God? I was in complete and utter awe.

A bit later in the drive, I asked God to show me His glory and within a few hours, it came much differently than in the past.

Pennsylvania, along I-78, about 60 miles west of Allentown about 7:30 in the morning, I was driving through freezing rain. Dozens of cars, trucks, and big rigs had already spun out. Some were smashed and upside down. Horns were stuck blaring in empty cars unrecognizable from the accidents and people were walking away from their totaled vehicles in the freezing rain.

"My glory."

Uhm, what? As I looked at the accidents everywhere around me, I did not see any glory. My hands tightened, gripping the steering wheel harder as I watched ice forming on the Jeep's antenna and side-view mirrors.

"I promised you no harm would come to you on this trip. You will be safe. I am with you. You will not get hit. You will not be hurt. Your wheels will not slide."

And they didn't. Not once. I felt God with me. Remaining calm, when the interstate lanes became too congested with smashed vehicles to keep driving forward I pulled onto the ice-covered median grass and continued the trek up the middle of the freeway. Even then, my tires did not slide once.

Finally, the ice turned into rain, and a bit later the rain turned into a downpour as I crossed the last state line. "We're almost home!" I exclaimed to Sadie. She looked at me and panted with her St. Bernard smile. In the early afternoon, I pulled into the driveway at home and came to a stop, tears sprung out of the corner of my eyes. "I did it!" God was with me the whole time, and I drove over 7000 miles on my own with Sadie!

Opening the door, I hopped out and stretched. Before I could stop her, Sadie jumped over the driver's seat and leaped onto the sidewalk, trotting out of reach on the path leading to the front door. She wasn't on a leash!

I shouldn't have worried. Sadie bounded straight up the pathway and up the steps to the front door. She looked back at me with her tail wagging, looked at the door, and looked back at me. She was happy to be home. Giggling, I walked to where she was waiting and let her inside, exhaling as the realism of being back to real life settled in. It was good to be home.

Monday, December 14, 2009

Except for lots of laundry loads to do it was back to regular life. I spent extra time with my cats who were not as peeved at me as I thought they would be for leaving them for so long with a neighbor checking in. My mind was so awake I could hardly sleep overnight even though I'd already been awake for two days straight of driving. I felt tingles of energy from within and around me—alive, awake joyful energy.

On my heart all night long from God was, "**It is time, Jesus throughout all religions.**" But I did not know how or why or what I had to do with it. I was all but bursting wanting to share what happened on the trip with my family and friends, but I couldn't yet. I didn't know how the story ended!

This was a sweet thought for sure. I'd already contemplated how it seemed as though God was giving me back a dormant life dream, I'd given up on it years ago. Ever since I first started writing outside of school when I was 13 years old, it was in my heart to publish my life story from my journals. Never once did I ever think anything awesome enough would happen in my humdrum ordinary life that would be interesting enough to publish and years ago I gave up on the dream.

All my free time outside of work had been devoted to typing up my journals and I worked on the manuscript through what transpired during the cross-country trip. The draft was nearly completed. There was just one little catch; now I was waiting for the happily ever after God had promised.

Thursday, December 17, 2009

Still bursting at the seams with the excitement of God working in my life and the prospect of my dreams coming true, I was joyful as I walked through the door at Sofie's shop for the next session. Not at all prepared for the scowl and disdainful looks on her face as I explained more details about what happened on the trip.

She nodded in agreement that she was proud of my discernment between the psychic attacks and God's voice, but then, she admonished me derisively, "You screwed everything up, Shannon!"

"What?" A pit formed in my stomach.

Sofie sighed, and in an exasperated tone waved away everything I was saying. She said she was going to have to do much more work now that I'd gone and made a mess of everything, and it would take much longer.

Internally reeling and taken aback, I listened as she spoke, "I will need to light a candle for you, Shannon. It is a very large, expensive candle. With all the work I need to do now plus the candle, it will cost much more."

I sat stunned as she told me how much money she was now charging for more work and sessions. I pulled my checkbook out of my purse even though it did not feel right. None of this felt right. I wrote out the amount while trying to fit broken pieces together in my head. I handed the check to Sofie, and she nodded and leaned over to her bag, dropping it in.

Almost as an afterthought as she was sitting back upright, Sofie glanced over to the side table. Her eyes landed on a necklace made of tumbled stones of some sort and she grasped it and handed it to me. "There," she guided, "pray every day while holding the necklace to help balance out all the negative energy you've drawn in."

Silence held the room as I held out my hand and she dropped the necklace onto my palm. The conflict within me was tearing at my stomach; this did not feel right at all. I placed the necklace in my purse and made my way out of her shop and into the winter chill. As I walked to the Jeep my thoughts were heavy. I unlocked the door and stepped up and sat in the driver's seat shaking my head, trying to pull my thoughts back together.

Drawing Sofie's necklace out of my purse, I gazed at it. The tumbled stones gleamed when the lights from the street caught the stones as I moved the necklace between my fingers. "This isn't right," I spoke out loud into the stillness.

As I contemplated, I realized that somewhere in me believed I did not need Sofie to light a candle to atone for anything I'd done and a warm knowing in my heart pervaded my senses. Nothing was screwed up; no mess was made. In the deepest part of my being, I knew everything happened the way it was meant to happen, for whatever reason, for some greater good in God's plans that were now emerging in my life.

The necklace felt heavy in my hand. I did not need it and I did not want to take it home with me. Hopping back out of the Jeep, I marched back to her shop and stopped outside as I saw another client was in session. I decided to wait outside in the cold, not feeling I could leave until this was resolved.

Eventually, the session ended, and I saw the woman get up to leave. As she came out of the door, I held it open for her and walked inside. Sofie looked up in surprise to see me. I sat down in the chair across from her and looked at Sofie, her eyebrows were still raised in question. I started with a soft but firm tone in my voice, "I know you don't need to light a candle."

She opened her mouth to speak, but I did not let her. Continuing, "I know I didn't screw everything up." Sighing, I shook my head, "And the worst part about this is, I did not even get to tell you everything earlier. In all that happened in this unbelievable story of God saving me from whatever harm they were trying to do to me, God gave me back my childhood dream of having my journals, my life story, published."

Sofie sat silently in her chair as I explained, "I've already written the manuscript up to this point. I so much hoped your role in my story would be the wise Christian Wiccan psychic who helped and was good..." My words drifted in midair; I could not find the right way to say what I was now questioning to be the truth.

Bringing my thoughts back in completion, "I know I don't need you to light a candle or fix anything because I didn't screw up. I did what God wanted me to do, I followed His will the entire time."

The room hung in silence. Sofie did not say a word. She leaned over to her bag and pulled out the check. Then held it out towards me.

"No," I said, shaking my head, "You keep it. You must need it more than I do." I got up and walked out of her shop; a burden lifted from my heart. No more would I seek wisdom from the world—from Sofie or anyone else—from now on it would only be between me and God.

Saturday, December 26, 2009

> It came to pass, when Jesus had risen from the dead,
> that he passed 11 years discoursing with his disciples...
> (The First Book of Pistis Sophia, Chapter One)

❊ ❊ ❊

On my way down to visit family in Virginia, I was in Pennsylvania and stopped off at a restaurant in Harrisburg to have a quick lunch. Sadie greeted me with a big wagging tail and expectant face when I hopped back into the Jeep. I navigated to the access road and made a couple of turns before slowing to a stop behind a vehicle at the red light. Looking up at the car ahead of me, my eyes landed on the New Hampshire license plate, "SHAN."

Bursting out in laughter, I grinned, "Oh what, what kind of sign is this God? What am I going to see next?"

I then glanced to the immediate left and saw the Pennsylvania license plate on the vehicle in that lane, and my jaw dropped in astonishment, "ROC STAR."

The cars in front of me from left to right had license plates that spelled out, "ROC STAR SHAN." I put it together, and I felt my energy tingling. It was a now-familiar, almost an indescribable sensation of awe mixed with an intuition that something was being revealed, even if I did not quite understand what it meant.

I remembered when Jesus came to me, he said he had big plans for my future. I'd also felt "famous" in my mind lately but kept pushing the idea away. Being famous was not important to me. But the sign smack dab in front of me was undeniable. I made the right turn and then turned left onto the interstate ramp, amazed chills still coursing throughout my body.

Sunday, January 3, 2010

In the last week since the ROC STAR SHAN sign, I'd been struggling, wondering about what God may have in store for the future. Questioning if it meant somehow being famous. Then, drawing in thoughts of concern it was all just my ego inflating. I brought it all to God in prayer today.

"God, I don't want to be disillusioned by thinking this is bigger than what You have for me." I repeated it, emphasizing my frustration, "I don't want to be disillusioned by thinking this is bigger than what You have for me!"

God answered, "**What are your dreams, Shannon?**"

"My dreams?" I tilted my head to the side and pondered. My dreams poured out of my heart, "To make a difference. To sing my heart's song. To be a shining light. To help and heal. To genuinely be me and not have to change or conform for anyone else in the world."

"**There are no dreams too great. I made you, I know your dreams. They will be fulfilled. It is all coming to you.**"

I kept sensing that God was telling me it would all begin with the book being published and everything falling into place from there. Of course, it all still meant I was still waiting for the happily ever after to complete the end of the story. On my heart in prayer lately was, "**One God. One Son, two religions, both in his name,**" but I had no idea what it meant.

Monday, January 4, 2010

I decided it was time to spruce up my house. Everything was laid out on the floor: photos, mats, frames, and the tools needed to put it all together and hang up on the bare walls. I turned on the television for some background noise while I worked. Flipping channels, I decided on the trivia quiz game show, Jeopardy. By the time the next game show, Wheel of Fortune, began, I was all but ignoring the television.

The host of Wheel of Fortune greeted the contestants as I cut along the edge of a photo. I heard a contestant say the names of his children and one of them sounded like Jeremie. Ha! I laughed and looked up at the television, saying out loud, "Just a coincidence. God, I'm not going to get any wild ideas and start to think there's something to do with this television show being a miraculous sign from you."

"Watch a little longer."

"Huh?" I was surprised to hear the response from God and familiar awe-filled energy tingles started running through my body. Not knowing what to expect and keeping an open mind, I went back to cutting the photo that I held in my hand.

The first puzzle was revealed, and I glanced up at the television and then just as quickly back down to my work, "Home Sweet Home." Then absolute craziness ensued in the game. The contestants tried to solve the next puzzle, and all three failed four different times! Even when all the letters were revealed they pronounced the names of Regis Philbin and Kelly Ripa incorrectly. "Regis Philgrin" "Regis Philbrin" "Regis Philmin" "Kelly Ripe-a" I could not decipher how this would be a sign—Regis and Kelly were a famous duo who co-hosted a morning television show based in New York.

I placed the photo and mat into the back of a frame, closed it up, and reached for the next one to work on as the next puzzle was solved, "Estimated Time of Arrival." I looked up at the television in astonishment with chills racing through my body again, jaw dropped, and scribbled the words on my notepad. "Estimated time of arrival?" Was God revealing when something was going to happen?

"Watch a little longer, Shannon."

My eyes were glued to the television during the final puzzle round. When the contestant correctly solved the final puzzle and won $25,000, I tried to figure out what the final puzzle meant as I wrote down, "Blaze of Glory." I knew it was significant, but it was not a date or time! I could not think what it could have to do with anything. Doubt filled my mind and I felt silly for watching the show and writing down the puzzle answers.

"It will be after. Watch a little longer."

Nodding and letting go of the uncertainty, I went back to work on the frames as a round of commercials commenced, then the show panned back to the host and co-host chatting together at the end. Suddenly, my ears heard the host say, "Next Week."

"Next Week?" I exhaled in awe. It felt complete, and I looked down at my scribbled notes and read it all together, "Estimated time of arrival, blaze of glory, next week." By the awe in my body, I knew this was a miraculous sign from God, but I had no idea what it meant.

As I walked upstairs to change clothes for a walk with Sadie it suddenly hit me. Glory. Blaze of glory. GOD'S GLORY! My knees went weak, and I collapsed on the floor. God's Glory! I was in awe. God just revealed on the Wheel of Fortune that there would be a blaze of glory next week!

I remained on the ground for a while in amazement, praying and thanking God, at least until Sadie decided she was not going to take my non-responses to her whining anymore. She galloped up the stairs and nudged at me until I got back up on my feet. I wrapped my arms around her in a huge hug, "Sadie, blaze of glory!" She cocked her big St. Bernard head to one side questioningly while continuing to pant, her tail wagging back and forth. All she knew was that it was time for her walk.

Thursday, January 7, 2010

With all my heart I believed God's blaze of glory was coming next week. What would it be? I scoured a calendar to see if I could figure anything out. Yes, sometimes patience still wasn't my strongest attribute. I kept looking beyond, and into February, and noticed a holiday I did not recognize, Imbolc. What was Imbolc?

Imbolc was a Gaelic feast day that represented the anticipation of spring and was also Saint Brigid's day. On the same day, two celebrations took place, one of the pagans for the "Great Mother" Goddess Brigid with the earned title of "wise one" with the Imbolc festivities and the other of the Catholics for Saint Brigid. I found some resources suggesting the goddess was made into a saint to ease the conversion of pagans to Catholicism.

As the Great Mother goddess, Brigid was said to unite the Celts who were spread throughout the area and people worked with her for intense healing, purification, and inspiration. I learned that as Saint Brigid, her nickname was "Mary of the Gael" for her ability to help the opening of hearts, with an energy akin to that of the Blessed Mother Mary.

On one Celtic mythology website, I stumbled over another name in addition to Brigid's, Sionainn. She was the goddess from whom the name of the ancient River Shannon in Ireland was derived. I never realized there was a goddess Sionainn (Shannon) and intrigue filled my heart. Sionainn was a mortal woman searching for the well of knowledge and when she found it she failed to honor the power of the well, believing in her inner strength to be greater than the well and protocols. Sionainn disturbed the tranquility with her overconfidence and superior attitude. When she opened the cover of the well to get the "Salmon of Knowledge" from inside, the water flowed out and she drowned in the river, named after her.

After becoming the river, Sionainn was reborn as a goddess, receiving all the wisdom and knowledge she originally sought in the well. The River Shannon in Ireland was known as the bridge between the west and the east and gave life to the land.

The mythological tale of Sionainn felt so familiar in my heart, it sounded similar to what I'd done by seeking knowledge in the world through Sofie and others instead of trusting my own inner wisdom from God. I believed through this I was truly the soul of Shannon, true to my given birth name by my parents in this lifetime.

Monday, January 11, 2010

In the last four days, my research expanded from the starting point of Saint Brigid. Growing up in the Lutheran tradition, I did not learn about the saints or what made people "saint-worthy." My heart was curious and never could I have imagined the revelations God would pour upon me.

As I read descriptions about the saints, I learned how they modeled exceptional holiness with lives of great charity and heroic virtues. Saints let God steer their entire lives and they fulfilled the definition of "bride of Christ," entirely attached, faithful, and dependent on God. Some were even known as miracle workers and healers.

From looking up the definitions of a saint, I moved on to research the apostles since they were canonized as saints. I read that an apostle was said to be a pioneer who went where no one else was willing or anointed to go to prepare the way for the rest. Similar to saints, the apostles bore the character, personality, and fruit of the spirit, living a life of servanthood for God. They manifested the qualities of Divine love and humility.

Astonishment filled my body as I read about the "death walk" which was said to be an intricate part in the making of an apostle. The death walk was the reason why apostles walked in such an awesome appointing from God, due to the degree to which they had to die to themselves. I read how the world could not do enough to brace itself or get ready for what God's apostles would do in His name.

"You're one of the first, Shannon."

God's words took me by surprise, and I pondered what it could mean. Then, I continued to research. The apostle was called, appointed, and ordained to the office by God and released into service with one specific purpose in life, chosen specifically for their calling before birth, not by choice, and trained in secret with a commissioned mandate from God and must ensure suffering.

"You will not suffer any longer, you've suffered long enough."

I noted what God said and kept reading. One perspective suggested apostles were "spiritual entrepreneurs," starting from scratch to build a brand-new foundation and setting things in order with God's direction. Another prophetic website mentioned the apostles of today, like the apostles of old, would turn cities upside-down for God, standing boldly against the religious system that kept people in bondage. Yet other websites contradicted these beliefs, stating the apostle anointing was dead because the church's foundation was already completed.

"It is fixing the foundation, making it pure."

As I browsed through websites, I saw many "apostle training" programs throughout the world. So many people named themselves or others as apostles. It seemed widespread. I wondered if I'd heard God wrong, "God if there are so many apostles already out there in Your name, how am I one of the first?"

"Undeniable."

Hmm, I was not sure how it would be possible and wondered if it might have something to do with the upcoming blaze of glory. I continued my research. Some websites included more than the original twelve apostles and Paul as apostles of God, describing apostle archetypes such as Moses, Joshua, David, Solomon, and even Jesus. When I saw Solomon I felt a nudging in my heart to look deeper, I did not remember much about Solomon from the Bible other than he was King David's son.

The description of the Solomon apostle archetype was one of wisdom, depicting how Solomon had the right pattern and principles from God and therefore entered into work without opposition because the apostle was building on new ground. The Solomon apostle archetype was to build a "New" church, bringing the power of God directly to the people paralleling Solomon's role as king in the Old Testament. The role of the Solomon apostle was to bring together the Old and the New in a new pattern that would establish the fullness of God's order for the church in the end times.

I recalled back to what I'd learned about the River Shannon in Ireland as a bridge between the west and the east, and questioned, "Sounds sort of like being a bridge?"

"Shannon, you still don't understand fully what I'm calling you for."

"What do you mean?"

"My glory, my glory is all around you. No suffering, you've suffered long enough, only glory."

I decided that I should learn more about King Solomon. He was wise, spiritual, and prayed for understanding of the heart, a "discerning heart to govern" and the ability to "distinguish right from wrong" (1 Kings 3:9) instead of asking for riches and treasures of the world. Because of this, God graced him with much more. During King Solomon's reign, the kingdom was established in peace; his father King David's preparations for the temple were completed in devotion and worship to God.

"Solomon's blessing on your life. You will never have want for anything."

I looked back at my journaling about the Solomon-type apostle. He was prophesied to be coming to rebuild the church in the right way for the New Millennium. In disbelief of how comfortable it felt in my heart, I wondered if my role was similar to this archetype.

"Yes, you are the first—it is you."

I shook my head in denial, "But God, others are already..."

"Have you ever heard of anything like this before?"

Staring at my journaling, I tried to comprehend what God was revealing.

"Yes, Shannon—it is yours. It is you."

"God, the Solomon apostle is bringing it back together?"

"You. My plans are so much bigger than you realize."

Still in disbelief, I kept reading. When Solomon was dedicating the temple to God, supernatural fire came down on the altar. Such a miracle as this was typical of the way God commenced any new phase of His teaching for the world, He introduced the sanctity of the temple by a solitary miracle of fire (2 Chronicles 7:1). I exhaled in astonishment as I remembered the miraculous sign God revealed last week on the Wheel of Fortune game show.

"Blaze of glory!" God introduced the sanctity of His temple built by King Solomon by a solitary miracle of fire and was introducing a new era with a blaze of glory. "This means a new phase of teaching is commencing that I will share with the world?"

"Yes, Shannon, you are correct."

I shook my head in disbelief and continued to research. I learned how each time humanity stepped into a new era, God drew our attention to it with a sign or great wonder. Some people believed no more revelations would occur until we reached the final stage of redemption in the return of Christ and then they would resume.

Hmm, I sat back in my chair in wonder. If this were true, it led me to believe the end times were not fulfilled yet, although they would be soon, and it would have something to do with the blaze of glory and with me.

"Yes, it will amaze you, and it has nothing to do with Jeremie."

Then it hit me, none of this was ever about Jeremie at all. It was about me. I had to give up my life, give up what I wanted most in the world, and put my life completely in God's hands. Trusting in God with my entire mind and heart through the tests and trials, when the wisdom of the world discouraged me from following what I felt in my heart God wanted me to do. Even when logic and rationale sense failed, and I could step forward only by faith alone.

I gave my life willingly—spirit, soul, mind, heart, and body—in complete trust in God whom I could not see or completely know, and as a result, I was reborn for God's greater purpose as an apostle in the name of Jesus Christ. Astonishment filled my senses, the revelations coursed through me, and self-doubt filled my mind, "Do you really think I can do this, God?"

"I made you for this. Walk in it. It is yours."

Thursday, January 14, 2010

Journaling began today where I'd left off with the apostles. I recalled there were three requirements to be an apostle in the New Testament. First, they must have seen Jesus or witnessed the resurrection. Second, they were specifically selected by Jesus. Third, they had the power to perform miracles. As I researched further I came across the title, "Apostle to the Apostles," from some of the early Christian writings. Mary Magdalene? What? I'd known her as the woman with seven demons who Jesus healed, but there was more to Mary Magdalene I'd never looked deep enough to see.

She was the first to see Jesus in the garden after his resurrection and the "Apostle to the Apostles" because she then announced it to the other disciples; thereby, the gospel messenger of Jesus' resurrection. Depicted as a leader, she comforted the disciples in their grief and provided spiritual instruction, "Let your hearts not be troubled." It was Mary Magdalene who initiated the good news of the living spirit of Jesus in the resurrection, establishing the foundation upon which the disciples set forth into their ministries as apostles of Jesus Christ.

Questioning filled my mind and I asked God, "If she met the requirements to be an apostle and if she was chosen as the messenger of the good news of

Jesus' resurrection… why wasn't she an apostle?"

"Corruption, perversion of man."

I contemplated God's response and the minimized role of women in leadership in the church over the last 2000 years. Then picking up where I left off in research, I read through some sources that mentioned after Jesus' resurrection Mary Magdalene traveled to Southern France, leaving the other apostles for her own ministry wherein she was said to have a prophetic mission filled with miraculous healings.

"Learn this."

Hmm, I read a little more… Gnosticism: teachings that some believe are the spiritual basis of Jesus' essential message to humanity. I'd never heard of Gnosticism. "And, she taught it, God?"

"Yes, it was lost."

Gnosticism was related to mystical esoteric inner knowledge, from a personal experience and direct connection with God. The teachings included love and communion with God and were some of the practices of early Christianity which emerged after Jesus' death. Feminine qualities such as receptivity, intuitive perception, inner wisdom, and the art of healing were marks of Gnosticism, but later it was deemed heretical by the Catholic Church. I saw the names of writings, Pistis Sophia and the Gospel of Mary Magdalene, among others.

"Read these."

"Fixing the foundation, making it pure," I tapped my pen on my page filled with notes, thinking back to what God said a couple of days ago. If the teachings associated with Gnosticism were part of early Christianity then certainly, if today's church was to be pure with the original essence of the teachings from Jesus that meant going back to all the teachings from 2000 years ago, not just those which were canonized in the gospels of the Bible.

In my heart, I felt God tell me yes, this was part of what I was bringing together; the feminine that was lost from the church. I gasped in realization, the phrase that had been on my heart and thoughts for days. I could not understand what it meant until now! "One God, One Son, two religions both in his name." This was it. This was what it meant. One flourished as the Catholic Church, and the other went underground as Gnosticism. One God, One Son, two religions, both in his name.

"The new season of your life is here Shannon. Let it unfold in front of you."

Friday, January 15, 2010

[Jesus said,] "My prayer is not for them alone.
I pray also for those who will believe in me through their message,
that all of them may be one, Father,
just as you are in me and I am in you.
May they also be in us so that the world may believe that you have sent me.
I have given them the glory that you gave me,
that they may be one as we are one—I in them and you in me
—so that they may be brought to complete unity.
Then the world will know that you sent me
and have loved them even as you have loved me."
(John 17:20-23)

❋ ❋ ❋

It was the middle of the morning, and I was working in my cubicle at the office. All of a sudden a light bulb went off in my head, "Check headlines for a blaze of glory." I opened a web browser and typed in the URL to Google news, but in mid-load, the page froze. I opened a second browser and in a split-second change of mind typed to go to Yahoo news instead. I wasn't sure what I was looking for or expecting to find. My eyes widened in surprise when I saw the headlining news article on the top of Yahoo News, *"Mass. Senate candidate looks for boost from 'rock star' Bill Clinton."*

I exhaled in amazement, "Rock star..." my mind reflected back in time to when I saw ROC STAR SHAN on the two license plates of the cars. "Rock star..." Could it really mean? "...the world?"

"Yes, Shannon, the world will know who you are, but it will not go to your head. I made you for this."

As possibilities popped into my thoughts, I scowled, "I'm not going to run for office or be a politician."

"No, you are not. You will be as well-known as the former president."

The feeling of awe caught me again as I thought back to what I'd learned about the story of Solomon dedicating the completed temple to God. A miraculous validation of the sanctity and holiness of the temple had come forth from God as supernatural fire on the altar like a blaze of glory. God's power and glory on my life? An unknown ordinary woman as famous as the former president in our nation, as a "rock star" for God?

I laughed and shook my head. Incredulous, unfathomable! Yet at the same time, I considered the fact it would truly be a miracle, and entirely beyond anything I could ever achieve on my own. If it came to pass, it would truly be the glory of God and would validate my authenticity as a messenger in the name of Jesus Christ.

The webpage froze again when I clicked to read the article. I force closed and reopened the browser and noticed the headline was replaced with another article. I gasped in excitement, *"Blazing ring eclipse races across Africa, Asia"* (Source: AFP), blazing ring eclipse! The eye of God!

This was an "annular eclipse" which occurred when the moon passed directly in front of the sun. A ring of sunlight flared around the lunar disk creating a ring-like effect because the sun was not completely obscured by the moon. I began to read the article, not expecting the significance of what I'd discovered:

"A solar eclipse that reduced the sun to a blazing ring surrounding a somber disk plunged millions of people in Africa and Asia into an eerie semi-darkness on Friday. The spectacle, visible in a roughly 185-mile band running 8,062 miles across the globe set a record for the longest annular eclipse that will remain unbeaten for more than a thousand years."

The duration the moon was in front of the sun was 11 minutes and 8 seconds, making it the longest annular eclipse of the 3rd millennium (2000–2999). It would not be until 3043 until this record was beaten. Amazing. Absolutely amazing, but there was more, *"The eclipse...temporarily put a halt to the world's biggest religious gathering in northern India. Temples in Haridwar, site of the Kumbh Mela, which sees millions of Hindus bathe in the Holy river Ganges, were closed for the duration of the eclipse because the phenomenon is considered inauspicious."*

What was the Kumbh Mela? I had no idea it even existed, so I researched and learned that the Kumbh Mela dated back many centuries in Ancient India. Its origin was connected with one of the creation myths in Hinduism and was observed at one of four sacred sites once every 12 years. In addition to ritual bathing in the Holy river, other activities of the Kumbh Mela included religious discussions and assemblies, devotional singing, and mass feeding of holy men and the poor.

"Hold up, wait," I stopped reading in thought. Millions of Hindus pilgrimage to the Kumbh Mela every 12 years and gather for massive festivals of repentance and peace? Why weren't Christians doing anything similar to this? How was it that millions of people in another country who believe in the same religion get along harmoniously enough to have a mass pilgrimage to the Kumbh Mela and yet there were conflicts and dissension in the many denominations of Christianity?

I thought about how this discovery might be related to my mission for God, especially as I recalled God telling me it was time for "Jesus throughout all religions," when I read that today was also Mauni Amavasya, a day depicted as a call of the inner self. Mauni Amavasya emphasized the emptying of one's self of worldly distractions to focus on an inner dialogue with the silence of God within, beyond images in the experience of "no thing," the state of existence which transcended sound and was boundless, dimensionless, and attributeless.

The spiritual practice of turning inward into silence in direct communion with God sounded much like the mystical inner path of Gnosticism, as well as other esoteric practices that were said to have gone underground centuries ago when they were deemed heretical by the church. Yet even saints such as St. John of the Cross emphasized the importance of silence, therefore the practice was not relegated to "heretics."

In fact, upon deeper review of the gospels, I'd noted multiple verses showing Jesus practiced this too. It was said that he would travel to a mountain, a lake, or another "lonely place" in solitude to be alone in silence and to pray, even leaving his disciples behind. Silence seemed to transcend religions, the importance of turning inward to the temple of God within, not a temple constructed of stone and wood in the world, but the inner temple directly connected with God in Spirit; similar in aspects with the inner work I discovered was also associated with Mauni Amavasya.

My mind raced as I sat back in my chair, how could this eclipse have been right where the Kumbh Mela was, in one of the four locations where it was held once every twelve years? How could it have been on exactly the day of Mauni Amavasya? How was it I just so happened to turn on the television and chose to remain on the channel after Jeopardy ended and ended up seeing the Wheel of Fortune show?

Astounded, the revelations of how all of the pieces were congealing as perfectly fitting puzzle pieces of co-creation between God and humankind held me in rapture. The precise significance was almost unfathomable: the moon and sun alignment to create the eclipse, Earth alignment to have the eclipse be over the area of the world's largest religious gathering, on the same day of the call for the inner spiritual path and turning within to silence and connection with the Divine. Humankind established the day of Mauni Amavasya! The Wheel of Fortune show televised the show in their established schedule! I watched television once in a blue moon and remembered feeling like I should stay on that particular channel.

There was only one explanation I could come up with: today's events were planned and set into action from before the day the moon and the sun were created, from before the day the Earth was placed in position and set into its rotation and tilt before time was conceived or existed. I found no other way to explain any of this other than it was of God, set into motion eons ago before the beginning of creation. In awe, I exhaled as the rapture released its hold, and said, "God, I think I'm beginning to realize how big this is."

"Yes, you are, Shannon."

It was blowing my mind. I could not even think of the right words to say. "God is...what?" Awesome, amazing, and great, did not seem to fit what I was feeling. "God is. God just is. God is infinitely above anything we can conceive or know or ever imagine." I thought, "And God is choosing to reveal this to a greater extent to us now in our generation."

Hours later, after arriving home from work in the evening, I was still blown away. It felt like when I was a little girl and I'd sit cross-legged on the floor and start thinking about infinity. In my mind, I'd think about where I was sitting on the floor, then I'd expand my mind, expanding, expanding trying to see how far I could get my mind to go, thinking about how big infinity was. At some point, I'd end up stopping because my brain hurt from trying to reach infinity. That, right there, beyond where my mind could reach in infinity, was God.

DISCIPLESHIP

...LEARNING AT THE FEET OF THE MASTER.

I want you to know, brothers and sisters, that the gospel
I preached is not of human origin.
I did not receive it from any man, nor was I taught it;
rather, I received it by revelation from Jesus Christ.
(Galatians 1:11-12)

❖ ❖ ❖

Saturday, January 16, 2010

One might think I'd be joyful and excited after everything that transpired yesterday, but I was not. I woke up frustrated. Here I was with a testimony of Jesus saving me, an anointing from God, and a message to share with the world—beyond anything I could have ever dreamed—at the same time, here I was waiting for God to bring the husband He promised into my life. It was difficult not to doubt the revelations over these last weeks about who I was and what I was called by Jesus to do, especially since there was no sign of my promised husband on the horizon.

When I called out in prayer, similar to when frustration consumed me while waiting in California, I petitioned, "God, if this is what You are doing, it is time for You to show me… to show me… to show me…" I kept repeating it because I could not make myself to say, "…or release me." At the point in prayer when I used to cry out, "I'm giving up, I have no hope left. I can't do this anymore, I beg of You to release me from this," now I could not say the words out loud, could not even seriously consider them.

"Do you see how much faith you have, Shannon?"

I was not sure what God meant.

"Your faith can move mountains now."

Reflecting on what God revealed, I realized my trust was so much stronger than it was a couple of months ago, especially last summer when in the confusion and heartbreak I could not decipher what next step to take or what decision to make. I believed with my whole heart that I was now on God's path and exactly where I was meant to be in life.

"You have faith that can move mountains," God repeated.

There was no doubt in my mind I was hearing God and that He guided every step I took, even with no evidence of my promised husband on the horizon. I believed because God promised it would happen, just like when God promised Abraham that his wife Sarah would conceive a son in Genesis 17:16-22 even though it seemed impossible because they were already elderly in years and Sarah was past the age of childbearing.

"You have faith that can perform miracles."

"I do?"

"Yes, you needed to know how far you've come. How strong your faith is now."

"Really?"

"Yes, you are ready."

"I have faith that can perform miracles?"

"Yes, and to heal."

Feeling a lot less frustrated and even maybe a bit encouraged, I drove over to a local bookstore and pulled into a parking spot. I planned to browse for any books on Christian Gnosticism to learn more about the pathway and beliefs. As I paged through the books in the store, I realized my experiences over the last few months with God were similar to the Gnostics.

The etymology of the word, "gnosis," was Greek, it meant "inner knowing," not an intellectual knowledge, but a knowing that came from direct inner experience and produced a wisdom of the heart. Gnostics sought to discover the true spiritual self through direct mystical experience with the Divine, through self-effort towards the spiritual flame within, to "know thyself."

The teachings honored the masculine and feminine aspects of the Creator, as well as the alchemical sacred marriage of these energies in restoration of harmony and balance within. I recalled Jesus taught in parables of the bride and bridegroom as symbols as written in the canonized gospels. The Gnostics believed it was this union that awakened the light of Christ Consciousness and allowed for the embodiment of Christ through a human while still alive on Earth. In doing this, Heaven would be brought to Earth to illuminate the world of matter through the light of Christ in the soul.

A further discovery was at my fingertips as I skimmed through another book and read about the uncovering of 52 early Gnostic Christian texts in earthenware jars in the mountains of Upper Egypt. They were discovered in 1945, although the texts were not published until the year that I was born, in 1977, "The Nag Hammadi Scriptures," I whispered with excitement and awe.

I'd already heard of the Dead Sea Scrolls, discovered in 11 caves near the Essene community of Qumran in 1947. The Dead Sea Scrolls consisted of more than 800 Jewish religious scriptures written between 120 BC/BCE and 50 AD/CE, predating the New Testament of the Bible. However, the scriptures found at Nag Hammadi were written later between 60 and 400 AD/CE and focused on the teachings of Jesus.

The 13 leather-bound books and 55 texts discovered in Nag Hammadi included gospels referenced in the early literature of the church and others never seen or heard of before. Some of the texts revealed philosophies at odds with Orthodox Christianity such as teachings about karma, reincarnation, and the existence of the Divine Mother.

Exhaling in delight, I realized, "Just like God told me, they were lost!"

Beyond the depiction of Jesus as a Savior for our sins, the Nag Hammadi Scriptures portrayed him as a spiritual master and guide to enlightenment. My finger ran across the words of one of the gospels in the Gospel of Thomas, *"Jesus said, the kingdom of God is inside of you."* This was almost identical to the Bible verse from Luke 17:20-21.

Yet, it appeared the Gnostic texts focused on a search for truth within one's self that seemed to go deeper than the Christian belief of being "saved" by Jesus. It was not just believing our sins were forgiven because of who Jesus was, or that he died for our sins on the cross, but an ongoing inner relationship and Divine revelation directly with God; a continual emergence of a new gospel through the Gnostic's life in the alchemical work and transformation in Christ.

Continuing to page through books along the aisle, I opened one that was not related to Gnosticism. One line jumped, catching my eye. The author described a vision when Jesus in very human and real form, came to him and said, *"Do not idolize me."* A little disturbed, I closed the book and set it back on the shelf.

Even as I moved to the next book, the human image of Jesus saying, *"Do not idolize me,"* did not go away. As I left the bookstore and headed home, the question burned in my thoughts: were we idolizing Jesus?

Sunday, January 17, 2010

Sleep was restless overnight, and I ended up arriving a little late for church, walking in during the middle of one of the opening songs. The worship music singers at the front of the church led the congregation, "One way, Jesus you're the only one I could ever live for…" I tipped my head to one side unconsciously and noticed a slight twinge of uncomfortableness within my body as I listened to the words of the song. I stepped into the pew as the chorus repeated. "One way, Jesus you're the only one I could ever live for…"

I thought to myself, "What about living for Father God? The one who Jesus said sent him? Where was the line drawn for worshipping Jesus instead of the Father?"

The worship music leader began praying during the bridge of the song, "We worship you, Jesus. We worship you, Jesus. Just tell your dad. I love you, Jesus. Just let God move through you. Yes, Jesus, we worship you." Someone near me repeated her words, "Yes, we worship you, Jesus." There I stood in the pew, not singing along, jaw slightly dropped, and taking it all in.

"He alone will be glorified in this church. We worship you, Jesus. We worship you, Jesus." The worship leader concluded as the song came to an end. She then motioned the congregation to be seated and as I sat down, I pulled out my journal and wrote the question, "How can the fullness of God move if we are worshipping the Son and not the Father who sent him?"

Still stunned, I looked at the notes I'd scribbled about what I observed and how it felt inside. Off the top of my head, I could not recall any verses in the gospels where Jesus told anyone he was God or asked for his disciples to worship him. In fact, I could have sworn Jesus directed all worship and glory to the One who sent him.

Before I could think on it any further, the sermon began. The pastor interchanged "God" and "Jesus" several times throughout the message as if both were one and the same. Was I never aware of this before? Did I just not notice? When I thought I was on the verge of being appalled, I in-so-much-as sunk entirely into it as the pastor prayed to Jesus at the conclusion of the sermon. I did remember distinctly in the Bible, Jesus instructed us to pray to the Father, not to himself. All I could do was scowl at my scribbled notes as the congregation clapped at the end, asking no one in particular in my thoughts, "How was I possibly going to set this right?"

"Wait for my directive."

"God, you're using me in everything that I do…"

"Yes, I am, Shannon."

"None of this is a coincidence?"

"You are mine; I am with you."

Walking out to the Jeep to head home, illumination ignited within me. Jesus was idolized by some Christians. I reflected back to a few days earlier when I questioned in my writings why we as humankind held onto idols. I postulated that it may be because we always knew what we'll get back from an idol. We cling to them because we know their aspects, their qualities, and we were comfortable with them and how they made us feel. Case in point, when Christians give their lives to Jesus, they believe that they know what they'll get back, eternal life.

Jesus was comfortable. He was predictable. What did we receive when we placed our hopes and trust in Jesus? Strength. Peace. Love. Comfort. Miracles. Healing. We knew exactly what we were going to "get" back. In doing so, we were clinging to the image of Jesus we created. We could rest assured all was well because we knew what he was doing for us and what we could expect to receive.

What happened if we removed the image of the human Jesus? We had the promise of eternal life, but no tangible proof. If we remove the "idol," we were left with the Unknowable, Great Mystery of God who was unpredictable and ineffable. If we removed the image of Jesus, we must have faith in what is unseen in Spirit, to the Father who sent him. Faith goes beyond what our minds know, what we "see" with our eyes, or what we feel with our hands. True faith is in what we cannot see and what we do not fully know.

Tuesday, February 9, 2010

As I drove along on the backgrounds to work this morning, I was startled when slowing to a stop at a red light. The SUV in front of me had a license plate from California. That was the part that first caught my eye, but then I read the license plate holder: "God is Love" across the top, and "St. Antony Monastery" across the bottom. I'd never heard of it before.

It turned out, St. Antony Monastery was the oldest Christian monastery in the world and associated with the Coptic Orthodox Church, one of the oldest denominations in the world. Suddenly, I appreciated how little I knew about the history of Christianity. This was my sign of where I needed to focus research next and it led to an entire week of journaling.

Dozens of scribbled notes and typed pages filled these days of research. Although I wouldn't include all of them here lest this turn into a history book, my heart felt the significance of what I learned. Honestly, I hadn't been aware of most of what I learned in all the years I called myself a Christian.

During the Apostolic Age (33 AD/CE to around 100 AD/CE) the apostles traveled across the west and east of the known world as missionaries of what was known as "The Way," the teachings of Jesus. Yet, even during this early period, a substantial number of sects, cults, and movements existed that had differences in theological and philosophical beliefs. In its infancy, the "church" was not a church in the way we thought about it today. Christians gathered in local communities in homes or secret meetings since they were suffering persecution by the Roman government.

However, when the Roman Empire adopted the Trinitarian version of Christianity as the official state church in 380 AD/CE followers were referred to as Catholic Christians. I found it interesting when I learned that Catholic meant "universal," as if it was originally meant to be the one and only "universal" church of Christianity. When the Catholic Church became the state Church of Rome, all other forms of Christianity were deemed heretical.

The differences of beliefs that existed before the establishment of the Catholic Church persisted into years of debate about the "trinity," that was, the nature of Jesus, through the Council of Nicaea in 325 AD/CE. It was settled at the Council: Jesus was Light from Light, true God from true God, begotten, not made, and of one being with the Father. Afterward, Correctores were appointed to edit and rewrite the gospels according to the outcomes. Some scholars believe this editing introduced paganism into the gospels to make it more palatable for Constantine and the Roman people.

Six decades later in 397 AD/CE, the Third Council of Carthage took place. This Council came to an agreement on the 27 books included in the New Testament canon. To put this in perspective, the 27 books selected were out of more than 500 gospels. All scriptures not included in the canon were deemed heretical.

The Nicene Creed, the church's statement of belief and profession of faith, was finalized in 451 AD/CE at the Council of Chalcedon. Yet, the debates and conflict did not end. For hundreds of years, the divisions and arguments persisted in further councils, edicts, and writings.

Almost immediately after the fall of Rome, splitting of the "universal" Catholic Church ensued. Most notable was the Great Schism of 1054, when the Roman Catholic Church and Eastern Orthodox Church divided due to political and theological disputes.

From my childhood in the Lutheran church, I was already familiar with the igniting of the Protestant Reformation in 1517. Martin Luther was said to have defiantly nailed the 95 Theses, otherwise known as the "*Disputation on the Power and Efficacy of Indulgences*" against the Catholic Church on the door of the Wittenberg Castle Church. The act was said to spark the Reformation, but as I looked over the historical timeline, it was just another division in a line of thousands of splitting off denominations away from the "universal church."

According to the <u>World Christian Encyclopedia</u> (Oxford) published in 1982, more than 20,000 denominations existed. This grew to more than 33,000 denominations in the edition published in 2001. I questioned in my journal, how was this the one, undivided church the gospels talked about?

In all my years growing up in the Lutheran Church, not once did I question the Bible. I'd never thought about: how it was written; by whom it was written; when it was written; or why any of that might matter to us thousands of years later. Nor did I ever consider the involvement of political or other power plays over the centuries which may have contributed to the outcomes.

Most of all, though, I realized that although I did still believe the books within the Bible canon were Divinely inspired, ultimately the sacred texts were all written, edited, translated, and published by man.

Friday, March 12, 2010

A sense of hopelessness began to overwhelm me. Frustration, emptiness, and a sense of detachment—the feeling this was all a dream and not reality. God showed me a path, but I could not walk on it because it was contingent on receiving my husband promised by God. Since there was no sign of any man coming into my life… was it real? Was it really God's will or did I make it all up in my head? What was the truth?

Why was God allowing me to remain stagnant in this desert land? Numbness pervaded my senses and it felt as though life was disconnected from where I stood, and all alone. I could not even willfully throw it away and say I was "done with all this" because I did not know what it was I would be done with anymore. I was uncertain what was of me or what was of God. I questioned what to rebuke or what to hold onto in faith. I did not see the light or know what was real versus illusion, in the dark night of my soul. Yet I knew I was not alone, and God was with me, guiding me through even when I doubted myself. My trust in God remained steadfast throughout every inner storm.

Out of frustration, I signed up on a Christian dating website. I wasn't sure what I thought I was going to get out of it. Even as I sat and typed in the "about me" section, I heard doors shutting in my head. Let's see… about me: "Hi There, I'm Shannon! Two months ago God shared with me the teaching for the New Millennium. Amazing but true, I'm appointed to share the news. But right now, I'm waiting for the husband God promised me before I announce it to the world in the publication of my journals."

Before going any further, I deleted the account without completing the profile. UGH! I sat there dumbfounded at myself. What happened to me? Where was all this darkness coming from? Why didn't I feel anything? Why did it feel like I was separated from reality? What was real? Was this my path or was reality that I did not know anything, and I was supposed to figure it out from here?

If I took away everything I focused on in the last seven months, what would be left? Nothing. My life revolved around God. I questioned how I could have made this up if I never expected it and certainly never asked for it. Never did I think God would call me for anything. And now as I questioned whether any of this was real I realized that without God's path, my life was nothing.

I'd discovered that was what faith was all about, believing in something that cannot be seen unlike an idol held onto for safety and protection. God was also in the unknown and in the times of darkness. I did not know what I'd be getting back after giving up my entire life to God. I was in the desert and the silence of the dark night. It was the most difficult experience I'd ever recalled in my life because there was no rational reason to continue holding on in faith to God's promises, and yet, my faith would not allow me to let it go.

As I signed off in my journal tonight with my regular closing, "Always, Shannon," I wrote right underneath it, "Although, I don't know what that means anymore."

Wednesday, April 28, 2010

When God told me I would not suffer any longer, I could now rule out that it meant I would never suffer in my physical body. It began with one painful welt on Sunday, a few more on Monday, and by Tuesday, my arms and chest were unbearable in pain and itching. The blistering welts felt like they were on fire. I was unable to sleep for the last two nights and went to the doctor today who confirmed it was a bad case of poison ivy. The worst part was that I knew God had warned me.

Before the onslaught of poison ivy blisters, I'd gone out to one of the back corners in my backyard to tear out overgrowth. As I reached in with my clippers and pulled out the vines and brush in both arms, I felt God tell me, **"Be careful."** I remember shrugging it off—what does that mean? Why would I need to be careful? I'd been doing yard work almost every day for three weeks and this was like every other evening.

I sighed at myself now in the realization, when I felt God say, **"Be careful,"** did I ask, "About what?" "Why?" "What are you trying to tell me?" Did I pay more attention to what I was doing to notice the "leaves of three?" No, I went on my merry way pulling out vines and branches believing there was nothing I needed to be careful about. Recalling back to that day though, I remembered I felt compelled to shower after coming in and throwing my clothes and towels directly into the washing machine. So somehow, in some way, I must have known even though I did not consciously know.

I had noticed in the suffering I'd been in; I wasn't praying. My focus was on finding ways to relieve the itchy pain—I was focused on "it" and not on God. As I thought about this, it was amazing how subtle the shift was until I saw it now in reflection.

I knew there was a reason why God let me get such a bad case of poison ivy. When I asked Him last night why I was going through this, He responded, **"Endurance."** It's not a word I used in everyday life, and I associated it with the endurance training of marathon runners. I knew this was a teaching moment. Endurance also meant the suffering was not going to go away quickly. I resolved myself to be strong and place my focus on reducing the swelling and pain as best I could.

Although removing my focus from God may seem trivial because I was still talking with God, what I was not doing was setting contemplative time aside in devotion and silent prayer like normal. What was my conscious-minded reason for not praying? "My arm hurts! I wouldn't be able to focus because of the itching so why should I even try?" And even worse… "I didn't feel like it tonight. I was in pain." What were these reasons? My own beliefs, feelings, and thoughts that I placed in higher importance than God, like an idol.

Idols in the Old Testament were depicted as bronze statues and representations of other gods. In the New Testament, idols were attributed to what belonged to our earthly nature such as sexual immorality, impurity, lust, evil desires, and greed. But it did not stop there, idols could be activities and pursuits of the world that take our time and focus away from our inner Divine connection: career and work; watching television or online videos; computer, electronic device, or video games; social media; overeating or undereating; drinking too much alcohol; gambling to the point of financial distress; any other hobbies that become too much of a focus in life. Idols could also be relationships, spouses, or children; and also attributes of ourselves, including any labels or definitions we form.

Unbelievably, the book I'd started reading discussed this very point, from <u>Will & Spirit</u> by American Psychiatrist and Theologian, Gerald G. May: *"All of us are to some extent idolatrous. If we are relatively free from mistaking image for reality in other areas, we at least idolize our self-images. When I speak of myself I am almost always referring to the image I have of myself, and I habitually assume that I am talking about something solid and objectifiable. I forget that my true "self' is mystery born of mystery."*

It made sense when I thought about it, not only could we not place God in a single religious box, but we could also not place our "self" in one either. We sculpted and molded these boxes of separation, the idols we hold up and say, "I know this is me," or "I know this is God," or "I am…" or "God is…" These separations divide us from each other, from knowing the truth about our self, and pushes us farther away from God.

From Will & Spirit: *"Proclaiming 'I am Christian' is every bit as self-defining and self-important as 'I am not a Christian' or 'I am an atheist' or 'I am a vegetarian.' Each time we define ourselves in such categories, we not only increase our self-importance, but we also separate ourselves further from those who do not fit within our categories."*

As I thought about the statement, "I am Christian," I envisioned a hypocritical Christian. One who constantly proclaims that he or she is "saved" and who tries to convert those who are "not saved" with the "only truth." One who clings to the Bible and uses it as a ready defense against non-believers. One who lives a "Godly, faithful life," doing "good works," and "loves others as Jesus loved them," but then does not love everyone unconditionally and divides by proclaiming other denominations or religions as wrong in judgment instead of unifying through common ground and in the Spirit of love.

In essence, I saw how at a deeper level the hypocritical Christian may be revealing, "You must belong to the box I've placed God in so that I can be comfortable in my beliefs, in the place where I am with God," instead of delving into the mystery of the eternal and infinite where the walls of separation and self-image crumble, this hypocritical Christian was blocked from knowing Oneness because of judgment in right versus wrong. It takes a lot of courage to question a belief, especially beliefs ingrained since youth.

If God is infinite and can do whatever He wants to do in the heavens and on the Earth, how can we think that we have it all figured out? How can we believe that we know the entire truth? How can we deem other pathways as being evil or wrong or not true?

"The Bible! The Bible is God's word!" says the threatened hypothetical Christian, as I roleplayed out this scenario on the pages of my journal.

"But… what was lost in translations? What words deleted, changed, or added in? Think about the differences even between different versions of the Bible which exist today? What was removed? What may not have been included that should have been?"

"The Spirit of God was with the authors of those books!" Retorts the hypothetical Christian.

"Perhaps the Spirit of God was present, but who can say that man did not corrupt it at any time over the last 2000 years? We can't know. We can't assume to know. We ultimately cannot put our faith in a book even if it contains the Word of God. Because what is it? Of this world!" I realized the Bible could be an idol, too.

I reflected back to last fall when I recited verses in moments when I felt like giving up or needed comfort. I was clinging to the words of the Bible, something tangible to help get me through. While there was nothing wrong with this, I recognized now that it was not enough to have faith in the words of a book. At some point, I stepped beyond holding onto the words on the pages. It came with the understanding that our Source, Creator, the All was infinite, uncontainable, and unboxable. God was greater than any religious box or image we'd created.

When one gets to the point of not just believing in God, but knowing God, with that knowledge comes the greatest unknowing fathomable. The fear in that unknowing dissipates with the experience of unconditional love that comes from within. The knowing opens the door to the mystery. The unknowing we must step into, beyond idols, images, tools, books, guides, and even the faith that brought us to the very moment. As one steps into the mystery, all fear subsides in the infiniteness of love.

It was not a leap of faith; it was beyond faith. Beyond anything I could describe, comprehend, or know with my rational mind. It could not be forced upon but was given by the grace of God when I turned inward and away from wisdom in the world. As Jesus said, *"Ask and it will be given to you; seek and you will find; knock and the door will be opened to you. For everyone who asks receives; the one who seeks finds; and to the one who knocks, the door will be opened"* (Mathew 7:7-8).

Wednesday, May 19, 2010

I tossed and turned all night, the details of my dreams were slightly beyond the edges of my conscious memory, but I knew they were spiritual in nature. I awakened to Sadie towering over me, her big St. Bernard paws next to me on the bed. She nudged my arms with her nose, telling me to get up, and when I did not move, she licked my face repeatedly until I pet her, "Yes, I'm getting up, girl."

I paused and asked God what I needed to remember from the dreams.

"Grace."

Hmm, off the top of my head, the one verse I could recall stated God's grace was sufficient. I was not sure if that was where God was leading. Before getting ready for work, I ran a quick Bible verse search in an online database for the word "grace." My eyes landed on one of the more than 100 verses that came up.

"Jonah 2:8," I exhaled out loud in awe, *"Those who cling to worthless idols forfeit the grace that could be theirs."* Any time we place idols or images before God, not only are we separating ourselves further from God, but we are also losing out on grace!

Before digging further, I wanted to make sure I had a working definition of grace. From M-W.com grace was defined as: "Unmerited Divine assistance given humans for their regeneration or sanctification. A virtue coming from God. A state of sanctification enjoyed through Divine grace, such as approval, favor, mercy, pardon, a special favor, or privilege. Disposition to or an act or instance of kindness, courtesy, or clemency."

Romans 6:14 advised once we were living in grace, sin was no longer our master and we were no longer living under the law. But what did living a grace-filled life look like? Other verses provided the answer: receiving one blessing after another (John 1:16); in all things at all times, having all that is needed (2 Corinthians 9:8); and capable of performing wonders and miraculous signs (Acts 6:8).

Did I even need to emphasize how huge this was? If we chose to self-willfully miss out on God's grace by having idols in our lives, we were missing out on so much (blessings, having all needs fulfilled, and the gifts of performing miracles)! Anything, absolutely anything could become an idol and separate us further from God.

The key then was a willingness to renounce everything of this world to reconnect with God within as described in the teachings of Jesus (Matthew 19:21, Luke 14:33; Matthew 16:24, among others). The treasure we seek is in our hearts, not in anything of this world.

Later in the evening, I walked along the street in my neighborhood with Sadie. I was in peaceful and silent prayer. I noted that periods of silence were more comfortable now, I did not need to hear from God all the time, and there was not as much frustration or struggling in the dry desert times anymore. No crying out for Heavenly comfort.

As I talked with God, I mentioned, "…it must mean I'm learning how to walk more comfortably with You."

"In grace."

"In grace? What does that mean, God?"

"I am with you."

This was what a grace-filled life looks like? Unshakeable peace, accepting of where I stood, comfortable with who I was. This was what I'd been trying to figure out lately because the sense of peace pervaded my being so often now. It was the grace of God.

Thursday, May 20, 2010

Driving along a bypass road, I was surprised to notice a church sign off to the side of the route. I hadn't remembered ever seeing it before in all the times I'd passed through the area. It was the "True Jesus Church." I heard God's soft voice.

"Go."

"You want me to go there?"

"You are ready."

Hmm, ready for what. I was not sure... But then I felt God impress on me a single word,

"Demons."

"Wait, God, and you want me to go there?" I asked with an incredulous tone in my voice.

"You are ready."

In disbelief of what God was directing me to do, later in the day, I searched online for more information about the church since I'd never heard of it before. The True Jesus Church was a nondenominational church founded in the early 1900s in China and then spread to other areas around the world.

As I kept browsing, I noticed their statements of faith, *"The God we worship is the true God. Thus, His church is the true church,"* and *"Jesus Christ... is the only Savior of mankind. The Creator of the heavens and earth, and the one true God."* Ahh, I realized they adhere to the Oneness belief there was no trinity.

I thought about the many years of debate over the trinity and wondered how anyone could state definitively what the godhead looks like if we could not see or know directly of what it consists of; for how could we know the fullness of mystery, infinity, and eternity? Our limited human thought and the boundaries of conscious perspective did not know the whole truth of God —or the trinity for that matter.

Yet, what had the "trinity" done? It separated Christians from each other for thousands of years and created turmoil, suffering, and inter-Christian conflict. The trinity fractured denomination from denomination time after time until we arrived at the shattered state that Jesus' teachings were in today. The fact that it caused so much conflict was amazing to me, especially because the word "trinity" did not even appear in the canonized Bible scriptures.

I wondered, what if we agreed that we could not know for sure what the godhead looked like because it was spirit and had no image? What if we agreed we could not ever fully know the whole truth because our conscious minds are incapable of comprehending the expansiveness of infinity? Infinity could not be boxed, and if one tried, only a part of the truth would be captured. And what did that do? It separated and divided Christians into boxes of belief, "We know the only truth!" How could anyone be so egotistical to think we had the absolute answer on the trinity?

Jesus said we should be one in the Father as he is one in the Father. Would it make it a four-person trinity if we add another person to Jesus, the Father, and the Holy Spirit? Or a five-person trinity if you add me too? Or wait… maybe an infinity-trinity if it includes all souls from the beginning of all time? If God is All and All is God, just as a trinity exists it also does not exist. If God is ALL, that meant God is all polarities, possibilities, and potentials.

To bring forth Heaven on Earth, we must remove the stumbling blocks that have too long separated us. We can argue sides of theology and philosophy for years and never get to a final truth on the trinity. The debates have been going on for thousands of years! How does our faith in God change if we let go of all the creeds and the scriptures and the thousands of years of theological arguments? If faith is within the expansiveness of God, and if life is filled with God's grace and the fruits of love and goodness, what is the problem?

It is part of the Mystery and having faith in the unknown through the letting go of idols and images in the world to establish a root of faith in what cannot be seen or fully known. That's where I was now, in the truth rooted in the infinite Mystery within my heart.

Friday, May 21, 2010

With an unshakeable sense of peace and obedience, I was about to go to the True Jesus Church. As I went to put on a sweater and black pants, my hand hesitated before reaching for a fuchsia-colored sweater. I did not want to stick out wearing a bright color.

I heard God's gentle voice, **"It does not matter what you wear. You will stand out."** I wasn't sure what to make of that. I began to question again whether I was truly supposed to go.

"Go," God answered. I threw on a darker sweater instead and grabbed my keys, Bible, and notebook, and gave Sadie a kiss and head pat good-bye as I headed out the front door.

Parking at the church a little while later, I tried to find the entrance. A kind-looking Asian American man came out of a side door of the building and must have seen the questioning look on my face because he welcomed me inside. He introduced himself and asked my name.

"Shannon," I smiled in reply, "I'm here for the church service tonight."

The kind man led me down a side hallway as he explained the Friday night service was smaller, so it was not held in the main chapel but in a smaller one. As we walked in, I noticed rows of pews with a podium at the front. The congregation was already singing a traditional hymn as a pianist played the melody. The man motioned to follow him into a pew and handed me a hymnal. I found the song and started singing, finding the notes from the melody even though I'd never heard it before.

It was then that I glanced around the room. The pews were filled up with members of the congregation and I realized I was the only Caucasian person in the entire chapel. All the members of the congregation were Asian Americans. I giggled inside and let a small grin escape my lips as I turned my gaze back to the front of the room. No wonder God told me I would stand out no matter what I wore tonight.

A few hymns were sung, and the pastor went up to the podium and asked the congregation to pray in silence. He then led us into the Lord's Prayer. After a couple more hymns, two pastors went up to the podium: one preached in English while the other translated in Mandarin Chinese.

It never ceased to amaze me when I knew God wanted me to go somewhere and I obey and go, and then received insight and revelations. This church service was one of those times.

The sermon discussed a parable in Judges 9:8-15, when a man named Abimelech wanted to be king over Israel, and the Israelites wanted a king to rule over them. In the parable, the trees went out to anoint a king for themselves. First coming to an olive tree, they said, "Be our king." The olive tree refused. The trees then said to the fig tree, "Come and be our king," but the fig tree also refused. This happened a third time when the trees said to the vine, "Come and be our king," and the vine also refused. Finally, all the trees said to the thorn bush, "Come and be our king." The thorn bush replied if the trees wanted to anoint a king, then they could come and take refuge in its shade.

The pastor described that the olive tree, fig tree, and vine all knew their places in God's plan. They knew God was ruler over everyone and everything and they remained steadfast in their purpose to serve God and others, not to rule over men. But the thorn bush was willing to be king over the trees, and the trees were willing to make the thorn bush their king because they wanted a ruler from the world. Yet there was no protection from the sun under the thorn bush nor protection from its thorns.

The pastor then related the parable back to the Israelites wanting someone to rule over them. They'd turned away from God and desired a human king. Awe coursed through my body in tingles of realization. In the story, the Israelites (that is, God's children) desired a human king because they did not want to turn away from their sins. If their king was human and ruled in a way that satisfied their desires, they would be happy.

In the story of Jesus leading up to his crucifixion, he rode into Jerusalem as the King of Israel, and later he had a crown of thorns placed on his head. I noted the symbolic parallel using the same words as the "thorn bush king."

Wisdom poured through me as my heart understood the teaching. I saw the similarities between the two stories, showing us that our desire for a human king was faulty; it was still desiring something of this world rather than of spirit. Images fall away, human kings and leaders die.

Images and idols of the human Jesus crafted by our minds and hands depicted him as king, savior, and messiah. When we placed the human Jesus up on a pedestal, he became the thorn bush king—even though that's not who he really was. He was One with God, the Son of God, sent by Love. He reminded us to turn within ourselves to find the kingdom of God, we were children of God like him, and we could do as he did, including healing and miracles which the apostles carried on after Jesus' death.

Clinging onto the image of the human Jesus was placing one's self under the protection of the thorn bush. It was not real protection because it was not the real living Spirit of Christ. It was evident when people did this because their lives were consumed by fire. Those people also consume others in the fire for not believing in the same king they do. I considered that if people believed in the infinite and eternal Truth that came from within, they would be like the olive tree, fig tree, and vine, who knew their places in God's plan and whose roots remained steadfast in faith, who knew we could not look to a ruler of this Earth.

I drew my focus back to the service as the sermon ended, and it was announced praying in the spirit would be next. The kind man leaned his head in close, "I don't know if you're accustomed to this." I followed the lead of what I saw the rest of the congregation doing and kneeled in the narrow space between where I was sitting and the pew in front of us.

As I bowed my head and folded my hands together, the congregation began praying in tongues all around me. The sounds of rolling "rRrRrRrRrRrRrRrRrRrRrRrRrRrRrs" and range of tones rose to loud crescendos of chaotic sound in the room.

Taking it all in, I kept my eyes closed. As time passed and there was no sign of an end, I peeked out of the corner of my eyes and gazed around at the people in the room. Some were swaying back and forth; others were bobbing up and down with their upper bodies and palms held upwards. A few did not seem to be as fervent in their praying, but undeniably most of the congregation were praying out loud in spiritual tongues with their whole hearts, basking in the presence of the Holy Spirit.

Closing my eyes again, I tried to focus on praying in my mind, but words and thoughts were lost in the loudness of the tones around me. Then I tried to focus on feeling God's presence. I felt nothing. Peaceful in the middle of all this, but nothing else. After what could have been five or ten minutes, someone rang a bell, which seemed to mean it was time to stop and sit in the pews again. After a couple more hymns, another gentleman went up to the front for announcements.

I kind of had a feeling this was coming, so it was not a surprise when the man at the podium welcomed me by name in front of the entire congregation. I smiled and waved in response to the applause and warm welcome. Thereafter, the service was dismissed and the kind gentleman who I'd sat next to asked what I thought about their church.

"It was different than other churches that I've been to in the past," I admitted to him. I said I was curious and had a question for him if he did not mind.

He welcomed the question, so I mentioned one of the aspects of their service that was different from others I'd experienced in the past was there was not an interpretation done after speaking in tongues. I'd thought that when someone prayed or spoke in tongues out loud within a church it was to be one or two people at most at a time and followed with interpretation.

He nodded and said, "Good question," and pulled out his Bible pointing to a marked verse where Jesus taught his disciples how to pray. The two types of praying were the Lord's Prayer and praying in the spirit. The kindly man emphasized after reading the verse from his Bible that this meant it was right to pray in tongues. He said that he was glad to do so because he did not want other people to understand or know what he was praying.

Nodding I reminded him with gentleness in my voice that God hears our silent prayers as much as he hears our spoken prayers. He agreed this was true and then he told me they worship on the true Sabbath. He asked if I knew Saturday was the true Sabbath and mentioned it was one of the distinguishing factors that made them the true church rather than the Protestants.

I listened to him, realizing as he spoke that their choice of Sabbath day worship was one of the labels on the box they've crafted for their beliefs. It separated them from other denominations. He went on to say that Sunday, named the "Lord's Day" by other denominations was not the true Sabbath and that those Christians were not going to church on the true day they should.

Smiling and with kindness in my voice, I reminded him that there was also a verse in the Bible that stated to not let anyone judge by what day of the week one holds as the Sabbath day. As other Christians should not judge him by what day he goes to church; that also meant they could worship on Sundays if it was what they were more comfortable with.

The gentleman paused in thought before responding. Then nodded as he said, "You've studied the Bible, haven't you?" Giggling, I grinned back as I said, "A little bit." Our conversation continued for a few more minutes. Before I headed back out to my car I thanked him and the small group of church members who'd gathered around us.

My first silent reflection as I drove toward home was filled with gratitude for God speaking through the sermon. Then, I burst out laughing as recognition of what I'd experienced settled in. God told me to go to a church where people were zealously speaking in tongues all around me. If there was any part of me that was still scarred from my previous Pentecostal and charismatic church experiences, any part of me that did not trust God at this point, I would have been so anxious, so afraid, so ready to fly out the exit. It was not one person speaking in tongues of various tones and words, but many people loud, moving, shaking, bobbing, and swaying back and forth from where they knelt. I'd risen above the fear. The demons of fear from my past were gone.

Tuesday, June 1, 2010

A while back I recognized I'd grown to be comfortable in my grace-filled life with God. Well, now I was beginning to sink back into the feeling that I could not do this anymore. It was difficult to hold a conversation with anyone whether it was at work or with family and friends. There weren't many ways I could get around explaining I would do whatever God wanted me to do, whenever God wanted me to do it, without sounding crazy. To state openly, "God was leading me in all things, and I would go where God sends me," was not of this world—at least the world in which I existed. Trying to articulate goals and plans was fruitless, too. I did not have desires anymore: for anything.

How was this normal? How could this not look insane to everyone around me? There was nothing I could do though; I was unwilling to turn away from God's will, which meant I'd continue on my path regardless of what others thought. My former life was destroyed, and my new life was devoted to God. What was even worse, this level of mystical obedience and devotion was not what the everyday Christian looked like.

Even in talking with other Christians, they did not understand the degree of humbling of my will and desires I did every day to God. I thought about the obedience of Biblical figures—Noah, Abraham, David, Daniel, Elijah, Samuel, Jesus, Mary, Paul, and the obedience of the saints. None of which was an ordinary level of obedience and devotion—if it were—the world would be a much different place.

As I wrote, I contemplated, okay, people thought Noah was crazy for building a gigantic boat. People thought Abraham was crazy for leaving his homeland for the unknown. They also surely thought David was crazy for going up against Goliath… Did I need to continue? Did that help me from where I was struggling with this? Not really, but I guess it put me in good company.

In my heart, there was no doubt I was on God's Holy path even if my mind kept questioning. Although, I did receive comfort recalling the stories of the faithful and righteous from the Bible, especially Mother Mary, who gave her life to the will of God in complete faith and trust. Even in the Catholic Church today, she was considered the Mother of all the faithful, closely associated with Christ in continuing the work of evangelization, redeeming humanity and dispensing Christ's grace to the faithful, teaching spiritual life for individual Christians, and known as a worker of miracles. She allowed herself to be guided by the Holy Spirit on a journey of faith to a life of service and fruitfulness. As much as I never thought I would say it, it appeared as though I was destined to continue walking a similar road of faith in what I did not fully understand, know, or could see in front of me.

But at the same time, I needed to face reality. In my solitary life with my St. Bernard and cats, I was basically a nun. Except I did not have a superior, I was not Catholic, and I did not live in a small cell. Okay, maybe I was not a nun. I was something though—something that wasn't normal, and my obedience and devotion were unwavering, but I also had moments of doubt. How there could be anyone who would be equally yoked with me? Why wouldn't God release me from the promise of bringing a husband into my life? Why not let me live my life alone like a nun in a convent? That would be normal from where I stood right now!

Being able to define myself would allow me to have some sort of label people could understand in the world. As I wrote this, I was sighing, because it went against everything I'd learned about not boxing ourselves in self-definitions or images or idols. I was box-less because there was no way to define "me." I was standing there, no husband in sight, no sign of God's promises coming true, and feeling like I was crazy for continuing to hold on in faith.

I was slipping—I felt it—I needed Divine help. I wanted nothing more than to bring glory to the light and love and to serve in my appointing, but I could not yet and did not know how long I had to wait.

Monday, June 7, 2010

It was when I least expected a revelation that it knocked me most to the floor on my knees. I needed Divine encouragement from where I stood stagnant right now, in the desert and waiting for God's promise to come true. This was beyond anything I could have expected, well, let me explain.

Every day I received more than a dozen daily devotional emails in my inbox. Skimming today's emails, the name of one caught my eye. It highlighted the Messianic Age and Christ's return. Clicking it open, it was not too far into reading the email when amazed chills flowed through my body... "Christ's return is with the *blazing glory*..."

Wait. Hold up. Christ's return in blazing glory? Could the words in the Bible which describe Christ's return include "blaze" and "glory"? Hurrying to my computer, I pulled up a Bible verse search database, I wanted to see if scriptural support existed for Christ's return using the words blaze and glory. I found Matthew 24:30-31; Matthew 25:31; Mark 13:26; Luke 21:27, and 2 Thessalonians 1:7.

The Bible said the return will be in "blazing glory!" Until now I'd never considered there might be biblical support, how did I not realize this before? I read the Bible every day! Amazed and in awe, I shook my head, not knowing why this revelation seemed to yank me out of passive sleepy disbelief of, "I have faith and believe God will deliver on His promises someday. I was steadfast although it seemed so impossible to think I was a messenger of the Messianic Age. There it was off in the distance somewhere in the future where God would bring my happily ever after, and my book published." To the awakened shock, "This was really happening. It couldn't be me! How could it possibly be me? How could God have appointed me for this?"

I finished putting the dishes away and let Sadie out one last time for the night. I walked upstairs still heavy in awe, repeating over and over, "It couldn't be me," this suddenly became real. Falling to my knees in prayer, I beseeched God, "Why didn't You reveal this until now? Why didn't You tell me?"

I felt God impress on my heart that the vision given months ago was now coming to life. Tears streaked down my cheeks as I thought about the mistakes I've made, the sins I'd committed, and all my imperfect flaws.

I cried, "How is it me? I've done everything wrong! Taken the wrong roads! Sinned again and again! I deserve to be sent out into the darkness and destroyed! God, how could you have appointed me?"

"Because I know your heart, Shannon."

Waves of humility washed over me. God knew. God knew from before I was born every step I would take. Every decision I would make. Every sin I would commit. God knew every decision I made before I made it and still appointed me. I was humbled by God's grace and love.

This was not of me… I did not deserve the honor of sharing this message with the world. This was by the grace of God.

Thursday, June 24, 2010

Sadie greeted me with a wagging tail and a heavy Saint Bernard lean as I walked into the house after work. I let her outside into the backyard and since I was not in the middle of a book right now, I went over to my bookshelves to find one to read. I scanned the titles of hundreds of books I'd amassed: Christian books, books on the saints, books on Mysticism, Gnosticism, and more than a dozen translations of the Bible and concordances.

The book that caught my eye though was the Qur'an. I'd bought it months ago in case I ever needed it for reference. I decided to do what I sometimes did with the Bible, open it, read one verse, and contemplate the meaning it had for me. Flipping open the Qur'an to a random page, my eyes landed on the verse: *"God speaks the Truth: follow the religion of Abraham, the sane in faith; he was not of the Pagans"* (3:95). The religion of Abraham? Wait, Abraham was in the Qur'an? What was the religion of Abraham?

Before I delved further, I felt it was important to admit my prior ignorance on this topic. Over the years, I'd learned that the Old Testament overlapped with the scriptures of the Torah in Judaism. I knew that Abraham was within the Jewish faith, but what I did not realize until this moment was all three major monotheistic religions claimed Abraham was their father: Judaism and Christianity (through Isaac) and Islam (through Ishmael) both of whom were descendants of Abraham.

Digging deeper into the Islam perspectives of Abraham, I found he was depicted as someone who believed in One God and was avidly against idols and idolatry. Due to the strength of his faith, the Qur'an attributes the one true religion to be the "Path of Abraham." The story of Abraham was about obedience to the will of God, not blind obedience, though. The stories showed he frequently challenged God and asked questions, but Abraham trusted this God who made extraordinary promises. In doing so, he formed a personal relationship through direct connection and experience through faith.

Hmm, this sounded quite similar to the Jewish and Christian perspectives of Abraham. The Jewish tradition viewed Abraham as the epitome of virtue. He was the founding father of the Covenant, which was the special relationship between God and His people. In Christianity, Abraham was the father of all believers. His trust in God and his willingness to sacrifice was a model for later stories about faithful obedience. Of course, although Christianity revolved more so around the story of Jesus, Abraham held a special place as the father whose seed included Jesus (Galatians 3:16).

Abraham was a model of righteousness and faith; the "father" of the three major monotheistic religions, but each seemed to exclusively claim him as theirs. This brought me back to my original question: what was the religion of Abraham? Judaism, Christianity, and Islam were not founded yet. Abraham's religion was FAITH, faith in the One God. There was no other similar religious doctrine during his time. He turned from worshiping other deities or other gods and worshiped the Ultimate Source, Creator, One True God who was imageless and in spirit. The scriptures show how Abraham was righteous before God. He was God's friend; he walked in grace with God, and he was blessed.

I kept in mind this was before the law of the Ten Commandments. The commandments were given because the people were not following God, with the purpose to direct them to turn away from their sins and re-orient themselves to God with concrete rules. Which as we know, did not work. It was not the end; it was the means to an end for that generation.

This was also before Jesus' crucifixion "made us righteous before God." I realized this meant it was possible for humankind to be righteous, receive grace, and walk as one with God as Adam and Eve did in the Garden of Eden before Jesus' death! This insomuch as proved it was not the law of the Ten Commandments or believing in Jesus, the savior who made us right before God, faith was what made us righteous before God.

Abraham was the father of faith and the unifying link, representing the ultimate in faithfulness for all of God's children, not just one religion. It went back to what I'd journaled so many times before, true faith was beyond the boundaries of religion we created. Not to mention, beyond the splitting of so many denominations and factions within each one of the monotheistic religions.

We created a division between ourselves and our brothers and sisters the moment we established the first decrees of what one religion was and what it was not. We created chasms due to beliefs and laws and rituals thousands of years ago and still perpetuate them today. Wasn't the truth that God was All, and All was God? Infinite and eternal? God was inconceivably bigger than a single religion, even all the world wisdom traditions and religions multiplied.

If we were connected from the same source and "father," why has humankind started countless wars and murdered our brothers and sisters in the name of God? Holy wars, turmoil, conflict, and chaos for thousands of years... why, if we all come from the same Source? Was it our Creator's will for us to kill each other? Did this bring glory? These discrepancies were even written about by the author of the gospel of John in chapter 8 beginning with verse 39 as said by Jesus, *"Abraham is our father," they answered. "If you were Abraham's children," said Jesus, "then you would do the things Abraham did. As it is, you are determined to kill me, a man who has told you the truth that I heard from God. Abraham did not do such things. You are doing the things your own father does." "We are not illegitimate children," they protested. "The only Father we have is God himself." Jesus said to them, "If God were your Father, you would love me, for I came from God and now am here."*

There was absolutely nothing "Holy" about harming or killing others. Fruits of the spirit were attributes like charity, joy, peace, patience, and kindness. If one believed God was a loving God, such as Jesus sent by God who was love, or as in Islam wherein two of the 99 aspects of Allah included peace and love (Salam, The Ultimate Provider of Peace, and Al Wadud, The Loving, the Kind One), how could anyone believe harming others in the name of God brought any sort of glory? It took away the glory of the One, True God, and did not honor love.

We came from the same Source and were all created in the image of our Creator, and thus, are all Divine children of God. In the Oneness that exists in spirit, there is no separation of religions or denominations, humankind has created those, and it was those very divisions that we must let go of to focus instead on what unifies humankind: the virtues and qualities that spring forth from roots of steadfast faith. Faith that goes beyond all boundaries and rests in the infiniteness of the God of Abraham.

Thursday, July 1, 2010

A couple of days ago I flipped on the television. Sadie was lying beside me on the couch with her big head in my lap. The cats were perched up on the top of the couch around my head. I caught the tail end of a show on the National Geographic channel, and then the next show began, "How the Earth Changed History—The Gift of Fire."

The documentary discussed the history of worship and deification of fire in ancient times. Most ancient cultures seemed to have some sort of fire god and/or "sun" god. For example, there was Ra, the sun god in Egypt, the Greeks had Vesta and Vulcan, and the Romans with Hestia and Hephaestus. The one I did already know about was Brigid from Celtic mythology, the goddess whose symbol was fire.

Suddenly the story of Moses and God speaking to him from the burning bush crossed my mind. I'd journaled some questions about Moses a few weeks ago and now was time to pull them out and to see what emerged. Biblical stories in the Old Testament depicted God speaking to the forefathers of faith and other faithful people in several ways: through angels, directly in visions, dreams, or revelations.

It was curious to me that Moses was the first person reported to hear God from a burning bush. What was even more intriguing was that up until Moses' encounter, Elohim was the given name in the Bible for God.

There seemed to be much debate over what the word Elohim meant. The consensus was that it was plural in nature, perhaps signifying a multi-aspect godhead. Alternatively, Elohim described the entire body of angels, spirits, and other lesser gods in the heavens as well as the One Creator God. Another description of Elohim mentioned being the sum of distinct parts that are the totality: the creative force of the universe, which was both masculine and feminine since we were created in their image (Genesis 1:26-27).

However, starting with the burning bush event, God revealed His name as Yahweh, the singular masculine Tetragrammaton, YHWH. This was what "Jehovah" was derived from. Curiously, in my research, I found that the name Yahweh was also associated with a pagan god. Specifically, Yahweh was known as a sky god of thunder and lightning and his manifestation was often as fire. Was this significant?

I needed to dig deeper. First, I searched for all verses from Moses onward in the scriptures that described God as fire or casting fire out from Himself. For example, the Lord went ahead of His people as a pillar of fire at night to give them light (Exodus 13:21). He descended on Mount Sinai in fire (Exodus 19:18). He spoke out of the fire at the foot of a blazing mountain (Deuteronomy 4:11-12). And was mentioned as speaking to His people out of the fire many times. Then I came to Deuteronomy 4:24 and stopped, *"For the LORD your God is a consuming fire, a jealous God."*

Was it possible Moses was not following the One, True, God, but a Lord God with attributes of fire like other fire deities? Could this be why the "Lord" God in the scriptures beginning with Moses seemed to be different in nature than the God of Abraham? The Lord God was an unloving, angry, jealous, tribal, fear-inspiring, law-giving, patriarchal God. He did not seem to display the qualities of love that we see earlier in the story of Abraham or later in the story of Jesus.

The following verse in Isaiah provided more basis for my review: *"See, the Name of the LORD comes from afar, with burning anger and dense clouds of smoke; his lips are full of wrath, and his tongue is a consuming fire. His breath is like a rushing torrent, rising up to the neck. He shakes the nations in the sieve of destruction; he places in the jaws of the peoples a bit that leads them astray."*

Anger? Wrath? Consuming fire? Destruction? Sounded more like the opposite of the God of Love, but then, there was more… I stumbled over another verse in 2 Kings 16. Ahaz, son of Jotham, became king of Judah. Beginning in the third verse, we learned he did not follow in the ways of David, he followed the ways of the pagan nations the Lord God had driven out for the Israelites to live in the land. Ahaz performed one of the "abominable" practices the pagan nations were said to have done, detestable in the sight of the LORD.

What was this abominable practice? He sacrificed his son. I checked every translation of the Bible I had access to, and the description was similar in each. This act was despicable and disgusting. It was horrendous to the Lord God for King Ahaz to sacrifice his son.

Really? This was something that the Lord God was against? It was an abomination? If this was a pagan practice and abomination, then most certainly, the very same Lord God would not be willing to sacrifice his own son. Especially not by sending him into the world to be sacrificed as a savior to humankind. Right?

And in fact, if that God did send his son to be sacrificed in the fire, it would go against everything we believed about the unchangeable nature of God, *"This is love: not that we loved God, but that he loved us and sent his Son as an atoning sacrifice for our sins"* (1 John 4:10). The word sacrifice is stated in several verses and was 100% contradictory to the "Lord God" in the Old Testament.

Questions brewed in my mind, did this mean the Israelites weren't following the One, True God? Did it mean maybe they were following a lesser fire deity Lord God? Was the story of Moses and the Israelites a founding myth that never actually happened? Or, on the flip side, did it mean the God of Love who sent His Son as a sacrifice for humankind was a pagan god because the practice was like the pagan practices?

These questions were not meant to be answered but to demonstrate how we build our faith in stories that were handed down through generations as the absolute truth, and we believed in them. Since there was no archeological or recorded evidence of a mass exodus in Egypt during Moses' time, it may have never happened. The story could be a founding myth, a story behind the origin of a ritual or group of people such as a nation or the spiritual origin of a religion or belief.

The stark differences between the attributes of the Lord God Yahweh in the Old Testament and the Creator God of Love in the New Testament were huge. Faith must go beyond all these—the myths, stories, scriptures, and all else that was of this world—everything that our generations have carried forward as truth.

During my studies of the Bible in the past months, I uncovered inconsistencies, without even trying! These caused me to question more and more the validity of the entire canon. For the sake of brevity, I decided to only include three examples here. First, there were two versions of the story of Jacob's ladder; one by the "Jahwists," and the other by the "Elohists," and only one version made it into the Bible.

Another example, in 2 Samuel 24 and 1 Chronicles 21:1, the same story about David is told. In one it states the Lord God directed David to take a census of his people. In the second story, the verses stated "Satan incited" David to do it. Which was the true story?

The last one was in the New Testament book of Jude. At least one non-canonical text, the Book of Enoch, was used to support statements Jude was making to a community of believers. The text was even referred to favorably, in a manner that made it clear the audience of early Christians would be familiar with the writings of the Book of Enoch. Yet the original non-canonical text mentioned was deemed heretical by the early Catholic Church!

I was sure there were many more discrepancies not yet uncovered in my research. None of this shook my faith because my faith was not placed in a book (even if it was the Bible). I could no longer place my faith solely in a collection of texts which were written by man, nor limit God to those specific scriptures alone.

My faith was in God, and God was infinitely greater than the Bible. Infinitely.

Sunday, July 4, 2010

In consideration of all that I'd learned recently about the Abrahamic religions, I wanted to understand more about what the word "religion" meant. It derived from the Latin word *"religio"* which meant to re-bind or re-unite to a source. The connotation of "religion" was much different in the everyday use of the word. It was not used in our vernacular with the meaning of a pure reunion with God through spirituality and inner work. Most, if not all, religions came with doctrines, creeds, rules, rituals, statements of belief, and conformity.

With more than 30,000 denominations in Christianity alone, it was obvious to see that this had created more separation than unity. Rather than turning inward to seek and reconnect with God, we'd turned to churches, temples, pastors, gurus, rabbis, scriptures, and sacred texts for wisdom. Religions served to conform from the outside, whereas true spiritual connection with our Source was as unique as each one of us from the inside, based on mystical and personal direct experiences with the Divine.

It was in faith that one stepped off the edge of what was known in the world into the depths of Mystery within. The true religion was spiritual, not able to be seen by our eyes and without form or images. It was boundless and infinite and could not be conformed because it was Oneness in unity. It did not rely on logical or rational proof, material evidence, or human reasoning. The true religion did not change as eras and cultures came and went, it remained steadfast eternally.

The word faith translated from the Aramaic word "*haimanuta*" described at a fundamental level that faith was related to a state of sacred unity, not a specific belief. Likewise, in Greek, the word faith was derived from "*pistis,*" meaning to trust, have confidence, faithfulness, to be reliable, and to assure. Translated from the Latin word, "*fidere,*" it means to trust. It was the core from which all our beliefs begin.

If we stripped "faith" to the most basic level, it meant a confidence, firmness, trust, and integrity of being in a state of unity with the Divine. It was not a "belief" in anything. True faith then came from personal experience with the Divine. I considered the differences between our outer and inner senses. That is, how we received intellectual knowledge compared with spiritual knowledge from within.

Listening to a sermon and agreeing with the minister's interpretation of a Biblical story was intellectual. Listening and experiencing an awe moment of, "Wow, this confirms how the Divine is showing up right now in my life" was spiritual, an experience of the Divine, with the Divine.

There were also varying levels of belief, those that were deeply rooted in faith gained through gnosis, or those that were easily plucked out of the soil without root, for example, if the belief was intellectual, such as, "Why do you believe what you believe in when it comes to God?" How many people would answer because it was what my parents instilled in them. Maybe shrug and say, "It's what I've always believed," or because it was what the Bible (or name of any other sacred text here) said.

Unless it was a personal direct experience with the Divine and growing of faith, there was no true spiritual root. If purely intellectual, the person was holding an image, not in true Oneness with God. The "true" religion was not a religion at all in the terms we used the term to categorize beliefs in the world. It did not have conformity, or compel or force change from the outside in. Nor was it changeable in different cultures or societies. It was within each one of us and could not be seen as described in Hebrews 11:1, *"Now faith is being sure of what we hope for and certain of what we do not see"* and *"...without faith it is impossible to please God."*

I considered whether I was on the right track with faith and inner spirituality being the "True" religion. This was a great example as to why we cannot solely depend on the wisdom we read. A book I was in the middle of reading, suggested love was the true religion. As I contemplated, it did not sit right with me and I recalled a couple of verses that addressed this very point, *"The only thing that counts is faith expressing itself through love"* (Galatians 5:6) and *"The goal of this command is love, which comes from a pure heart and a good conscience and a sincere faith."* (1 Timothy 1:5).

It appeared, at least from the Christian New Testament perspective, love springs forth from faith, not the other way around.

✳ ✳ ✳

This is what we speak, not in words taught us by human wisdom
but in words taught by the Spirit,
explaining spiritual realities with Spirit-taught words.
The person without the Spirit does not accept the things
that come from the Spirit of God
but considers them foolishness,
and cannot understand them because
They are discerned only through the Spirit.
The person with the Spirit makes judgments about all things,
but such a person is not subject to merely human judgments,
for, "Who has known the mind of the Lord so as to instruct him?"
But we have the mind of Christ.
(1 Corinthians 2:13-16)

Sunday, July 18, 2010

This was so difficult to write. Sitting here in the church that had been part of my path for ten months, I did not feel God here at all. Every time the worship music leader said, "We worship you Jesus" or talked directly to Jesus or interchanged "God" and "Jesus," my worship stopped. Over the months, I'd become familiar with the sensations and feelings of when I was connected in God's presence and graced with conversations with God. I used to feel that when singing songs in this church, but today there was nothing but stillness and peace within me.

It had been a while since I'd come to church here and I was drawn in my heart to come back today. Understanding poured over me as the service continued, my time coming to this church was done. It did not fit where I was with God anymore. I knew it was not that I was incapable of feeling the Holy Spirit move. Yesterday I sat and prayed at the ocean for a while and I felt God with me as the wind whipped through my hair, and the roar of the waves crashed on the sand, and I'd explored other church services in the local area and felt God's presence in those sanctuaries, too.

This was another step in faith. Faith that where I was right now was right for me. Trusting in my inner connection with God that if something unbalanced my sense of inner peace, it was not right for me. After the service was over, I pulled out of the church's driveway and looked at the church sign. Tears began to fall. Why was saying goodbye so difficult? In faith, I was moving onward although I did not know what was ahead. All I knew was God would lead and would shine His light where He wanted me to walk through.

With wistful tears in my eyes, I drove around the circle and onto the highway heading south. I looked up and saw the license plate frame holder on the vehicle in front of me. The top said, "Follow Jesus," and then underneath, "THIS CLOSE." I laughed through my tears. Yes, I was still following Jesus THIS CLOSE.

Autumn 2010

It was official, at least on Facebook anyway. Jeremie's girlfriend, err, well, his wife, changed her last name to his. Surprised? I wasn't. I'd known they were engaged for months and since my will was for whomever God had as my husband to come into my life, I remained unattached the entire time.

Were there tears today? No, my heart was not broken or torn at all, which proved to myself that I was not holding onto the man. The only thought in my mind: it was God's will for this to happen. I was detached from him before and remained so now. Would he wake up down the road and remember how unhappy he was? I hadn't a clue, and it was none of my business. All I knew for sure was, I would not in any shape or form covet a married man. I was completely done holding onto the tiniest bit of hope he would come back into my life.

It was quite an exciting thought that inspired a bit of giddiness inside my heart and mind. I already believed God could make my dreams come true in ways that were greater than anything I could ever imagine and that included whatever happened next in my life. How silly would I be not to be willing to give up everything to receive what God wanted to give me in my promised land? Rather than seeing this as negative, excitement filled me as I thought about what might happen next. No longer would I live in the past or carry its burden with me, and the indescribable feeling of freedom expanded within as I realized infinite miracles from this moment onward were possible because I fully let go of the past.

I went outside into the moonlight and gazed upward to the heavens as I prayed,

"Dearest Heavenly Father,
You saved me, You called me Yours. You know my name.
You made me and began a work in me.
You know how You want me to serve You.
Do not stop, do not leave my life undone.
I am clay in Your hands, willing to be molded and used,
willing to take any risk in Your name.
You are the God of the impossible, the God whose love is unfailing.
The God of mercy, and justice, and peace, and good.
I beg of You God to shine Your compassion on me,
for You to not let evil prevail, to not let the selfish and the prideful succeed.
Victory belongs to those whose hearts have sought You,
grace is bestowed on those who have followed Your lead.
Here I am, arms open to whatever future You have for me,
waiting as long as it takes,
for Your mighty power to shine down into my life,
for You to bring this all together in only the way that You can.
Your glory. Your honor. Your power.
Your kingdom, Heaven and Earth,
forever, and ever.
As Your love is ever unfailing and eternally faithful,
give me wings, lift me up to where You want me to be—and let me fly
in the skies filled with dreams come true
and the happily ever after You've created.
Your love be known, Your glory shine, Your power unmatched.
My dreams are in Your hands, and my future is up to You,
Yours to direct and command."

I felt the cool breeze against me in the darkness, so strong, so peaceful, and in God's hands. I was waiting, hoping, enduring, persevering, and remaining steadfast in faith. No matter how long it took, I would wait. Time was meaningless because it was all in God's timing. What was next? I didn't know, but I was ready for anything.

TRANSMUTATION

…PREPARING THE WAY FOR CHRIST IN THE HEART AND MIND.

Summer 2011

I felt released to dive into the dating world and signed up on one of the popular online dating websites. It seemed like time over the last year was in a cycle stuck on repeat, I kept discovering each man I started dating had an alcohol or drug addiction.

In reflection, I realized that I stepped into the wilderness. I learned so much about idols and the real-life struggles of addicts. I noticed how God was not in the minds or hearts of the men I dated. None of them even had a willingness to go to a recovery group such as Alcoholics Anonymous (AA), the chains of addiction bound so tightly. I tried to help each man I dated to look inward towards God. When that did not work, I suggested at least looking up to some sort of a higher power, but nothing changed. They did not join a dating website to heal from their addictions or for a friendly support in recovery.

Yet life unfolded from one season to the next and on the eve of the first quarter moon with its beautiful yellow-orange illumination hanging low in the twilight sky, I found myself on another first date with a man named Craeg*. We were seated outside at a restaurant table next to a flowing river in a quaint town. I smiled as I gazed across the table in amazement at all I'd gotten to know about my date so far.

If I didn't know any better, I would have said he was my soulmate. We were literally like mirrors of each other: both owned our own houses, made around the same salary in different industries, each of us had a dog and cats, and we were both left-handed. To top it off, he even tied his shoes with two loops like me. It was comfortable and fun. I felt a little like I was back in high school, when my biggest crush was a friend who was learning to be a mechanic, drove a big truck, and was a bit of a country boy. It was almost as if I was now sitting across the older version of him.

We delved into discussions about previous relationships and spirituality, topics typically off the table during a first date. Later on, I was driving along the freeway back home. In wondrous joy about the chemistry and connection, and I felt God say, **"He is who I have for you,"** with a strong sense of the now present moment inner woven with the words. It made me so happy.

But the happy feeling was short-lived. On one evening a couple of weeks into dating, I answered an incoming call, and Craeg's voice sounded different. He sounded troubled. I inhaled and held my breath as I heard him say, "There's something I need to tell you." Before he could say anything more, I heard screaming in the background followed by a tirade of crying and anger.

It turned out that Craeg never actually broken up with his girlfriend of many years before setting up a dating profile online. Because of meeting me, he decided to break off their relationship for good, and the fury I heard was her coming to get her belongings out of his house and demanding that he call me to tell me the truth. In the middle of the explosion, I knew he was not ready for a serious new relationship. I did not want to deal with the drama that surrounded his situation. Part of me knew if we continued dating, I would end up being the transition rebound. I was aware of my inner self pushing away, not wanting the heartache I knew would come.

The memory of God's recent words, **"He is who I have for you,"** stopped me from walking away. If it was God's will to continue dating Craeg, I would. Later the same evening, he came over to talk things through and to tell me more of the truth he hadn't shared before. Since he was honest, I decided I needed to do the same.

I told him that if he wanted to be in a relationship with me, he must understand that I would follow where God led me no matter what. If God told me to go somewhere, I would go. When God told me to leave, I would leave. I acknowledged sometimes it was difficult and not always an experience that led to happiness but through suffering, but no matter what God asked of me, I would do. Craeg said he liked the fact my faith was so strong. He hadn't grown up in a religion and his spiritual practices were using the law of attraction. He introduced me to the book, The Secret.

Autumn 2011

As the weeks went on, Craeg learned about Jesus from me, and I learned the basics about manifesting and dream vision boards from him. We had fun together, and both of us had vacation time coming up before the end of the year so we decided to take a spontaneous road trip cross-country. I'd already done it once and was all set to go again.

We crossed the eastern states into the cornfields of the Midwest, traversed the continental divide over the Tennessee Pass in Colorado, enjoyed Las Vegas, and then kept heading west to California over the Amargosa mountain range and into the desert of Death Valley.

Noticing the flora diminishing the further down we traveled into the valley, I was surprised that the desert was not completely, well, dead. We saw two coyotes running alongside the road, and small shrubs decorated the desert. Slowing the Jeep to a stop, I opened the door and hopped out to take in a better view of the landscape. I was stunned, I could hear the silence.

I stood still and closed my eyes, noticing the tiniest of a breeze across my skin. It was the greatest nothingness I'd ever experienced; I could feel the silence penetrate within me. It was not dead; it was filled with imageless creation. I imagined as if it were the great silence before the beginning of time and then opened my eyes to once again see abundant life in the desert all around me.

Driving further along the highway, we came to Badwater Basin, the lowest point below sea level in the Western Hemisphere. There were quite a few tourists there. I hopped out again to walk out to the salt flats and sensed the difference as I stepped away from the Jeep. I could feel the energy buzzing from each one of the tourists as I walked past them. Some had joyful light energy, others were more at peace, and some were more phrenetic and anxious or had a heavy sensation of energy. Closing my eyes on the flats around all the tourists, I felt the bustling and moving of energies that surrounded me.

The contrast was amazing, and I realized how much our energy affects the environment and spaces we live in, not to mention, our internal wellbeing, in ways we don't even think about. In the hustle and bustle and distractions of everyday life, I'd never stopped long enough to become aware of the energy around me.

As we drove up the western mountains that surrounded the valley, night had already fallen. The stars appeared, and we stopped to take in the sky. Twinkling stars of white and other slight shades of blue and red hung everywhere in the heavens above us. I could see the stars in three-dimensional form, some closer and some farther away. Clusters of stars in the cloudiness of the Milky Way shone brightly. Standing under the incredible sky, I felt so small, but at the same time, connected with the entire Universe as if I were one with the heavens above.

Before the long drive back east, our last stop was Sedona, Arizona. Craeg heard about energy vortexes from his family who practiced metaphysical and more of a New Age-type spirituality and wanted to visit one. From a map, I figured out the location of a vortex in Red Rock Crossing State Park, and we set off to find it.

Enchantment surrounded me the moment I stepped into the wooded area of the park. Rays of sunlight danced between the branches of the trees with leaves of every shade of autumn and more of the fallen leaves at our feet along the path, guiding our way towards the creek. The deeper we walked through the woods, the more a sweet aroma pervaded my senses. I felt inner cleansing with each breath I took.

The creek babbled and flowed alongside the trail we walked along, I spied an open area across the creek and another river beyond. Balancing across a fallen log, we crossed and found a shallow area near the bank of the river to venture through the water. I held my shoes in hand as I walked through the flowing river towards a red rock platform in the middle. The water was crisp and cool against my legs and undaunted, I crossed to the center, feeling guided in the direction.

As I stepped up and onto the red rock, I breathed in the rejuvenating air and took in the sound of the river. Little waterfalls flowed through the rock and down into the creek around me and I gazed out to Cathedral Rock and other formations lining the nearby horizon. I motioned for Craeg to continue onward without me. Whether we were at the actual energy vortex site or not didn't matter. I knew I was where I needed to be to pray.

Beneath my bare feet, the rock felt cool and hard. I stepped to the very edge and watched at how the creek coursed from behind me, split around the rock, and came around either side before rejoining together again. I planted my feet where they were and sensed a powerful renewal in my spirit.

I bowed my head to pray, but no words came to mind. This seemed odd at first to be in such silence, but then I settled into the experience and let the oneness pervade my senses with the creek, with the air, near the trees, and on the rock. A moment transcending words. Focused on the sound of the water, I allowed my mind to drift in meditation beyond the edges of where my thoughts came from, in silence.

Time stood still as my awareness expanded beyond the boundary of my body. My senses heightened as if I were one with the All. I lost track of where my feet ended and where the rock began. My spirit filled with the energy of Nature and God's presence flowed through my body. I sensed a peace-filled strength within.

In the embrace of the silence inside and as one with Nature, I heard a gentle and loving tone speak, **"Reclaim your Goddess power."** What it meant or where it came from, I was not about to guess, but I felt it was significant on whatever would appear ahead on my path.

Winter 2011

After not smoking, let's call them, "sacred herbs," since before we met, Craeg decided to start smoking again. We were hanging out in his living room watching a movie, and as he lit up, I asked if I could try so I could experience what it felt like. Of course, I pulled my journal out to have handy in case I wanted to record any insights.

I did not recall the exact moment when the shifts to higher consciousness started, but I did vividly remember becoming much more aware of many dimensions surrounding me. I sensed my energy field vibrating outside the edges of my physical body, and I expanded my awareness to the energies in the room. I felt connected with the spiritual realm behind the veil. Whoah!

"This is the dimension spells are cast from," I thought, and fear struck me in the realization of the sheer amount of mental power I was sensing. It was radiating out from my consciousness.

I gazed around the room in awe of the sensation, thinking that in this state of elevated consciousness, a person was powerful and directly connected with the universe. A direct line to the All. I wrote my observations in my journal and hypothesized that if people casted forth harmful or evil intentions in this consciousness state of mind, they would manifest on all the lower realms of existence. Then I reflected and remembered we must have the same power even when not in higher conscious states. Other than observing these higher dimensions, I was still in my body and that meant I was still creating in the outside world just as much as I was in my mind. I realized we continually cast out energy like spells with our thoughts, words, and actions. The only difference was now I was aware the ripples were creating through the unseen dimensions of the universe too.

Exploring further, I narrowed my focus and visualized the room as being dark and sinister. With surprise, I noticed how my imagination began adding in features like belfries and bats and darkened shadows that were not there before. A feeling of increased darkness pervaded my senses. Then, I changed my focus and visualized the room as Holy and sacred and light and bright. I noticed that all the shadows disappeared. The room felt gloriously filled with light streaming from Heaven above as if I'd entered a sanctified temple.

In amazement, I understood we are co-creators of our environments and experiences starting with our responses to thoughts and the intentions we chose to visualize in our minds. I opened my journal and wrote, "If people focus on love in this dimension, connected with the spiritual realm, they can do anything on Earth."

Aches of pain pulled my awareness back to my body. Earlier in the day, I'd fallen and twisted an ankle and landed on my shoulder on the ground. Recalling that some people use herbs for medicinal healing purposes, I wondered if it would work if I focused healing energies on my injuries.

I held my hands over my ankle first, sending thoughts of restoration of full motion and balancing of energy, and I was astonished when the pain disappeared. Rotating my ankle around in little circles, it was painless as if there was no injury. Then, focusing the same healing intention on my shoulder. I repeated the process, and the pain disappeared. With a little gasp of glee, I rotated my shoulder in a full range of motion and giggled in delight because I could not have moved it like that a few moments ago.

Amazed with my experience in elevated consciousness so far, I turned my attention to Craeg and asked him to share about his experiences. He told me he enjoyed connecting with his inner self, hearing his inner voice, and being more aware of his thoughts. Craeg mentioned taking a focus on a single thought in his mind and running with it to see where it led into the future. He acknowledged how he'd made several life decisions about the direction of his path from exploring within.

I nodded in understanding and turned back to my journal. With a deep breath in and out, I cleared my thoughts and began to write what came as a stream of consciousness,

"We have the power of creation from the spiritual to the physical realms. This was why humankind was appointed to take care of the Original Creator's world, like Adam and Eve. We must create in the light, with the intention of love and healing. We must question motives for all we do and intend to do everything out of love. If it does not glorify love then remove it from life. Anything not done in love is in darkness, seek only love.

Now into this world comes an age of healing, showing the glory and the power of love. Each person must guard oneself against evil and sin until reconnecting with Christ within, thereafter becoming an expression of love into which evil cannot enter. There will be great turbulence in the world as this shift begins, with shaking and great joy like the prophecies in the scriptures.

Ultimately, wars will end. Harmony and diplomatic peace will be ushered in as people will want to help one another for a better world for all. Conflicts will resolve in healthier and mutually beneficial ways. Money will be useless; food will be so abundant that money systems will be obsolete. Healing will be done through the creative power and intent of love.

One day, the last bit of darkness will be destroyed, and Earth will be fully united with Heaven. All matter will be destroyed. The length of time it takes for this to occur brings Love the greatest glory and it will go on in eternity once the darkness is gone. The end of the world is here... and the world ends with Love."

As I read over what I'd written, the vision felt like it was describing the New Heavens and New Earth prophesied in Revelations.

Winter 2011 (Continued)

The next weekend we were hanging out in his living room again and Craeg pulled out his stash to smoke. Excited to see what insights I'd receive this time; I kept my journal by my side to scribble notes as the evening drew onward. Elevating up in consciousness, I observed a blue haze around the room and us. I noted this was beginning differently than last time.

It felt like a perfect Heavenly image of regular life, and as we spoke back and forth, it seemed to flow melding into each other in harmony and perfection. I noticed my fingers felt tingly when I touched his arm and as I focused on the sensation it increased until I felt a crackling vibration of electrical energy between us, and it did not go away. For some reason, I sensed our souls linked and it felt like we were somehow connected as "one" with each other in higher dimensions, even just sitting next to each other on the couch.

I leaned into the sensation to explore further, suddenly I sensed that I was a lower, exceedingly small being. I was taken upwards in my consciousness along a string that kept going and going and going to a great height, higher than I could imagine. From this height, I looked down, onto what I knew was my body down at the very bottom, although my body was like a speck of dust.

My awareness shifted to the brightness of all the levels between. I saw what seemed like a puppet finger in an avatar of my physical form through ripples of layered blue haze from this great height, the view of all the dimensions and planes and realities was beautiful. It seemed to glow a blue light on the edges of the stream that I'd risen to on the height.

Coming back into my body, I reached out with my hand and touched Craeg's elbow and felt grounded back in my physical form. Removing my hand from him, I accelerated upwards in consciousness again. I sensed the string was more like a pillar shooting straight up and down. I comprehended my physical body was the lowest part of my being and the "crown of life" from the scriptures was when the soul ascends to the height from which one was from in the heavens.

Testing this experience, I touched Craeg's arm and came down from the height into my physical body. And once again, removing my hand, I felt myself accelerating back up into the height. I contemplated that my "true self," my light being form was up high where there was Heavenly perfection. We can ascend and travel into the dimensions. When we focus on something in the physical world it grounds us back into the lowest realm of Earth.

Yet at the same time, I pondered, "If we were always narrowly focused on the physical world, then we prevented ourselves from opening up to the wisdom and experience from the higher realms within our consciousness."

After grounding myself again and coming back into my body, I inhaled deeply and exhaled to clear my thoughts and then scribbled in my journal the stream of consciousness that came forth, "If the Creator projected a thought, it existed. Intent automatically creates waves like ripples and manifests. The bigger the power creating the intent, the greater the effect."

Sketching a diagram, I drew a horizontal line separating Heaven from Earth (the physical realm) and labeled the line "confusion." Then, drawing a stick figure, I drew an arrow pointing upward across the line of separation and wrote LOVE. Turn inward and upward into the spiritual realm with the intention of love and break through the veil of confusion about who we are, then receive love.

Feeling a shift to another dimension, I paused, and wrote, "Love will not hurt you." Shift again, "believe in love," shift again, "release your fear and be free." Shift again, "you know what love is, you know we are one." Shift again.

Suddenly the shifts amplified in speed and intensity, with a powerful force as the energy of the words coming into my comprehension was so rapid that I was writing as quickly as possible on the page.

My forearm became warm, and my muscles felt compelled to write down the words as they came:

"We go through every emotion all of the way up the intent. All must be aligned at every level through the dimensions to open the gates to reach the Father. Rooms through every life, on every one of the many planes of existence. The writer is the goddess because she is receiving messages all the way down the chain into the very bottom level. In every life, she had to remember love to be able to take the pen and write in each lifetime. So, it made sense on every plane back down to the physical world. Where Shannon is writing this in her own hand."

It was so intense without pause. As I wrote, there were three separate jolts of electric sharp staccato. Almost as if time were "hiccupping." In my peripheral view, it seemed like the whole room—including Craeg watching television—moved together, connected as one.

Sensing the shifts of dimensions slowing, I noticed a feeling of descending coming over me. The shifts drew me downward through each stronghold lower than love. Some shifts were instantaneous. At times it felt like I was falling down a dark tunnel with bright edges; other moments felt like a staccato pause.

The shifts through each emotion clicked like a photo snapshot of a camera until I returned to normal consciousness.

Later that night, as I tried to sleep, and sleep did not come, I pulled out my journal again: *"The Father had the first thought (intent), and the Mother received it. It was she who created in her womb of the All. Think of this as a ripple, creating a new world as the ripple continues outward. These creations have an energy source. Like how a seed develops and grows with nutrients and energy.*

If my intent is of Love, it is created in the energy source of Love. Then Love ripples out love through every dimension. If my intent is anything other than Love, it is, likewise, created in its energy source and creates new worlds separated from Love.

Every one of the multitudes of dimensions is a reality. Each is created with a single intent and ripples outward infinitely. Linear time exists because we created it, running every which way through all the planes and dimensions. Time is infinite without linear form, but because we've created linear time and projected it across dimensions, it crosses every which way on the ripples we've created like a matrix.

This matrix exists in us too, because we create worlds out of the infinite Universe of thought in our consciousness. From different intent sources (that was, Love or not of Love). They contradict each other..."

And I fell asleep on the journal's page.

Winter 2011 (Continued)

What my heart knew all along came true. After a few months of dating, Craeg began to question what he wanted. How I wish it would have been a clean and tidy break-up, where he just ended it and did not waffle back and forth.

My heart endured weeks of his indecision. Craeg would say his heart was not in it and that he was not ready for a relationship and restarted his dating profile online. Then he deleted his dating profile and called, texted, and invited me over to spend time together, saying how special I was and that he knew if he let me go, he'd be losing someone with who he felt a deep connection.

In the final throes, Craeg told me he knew I loved him, and I was ready for a husband and lifelong commitment. He knew I was going with the flow and never demanded commitment more than what we had together, but ultimately, my future was God's path and that meant marriage, happily ever after, and completing my book. Craeg admitted he did not feel in his heart the way he thought he should feel and could not look that far ahead yet to know if his path was going in the same direction. Then he would counter it with, he did not want to let go of what we had together.

The roller coaster ride sent my heart through the wringer and became a test of my beliefs about love. Everything I knew from the teachings from the scriptures was to remain steadfast, to show love in all I did, which meant if Craeg kept the door open in a "maybe," I waited, because love was patient, always there, and never failed.

It was almost too great of a burden for my heart as the weeks drew onward, resolute with open arms each time Craeg changed his mind again and again. I cried out to God for a miracle to relieve my heartache and suffering, but no answer came.

My prayers were constant, deep, and humbled on my knees. I wanted God's direction of whether to continue waiting with open arms on the roller coaster or to walk away. And all there was, was silence. I was frustrated for not receiving the miracle sign that I was waiting for to know from God what I should do in the name of love.

During one of my prayers, the thought arose to fast from all solid foods, including biting or chewing any food, to show how dedicated my will was for God's path. I agreed with the idea and decided to fast until the day it was clear whether the man I'd been dating was the husband God had for me, or if there was another man destined to cross my path as my promised husband from God.

This was a sacrifice and offering to show my devotion in faith of God's promise and in adherence to what I believed love was. God would answer, though I did not know how long it would take. My willpower was unwavering, although my mind fought the decision in fear. I'd done fasts every so often over the last couple of years, but they were three days at most.

This time I would limit consumption of food to smoothies, protein shakes, other drinks, and lots of water for an indefinite period into the future, as long as it took to hear from God. Doing something this extreme never crossed my mind before, but it felt right in my heart to do now, however long it took waiting for my happily ever after from God, I committed to not eat any solid food.

Winter 2011 (Continued)

Within three weeks of initiating my fast, Craeg stopped contacting me. It was between just God and me again, and solitude surrounded my world now that none of my focus was distracted on dating anyone. I did not rejoin the dating website. The pages of my journals, parched for over a year while I was dating one man or another, poured forth with insights and revelations as if floodgates exploded open.

One day I was sipping a smoothie during lunch in the cafeteria at work in contemplation. We become what we eat, isn't that how the old saying went? Eating through the mouth was symbolic of what we "eat" of the world through all our senses. What if we took in false truths or harmful statements? What if we ingested toxic beliefs or stewed on and consumed thoughts that were not Holy?

I recalled the story of Adam and Eve in the Garden of Eden. They were told not to eat of the tree of the knowledge of good and evil, or they would "be like God," but what was good and what was evil? They were judgments. If everything God made was good… then there was no evil. Evil wouldn't even have existed. So, even though the tree of knowledge of good and evil was in God's GOOD creation, it was still bad to eat the fruit. This was leading me somewhere.

I considered the arguments I'd studied; some Gnostics and other esoteric traditions believed the serpent in the story of Adam and Eve was not Satan or evil at all but was Wisdom. In the traditional interpretation of the Genesis story, though, the serpent in the garden was viewed as bad. Eve was scorned because she listened to the serpent and "tricked" Adam into eating the fruit from the tree. But the tree was part of God's creation and all God's creation was good, so this led me back in a circle.

Then it struck me. Leading up to this, we saw Adam and Eve talking with God in the Garden of Eden. We knew God was walking alongside them. In this singular event, Eve listened to wisdom from a creature in God's creation, that was, of the world. She ate the fruit of a tree for knowledge instead of seeking within herself or asking God. Adam followed her lead and did the same thing. It led them into judgment of what was good and evil, and they became what they ate, their minds were filled with it. They judged themselves even before God approached them by feeling ashamed for what they'd done against God's rules of right and wrong.

As I was in thought about the cycle of death and resurrection, Jesus came into my meditation. I saw him in a whole new light. Jesus was the greatest teacher of love who ever walked the face of this Earth, not only because he showed us the power and glory of love through his ability to heal and miracles, but also, the path of what we needed to walk upon in the name of love for God. Jesus let go of his physical life for his true spiritual nature, following God's will obediently to his death.

He must have been a wise sage to understand and articulate to his disciples why he had to do what he did, he knew it was for the good of all people for generations to come. He demonstrated with his life what he taught, thereby practicing what he preached and renounced desires and treasures of the world—even walking willingly to the crucifixion of his very life. Some referred to Jesus as the New Adam or the Last Adam and this made sense. Instead of listening to the wisdom of the world, he remained true to who he was and his mission on Earth in the name of the Father God of Love.

My mind went back to the story of Adam and Eve. After they were kicked out of the Garden of Eden, they must have believed they were separated from God, but it didn't have to end that way. When the gates closed, they could have kept knocking and turned their will, intention, and focus back to God. I guarantee like in my own life, a loving God would answer. I thought about the truth found in the story of the prodigal son (Luke 15), if a loving God, like the Father in the parable, would not have open arms upon the son's return, what truth would there be in Jesus' teachings?

But instead, in the origin stories across Judaism, Christianity, and Islam, Adam and Eve turned their attention wholly on building a life outside of the Garden of Eden. They created physical children of their own, and we know the story from there on throughout the ages. All they had to do was turn back to God. Perhaps they no longer had faith in God, or themselves. Whatever it was, it defined our course in history. Billions of people over time believed in the story told of Adam and Eve.

And what was a belief? Per M-W.com, belief was an acceptance of a statement or a thought as the truth. Does that mean all beliefs are factually true with evidence? Not necessarily, but all beliefs are true in the sense that inherent in a belief is a trust and confidence that something exists and is true. The world is shaped through the lenses of beliefs people hold as the truth.

Let's say in a math class I thought I knew the right way to solve a problem. I believed I had the correct formula and knew how to work through the steps to arrive at the solution. If I believed, then that meant I projected my confidence into the universe as my reality, certain I knew the process to use to obtain the right answer. But what if there were errors? Maybe I used the wrong formula, forgot one of the order of operations, or introduced an error in my calculations? If I didn't stop to question my belief that I "knew" the way to solve the problem or double-check my work by working through the problem a second time, there was a good probability my answer could be wrong.

However, if I'd stopped to question, "Was this the right way to proceed?" My mind would open to receive truth beyond my beliefs from higher levels of consciousness. Likewise, any time I believed in the truth of something false, I inadvertently created confusion and contradiction in my mind and prevented myself from seeing what was true in reality.

I realized this was what it meant in my stream of consciousness weeks ago when I wrote how we create new worlds, dimensions, and realities within our own minds. We project out all over the place. From the past to the future, rehashing, replaying, revising, and worse, creating alternate realities based on desires of the mind. No wonder I used to get so frustrated, the worlds I'd created in my head were constantly colliding and clashing with each other against the truth of what felt right in my heart.

In the nature of our minds, I noted that we form beliefs all the time, we could not help it. Every decision or action had a root in a belief, every single thing we did. A belief that it was cold, a belief being hungry, a belief that a room should be bigger or smaller, et cetera. We use the knowledge in our experiences and exploration of the world in the formation of beliefs of truth from what we "know to be true." Unless we question our beliefs, how do we know whether they are the truth for our own lives?

What if I started all over at the beginning with the belief that everything I knew to be "true" may be, in fact, false? With a grin, I knew—this was my next practice.

Spring 2012

Instead of getting up on this weekend morning, I stayed in bed, stewing on thoughts. Negative thoughts. Practicing what I'd been working on lately, I kept telling myself I was not going to be attached to them or believe they were true. I tried focusing on love to stop thinking the thoughts, but they kept returning. Okay, so that idea wasn't going to work. In observation, I became aware of the essence of the thoughts, one rationalization after another.

As a general example, projecting possible futures or playing memories on repeat and turning them over in my mind for new insights or to glean more information out of them to determine what was true. I was not asking questions, and I did not hear God's voice in any of the thoughts.

I wondered if it meant all my thoughts were false. What was I doing right now? Analyzing. Where was it getting me? Nowhere. I was going in circles in my mind because I kept picking apart the past or the future over and again. But in awareness, I beamed at the fact I must be detached from my thoughts because I was observing and holding them up under an investigative lens. Staying in contemplation, I wondered: how could I know whether a thought was true or false? The answer came to mind: by the fruit that it bears within me.

If I tested every thought, weighed it, tried it on, and considered it while remaining detached, I could also observe at the same time how it made me feel inside. If it brought frustration, fear, anxiety, or other negative emotion, thought, and/or physical reaction, then I would know it was false for me. If it inspired, encouraged, brought wisdom, joy, and peace, then it was of God and was true for me. In awe, I gushed, "It can't be that simple…"

"It is that simple."

"If I can determine whether something was true or right for me by being aware of how it made me feel inside, then that gives me knowledge of the truth from within?"

"Power."

Gives me power? I pondered for a moment if this knowledge through understanding came from recognizing the experience I was having and gave me power, what did that mean? Was I receiving wisdom? I practiced by thinking about all kinds of negative thoughts. I observed each as it crossed my mind. How did it make me feel? How did my body react? How did my emotional state react? Then I named the feeling whether it was worry or fear or something else. Quickly, I noticed a pattern that when I identified and "named" the fear or negative emotion, it disappeared.

In the moment, I then realized the thoughts were gone. I tried to think of them again, and they were not there. None of them. The fears disappeared from my mind, and I could not summon them back. They were almost, seemingly, transformed into nothingness. "But what does that mean?"

"It means you are powerful."

In awe, I comprehended the negative thoughts and fears were not even entering my awareness anymore. My mind was not allowing the consideration of them once I determined that they were not true based on how I felt inside. They were obliterated from my world; did I transmute the thoughts with love? Did this mean I was channeling love through my consciousness and the wisdom in my heart? "I can control fear…?" I said as the realization poured over me.

"Demons."

"I can command demons to leave…?" Shaking my head in amazement, I stopped again, "Help me, God, I have no idea how I am going to do this."

"I will show you."

The answer poured over me from my inner wisdom, "…by channeling love… I can do this!"

"You already knew that."

"If this is what You wanted me to learn, to be able to transmute fear. Let this be done!"

Contemplating this further, I wrote in my journal that having a thought cross through the mind does not in itself create issues. It was when we attach to the thought by either dwelling or stewing on it or immediately believing that it is true. Thus, charging the thought with focus, energy, and emotions, and then it becomes an intention. An intention is an act or instance of determining mentally some action or result, it is the "end" that manifests. When a thought that inspires fear becomes a projection of, "it is going to happen," it manifests. We create it. We bring it to life in our minds and then it comes forth in our world.

When we have thoughts that make us feel afraid, it is like a wound we keep tending, trying to soothe our mind by filling in the gaps until the fear goes away. Like a black hole of darkness in our minds, the opposite of the light of illumination and wisdom. Wondering, I questioned, "What was the benefit of being able to remove fear in consciousness?"

"Healing."

I nodded, as it made sense, through the healing of the mind, fears were transmuted and transformed. In this moment, my mind could travel anywhere in the past, present, or future, to any place, space, or time. TIME! Realization coursed through my body as I scribbled a drawing in my journal. Our minds are not bound by time, they can go backward, forward, sideways, and in any dimension or reality or dream that we created.

This seemed essential for healing, for how could a person heal from an experience if she could not remember and transform the memory? If one could not go back and fill the darkness with light, it remained in darkness. I noticed my mind was calm like the surface of a pond with no ripples. Wondering aloud in awe, I asked, "Where did all my thoughts go?"

"You eliminated them. You realized they weren't true."

All that was left was stillness. My mind was a blank slate. I could not get myself to think anything. No thought at all except the little intention to write what I was experiencing as it happened in my journal, "The openness and peace are amazing."

"See how much focus you used to give every thought?"

"Wow, yes," Without focus on or observing anything in my mind, I was fully immersed in "being" in the moment. Was this what people spend hours in meditation to achieve?

"Yes, but it does not heal the heart."

Light in the mind from the practice of meditation and mindfulness was the stillness and silence. That meant light in the heart would be stillness and silence within the heart, peace of mind, and peace within the heart. I scribbled more diagrams on the page: all creations in the past, present, and future must have an intersection somewhere if everything was connected. If it was all an infinite continuum of One, there must be a place where all united as One. Then it hit me, the now. Which meant the potential for healing was the most powerful in the present moment through the light in the mind and heart.

Wherever we were, in whatever present moment, was where our power existed to observe and focus intention to create and heal. Therefore, if we drew forth from the energy of light in our minds and our hearts using the power of love… I stopped writing as the reality poured over me, and God finished my sentence, **"You can do anything."**

Spring 2012 (Continued)

Four months had passed, and I continued to fast. I did not encounter any thoughts or feelings of suffering and there was zero desire within me to break the fast before it was complete in God's timing. I hadn't even come close to giving in. It was not even an option. This was not me throwing a little kid tantrum to get my way. I was humbling myself before God, "I am willing to lay my life down to receive the happily ever after you have for me." So far, there was no sign on the horizon of a husband coming into my life and I waited with patience for God's promises to come true.

Throughout the last weeks, I'd spent every bit of spare time studying texts, reading through the Gnostic scriptures I hadn't yet had a chance to delve into, and then expanded beyond Gnosticism. I learned more about alchemy, hermeticism, and other esoteric texts related to purification and transmutation and the Philosopher's Stone. I contemplated the deep meanings of "As above, so below," and realized fully that in my journal writings and testing of my own inner mystical experiences, I was without a doubt, a practicing spiritual alchemist. These concepts helped to fill in some of the gaps left out of the Bible, although I did note at least one brief glimpse of Jesus as an alchemist when he transmuted water into wine.

Alchemical transmutations did not always follow the scientific laws of physical Earth nature, because they also followed the laws of spiritual nature, and thus, some were miracles. Jesus, the disciples, and saints, among others, were said to have performed these miracles. They could heal diseases, mental illnesses, and physical wounds, raise people from the dead, and exorcise demons.

I began writing out all the acts of miracles that Jesus and the disciples were reported to have done. Then as I remembered another one and wrote it down,

I said out loud, "Jesus commanded the elements," as my mind envisioned the story of when Jesus walked out on the water and calmed the storm while his disciples were afraid.

"So did you."

Memories flitted back to the cross-country trip that seemed so long ago now. I recalled when we drove through the middle of California, there was soupy fog so thick it was impossible to see the lines on the road. We could not see anything at all, not even the front of the hood of the Jeep. In those moments, I'd closed my eyes and commanded the fog to part across the highway in the name of Christ. When my eyes opened, I was stunned the fog had dissipated and did not come back. Hmm… I pondered what that meant.

"See how much power you have?"

Okay, so the power of commanding the elements of Nature and performing miracles was within me. What was preventing me from accessing my full power? What was preventing me from doing all the things they did on Earth? Tapping the end of my pen on the side of my journal I questioned my inner truth and beliefs. I was not willing to move on with my day until I got to the bottom of this.

I began to think about rituals, I believed there was a possibility of depending on a ritual as a crutch; thereby creating an idol. Believing that the ritual itself had the power instead of the truth that it was the intention and the energy that comes forth in performing the ritual. As crutches and idols, they had the potential to take away one's power. "Having to do it in a certain way to get a result? Depending on an idol. Having to pray a certain way to get a result? Depending on an idol."

My writing slowed to a stop as I realized where this was going as I put it all together. Inhaling deeply, I wrote, "Having to ask in Jesus' name to receive a miracle? Depending on an idol."

I stopped and stared at what I'd written. Anytime we relied on an idol, we were placing it between us and our direct inner connection with God it also meant we were then placing an idol above our Divine sovereign birthrights as children of God and the Universe. We all have the same capacity for channeling love and performing miracles and healing as Jesus did, he even said so himself.

Realizations poured over me; I'd limited my own power because I'd idolized Jesus all this time even though I thought I was so careful not to idolize anything! I'd relied on praying "In Jesus' name." It was how I was always taught to pray, but by doing that, I was relying on an external image. Something inside of me shifted as I started to learn to believe in my power, but I did not fully embrace my inner Divinity as a child of God to do what

Jesus did on my own. Oh… it was like the thorn bush king! I'd been idolizing Jesus! He was my constant dependable crutch. It felt like I was losing something, a piece I'd held onto so tight. Yet, I knew I was gaining so much more.

If naming a specific fear transmuted it into the light, then my prayers should be naming Love itself as imageless spirit, not the image of love that came to Earth over 2000 years ago in human form. Jesus showed us what love in action was to the fullest extreme with his life. He taught us what love was. Love was one of the infinite aspects and names of the Omniscient One that is Everything, Eternal, Infinite, and All, but that same Divinity was within me.

By holding onto the last vestiges of the religion I'd believed in since it was drilled into my head as a little girl, I was denying my own Divinity. It was one of the many times when part of me wanted to smack my head in disbelief while the other half of me was joyful and praising in the moment of spiritual growth and greater illumination of sorts, even if I did feel quite silly that with all the studying I did about the thorn bush king and idols, I hadn't put two-and-two together until now.

I suddenly saw Jesus in a different light. Yes, his name brought glory to the God of Love. He walked and talked love during his entire ministry as a healer and a compassionate, merciful teacher of forgiveness, and let go of his physical life to show what love looks like in action, the willingness to sacrifice himself for everyone else. Yet, there were other sides of his name I'd not considered before. As the next weeks drew onward, these pressed upon my heart in contemplation.

I thought about the multitude of occurrences throughout recorded history of the extreme opposite of love spreading across the world in Jesus' name: the Crusades, the inquisitions, the killing, and torturing of millions of people over centuries. Not only that, but also what I'd mentioned about the fractured "universal" church into tens of thousands of denominations. It was not what love was supposed to look like in unity as One.

In my mind's eye, it became clear. The name of Jesus as the Son of Father God, the aspect of Love on Earth with the enlightened mind and open heart for the salvation of all was defiled after his death. The religion that formed as Christianity performed harmful acts on millions of humankind, not only by physical torture and murder, but also the emotional and mental damage that was done by Christians who inflicted their beliefs on others, even in the world today. The energy within the name "Jesus" was no longer filled with the pure power of love energy from the Holy Spirit.

I envisioned what looked like a circular yin yang, the light of Love on one side in the pure essence of Christ Jesus and the darkness of war, murder, torture, and fear on the other of what was done in Jesus' name. Between those two sides in opposition, I perceived a balancing point and in the middle of the balance was me, letting go of the name of the man. That was where I now stood, on the threshold jumping into the unknown, beyond Jesus—beyond the boundaries of everything I'd ever believed in my life.

Where I stood now was where faith truly began, when every image and idol were removed, and I was frightened because I did not know what was on the other side, but I knew there was no going back. How would one unring a bell once it has rung? Without Jesus as a crutch, I stepped into the realization that the power within him was also within me as a sovereign daughter of God and a co-creator in the world.

Now there was no line drawn in the sand between light and dark, and no trace of separation rested within me. No image or law or teaching to show me the Truth or the Way because all was One and existed within and without. There was no right and no wrong, no good and no evil, for All was God, and God was in All and through All, within me and around me. Anything was possible and everything could be true as much as it was false.

My mind was so scared. I did not want to create darkness in the world. What if I did not speak or act in the highest of light and love? What if I harmed someone in my intention of love? I believed that there was a power greater than me orchestrating the Universe, this I knew through the synchronicities and miracles I'd already experienced, but now I was in a free-fall beyond the edge of everything I knew. And I did not know where I was going to land, like Alice tumbling down the rabbit hole.

❊ ❊ ❊

Meeting the True Guru, we are shown the way to die.
Remaining alive in this death brings joy deep within.
Overcoming egotistical pride, the Tenth Gate is found.

Death is pre-ordained - no one who comes can remain here.
So chant and meditate on the Lord, and remain in the Sanctuary of the Lord.

Meeting the True Guru, duality is dispelled.
The heart-lotus blossoms forth, and the mind is attached to the Lord God.
One who remains dead while yet alive obtains the greatest happiness hereafter.

Meeting the True Guru, one becomes truthful, chaste and pure.
Climbing up the steps of the Guru's Path, one becomes the highest of the high.
When the Lord grants His Mercy, the fear of death is conquered.

Uniting in Guru's Union, we are absorbed in His Loving Embrace.
Granting His Grace, He reveals the Mansion of His
Presence, within the home of the self.
O Nanak, conquering egotism, we are absorbed into the Lord.
(Consensus, Khalsa. Shri Guru Granth Sahib: Khalsa Consensus Translation)

JOY ALCHEMY

...LESSONS IN MIRACLES THROUGH THE
LIGHT OF CHRIST IN THE SOUL.

Spring 2012 (Continued)

See, I will create new heavens and a new earth.
The former things will not be remembered, nor will they come to mind.
(Isaiah 65:17)

❉ ❉ ❉

Maybe it was because I was in the middle of the free fall or maybe something was pulling me in a new direction. Whichever it was, I signed up on a dating website. Perhaps it was a bit of both working together to move a step forward. And oh wow, it was quite an interesting experience this time around. Each first date had me trying to find ways to avoid explaining my four-and-a-half-month spiritual fast from eating solid foods.

On one of the first dates, I drove out to a chain restaurant and bar somewhere halfway between home and where my date, Erick* lived. When I arrived, he was already out on the patio enjoying a beer. Side note, by then I'd figured out meeting for drinks on a first date worked well. That way, I could bypass the whole fasting from solid foods conversation.

We delved into getting to know each other. I noticed his honesty about being in the middle of a divorce. He even admitted that he'd moved back home to his parents' house a week beforehand, so it was a recent major life transition. Inwardly my heart knew he was embarking on his own healing process and I sensed no long-term future for the two of us, but I enjoyed his company. He did not seem to mind the fact I was not eating solid food, so we planned another date where Erick introduced me to ice hockey.

We went to a Stanley Cup playoff game at the Prudential Center in Newark, and I loved every moment of the game. How was it that I'd never watched hockey before ever in my life? Erick played hockey throughout his youth and in college and then moved on to playing in adult leagues and tournaments. He taught me a bit about the rules while we enjoyed the game.

The second date turned into a third date, and it was increasingly strange how certain aspects about Erick reminded me of my ex-husband Paul; not personality-wise. They were quite different in that respect, but in the types of hobbies he enjoyed in his spare time, the major he pursued in college, and the craziest commonality of all, he drove the same make and model car that my ex-husband used to drive.

If it was just one of these I wouldn't have given it a second thought, but when symbol after symbol appeared, I knew they were indicators there was something important for me to learn from this relationship with Erick, whatever it ended up being. At the same time, though, this was not what I was expecting for a happily ever after. My heart knew he was not the promised husband from God.

The fourth date turned into a fifth date, and then I lost count. Part of me wanted to push Erick away and be on my own again, waiting for what I believed was coming into my future: my husband, my marriage, publishing my story. I did not believe this was how the story was supposed to end. The other half of me was observing at a higher-level vantage point. I saw myself attached to the promises from God that I believed would come true while clinging to a future that might never come.

With this in mind, I realized if I kept waiting, I would potentially be forevermore in a perpetual holding pattern waiting for my "happily ever after" from God. At the same time, I knew happiness was not a time point in the future for me to postpone joy, it was right here, right now, in this very moment. Everything I'd learned and practiced over the last months showed me this was true.

I could no longer hold onto anything from the past and projecting a "happily ever after" onto an outcome in the future was doing exactly that, possibly even counteracting the process of manifesting into my reality, as I'd learned through the teachings in hermeticism through The Kybalion, The Emerald Tablet, and other texts which described the laws and principles of the universe.

In solitude, tears formed at the corners of my eyes as my mind comprehended what I was about to do. I had to let go of God's promises completely, not just let go of Jesus. The tipping point hit me in waves. The truth that my happily ever after—Heaven on Earth—was not in the future, it was now, in the present moment where co-creation in life crisscrossed with infinite possibilities.

I had to lay down my life story, including every promise from God about my future and everything I believed would come to pass. At the same time, I realized if I let go of God's promises, there would be nothing left of my life.

The chains of belief yanked, snapped, and whirled into chaos in my head as if I was caught in the funnel of a tornado. Having held my beliefs so strongly for the last few years, I questioned inside, "What if this was my happily ever after and there was nothing more? What if this was it? If this was all there was for me?"

Whirling and twirling, my mind descended into a tunnel of despair. I held onto the fringes of reality and what I'd thought was true while my consciousness released the rest of my beliefs into the void.

My entire being was suddenly struck with immense trepidation and shock. I found myself spiraling deeper into the darkness. Questioning if I had ever heard God's voice at all. What if none of this was true? What if it was only my imagination? Was I led astray? Did I trick myself? Was it a lie? Am I nothing but shadows and delusions? Who am I?

My soul sunk to the depths of the darkness. I was nothing at all, filled with only the dust in the cosmos of what I used to believe and the story of my life that was no longer mine. My universe stopped; I was dead inside—in my heart and mind—full stop, nothing left in the past, and the future erased from potential existence. Darkness was all I could see, everything ripped and shattered into pieces, with nothing to hold onto—not even Jesus.

I did not crumble, nor did I cry out to God for help, I'd entered this realm of psychic death willingly on my own, and there was no going back. I closed my eyes and inhaled through my nose and then breathed out, through the death of me and all I knew to be true in my life.

Then, I remembered I was still alive. And my mind cleared as a single thought floated in... Be happy: wherever I was in the present moment, just be happy. There was nothing left in the past, there was nothing in the future. There was only what was real—right now—existing in this very space and time. From now on, I would seek experiences that brought inner peace and joy, my happily ever after was now.

Later in the evening, Erick was grilling himself dinner on the deck in my backyard. I relaxed, Sadie lounging on the deck beside the chair I was sitting in. While whistling a tune and without saying a word, Erick went inside the house to bring out more of the groceries he'd brought over. He pulled out a baguette and started cutting it into small slices and spreading fig jam and brie cheese.

Looking over at me, he said matter-of-factly with a small grin, "You're going to eat tonight."

It was almost as if he knew somehow, but he could not have known. I'd never told him about Jesus saving me years ago or how I was an appointed apostle, or I was waiting for my promised husband from God or that I'd died inside earlier in the day and now did not even know who I was anymore or what I was supposed to be or do in the future. The inner vision I'd held in my heart since I was 13 years old that someday I was meant to shine my light and make a difference in the world through the publication of my writings was now destroyed.

Erick went back to the grill and brought over a plate of what he had made, and then sat down across from me at the patio table. He picked up one of the baguette slices with fig and brie and drew his hand towards over to my mouth. I took a bite and ate it. Without a word or explanation, without letting him know what transpired earlier in the day or how my mind walked through death, but I was still somehow alive.

I smiled at Erick, after almost five months of fasting, it was over just like that. I had no idea what the future held, but all of the burdens I carried were gone. An almost indescribable feeling of immense peace and freedom poured forth from somewhere within me, and I felt as if I were walking in the Garden of Eden.

After dinner, I brought the dirty dishes into the kitchen and put everything in the dishwasher. My eyes landed on one of my Bibles strewn out on a table with other books from where I'd left them last. Knowing I was not going to need it anytime soon, I picked it up and carried it over to the bookshelves to tuck it away.

Before sliding it into place on the bookshelf, I hesitated and grinned, "Oh what the heck, I'll do this one more time," and with a flourish of my hands, I ceremoniously held the Bible in both hands, then flipped it open to whatever page it chose to reveal, something I'd done so many times in the past to receive a special message from God.

My eyes landed on the first verse I saw on the page of Hebrews 5, "*Anyone who lives on milk, being still an infant, is not acquainted with the teaching about righteousness. But solid food is for the mature, who by constant use have trained themselves to distinguish good from evil.*" My jaw dropped in awe, astonished, and amazed. I closed the Bible and found a place for it on the bookshelves and then went to rejoin Erick out on the back deck to watch the sun set behind the trees.

When Erick left the next day it was time for me to clean house: I recycled every printed-out typed page of the draft manuscript I'd left uncompleted years ago; I tossed all my notebooks and every single one of my journals, including all my journals from when I was a teenager; I shredded the pages of my drawings and diagrams of the spiritual alchemy transmutation process. Everything I'd written onto paper was now gone.

Then I sat at my computer and deleted every electronic file of my journals, notes, and manuscripts from the hard drives, online clouds, and emails that I'd sent to myself over the years. Whatever I had been holding onto from the past for the future was destroyed: no longer a Christian, no longer an anointed Apostle, no longer the herald of the Messianic Age, no longer would my story be published, all of the pieces of my former self ceased to exist in my world.

Instead, I chose a life of rejoicing and happiness in whatever may come, to follow what filled my heart with peace and joy, because that was all I knew to be true. I felt freedom and full acceptance of this new direction. The past was dead, and my new life was birthing, but what it would look like in the future, I hadn't a clue.

I dared to stare directly in the face of the unknown without fear, for I'd found where the light of life came from within my heart.

❋ ❋ ❋

Be inspired by love for life
And let my inner sun shine.
If I dare to dream beyond boundaries,
I am abundantly graced by design.
(2012, age 35)

Summer 2012

Admittedly, there were moments of uncertainty without a mentor in my spiritual practices and development. It remained of utmost importance to me that I did not create harm or darkness in the world, especially in the newfound freedom I found myself in.

I remembered books I'd read that suggested Jesus was a shaman. Not really knowing where else to explore, I decided to investigate the path and found a shaman a few hours away who was willing to educate me about the tradition. It was during the second session that she had me lie on the floor for a guided journeying meditation.

She drummed and led me into the meditative space in my mind. The drum beat rhythmically, and I sensed the edges of my focus began to merge with the oneness of reality around me, deepening in meditation. The shaman guided the journeying experience and told me to visualize the medicine wheel, and then to focus on the center of the wheel in my vision. There, she said, was a wise woman who was emerging from the center of the wheel and she had a teaching for me, and to listen for what the wise woman may have to say.

The drumming continued as I imagined the medicine wheel and I sensed a presence in the center of the wheel and noticed a woman with long straight brown hair in the circle. She felt oddly familiar as I approached more closely in meditation, and then I realized in surprise, the woman in the center was me.

The meaning was instantly clear in my mind and heart. I knew this was a confirmation I should not seek outside of myself for guidance and direction during this time of my life, it was the season to listen and learn from the wisdom in my heart.

During this season, Erick moved most of his belongings into my home. Still not seeing anything long-term or permanent, I went with the flow with whatever came to pass.

Then a couple of months later, at the end of the summer when coolness in the air hinted at autumn's arrival, Erick's divorce was final, and he changed his mind and moved his belongings back to his parents' house.

Continuing in the flow, my heart did not skip a beat. I drew upon the lessons I'd learned and chose to change my response. Instead of remaining steadfast with arms wide open in an unfailing demonstration of love that led to inner suffering as in the past, I decided on a path forward that was a little bit less like being a doormat. As Erick left, I told him if he wanted to be in a relationship with me again, I would be open to it. But, at the same time, I was moving on too since he was choosing to break up with me.

It felt like a middle way, it felt right, and peace filled my heart.

❈ ❈ ❈

If I believe there's no way out and nowhere to turn,
I am right, for what I believe creates my reality.

I detach the emotions I am feeling from what I think is true,
to give myself some space to breathe.

What is possible from where I stand right now?
What do I "think" will happen?

*Now I move that possibility to the side
and consider the opposite of what I "think" will happen.*

What is the opposite of what I believe?

*I have two opposite gateways of possibility, and I can fill the space
in the middle with all of the rest of possibilities from A to Z
and back from Z to A
in every combination of letters, colors, sizes, shapes, and outcomes.
Everything is possible because the future hasn't happened yet,
and I do not limit myself to what I "believe" for my belief may be untrue.*

*I listen to my heart compass
and consider the possibilities that appear in my mind.
Which of them feel right as I contemplate them in my heart?
The one that feels the most right – bringing peace and joy inside—
that is it! Right there! That is the way.*
(December 25, 2019, age 42)

Winter 2013 ~ Summer 2013

Imagine my surprise when Erick came back into my life a few months later. He moved his belongings back into my house, and it was back to being a comfortable relationship. In reflection, I felt this was somehow balancing the energy and karma from my past life. What that meant for the future, though? I did not know, and I was not about to project ahead. Erick would travel to Pennsylvania often to play hockey, and I used the time alone to meditate and write. It was a content existence.

On the nights when it was quiet in the house, I sat down with my journal. With me were my cats and new St. Bernard puppy, Lily, who I'd brought into my fur-family after Sadie passed on at the grand age of 11 last July because life was just not the same without a St. Bernard.

So, where was I now? No longer did the cycle of focusing on the past have a stronghold over me. Not once did projecting the future entrap my thoughts. Gone were the "should-haves" and the "could-haves." Erased was the shame of mistakes and "bad" decisions.

It felt as if I was a young child skipping along in life with curiosity and wonder of the present moment and seeing so much more than I had ever remembered seeing before. Until I let everything go, my mind was too cluttered to see all the possibilities in existence. I realized now that everything was possible without beliefs binding my self to a previous or future life.

From a balanced space of stillness and peace, my awareness opened to intuition, visions, and dreams, wisdom from the Divine light within, and leaning into only my heart as a compass to determine: what was True North?

In this space of the heart, I examined thoughts that expanded possibilities and recognized others that narrowed into decisions, judgments, and beliefs. I explored how when new ideas presented in my life and at times my being rejoiced in a triumphant, "Yes!" and to others, I felt, "No."

In amazement, I noticed how my life aligned in the flow of Nature and the entire Universe as my practice deepened in attunement. My thoughts consistently foreshadowed what would come to pass, visions sprung forth out of the stillness of my quiet mind, and intuition—which I recognized as a sense deeper than emotion—became a gauge of resonance and flow.

I noticed how questions were answered before I prayed about them. This became stronger as I drew from this profound inner knowing within my heart as my source of truth. Until the day I realized I no longer prayed or petitioned to God anymore at all.

In this co-creative flow, I experienced more little everyday miracles than I'd ever recognized in my previous life. I was not asking for them, the miracles manifested on their own. I began seeing ordinary items, experiences, emotions, and relationships as symbols, continually revealing deeper meanings. It was as if the veil had lifted, but I could not pinpoint exactly when I began seeing so clearly from within.

The heart knows what course is right,
follow the heart always.

In the times of choosing between two options in a decision, I began to see how sometimes it was not yet time for the decision to be made. Instead, by allowing the flow of life to continue emerging, I noticed how more possibilities opened and new knowledge appeared. The wisdom within my heart was always certain of the best decision in perfect timing when it felt completely right inside without hesitation.

There were instances when several options seemed like a potential fit; I'd notice how I would be drawn to one option more than the others. It presented itself as a feeling and inner knowing, and with a sense of contentment, with less resistance.

Sometimes I tried on the decision in my mind's eye to see how it felt by stepping into the experience. It was amazing to realize the power of visualization and exploring within, and then to step back into the present moment having a greater sense of knowing where I saw the path leading in the future. Not projecting it as certain, but as a potentiality.

If one thing existed, then it's opposite always also existed. Yet, it was not only these two polar extremes but all of the infinite possibilities and potentials in-between. I found that so often I used to narrow my decisions to two without opening to the sky of possibilities, one of which might hold a higher and more joy-filled outcome than I could have imagined. Each time in the moment of decision, my heart knew the decision and my mind agreed.

We find exactly what we seek,
always endeavor to seek that which brings inner peace and joy.

When contemplating a decision or a potential pathway, I learned not to focus on the steps from here to there or the details or the "how." My role was to imagine the highest possible outcome, that was, one that invokes inner feelings of peace, joy, freedom, light, inspiration, bliss, and enthusiasm. Then, I stepped back and let the Universe do the rest.

This was true co-creation. I found that all I needed to do was hold the vision while remaining detached, allowing an even greater experience to spring forth. Saying "yes" or "no" to opportunities that presented along the pathway depending on how it felt in my heart, and every time, the vision was fulfilled.

I thought about how many times I used to believe what I wanted in life was what was "best" for me, but then when I attained the outcome it was less-than-joyful in experience. I learned to listen to my gut, emotions, intuition, and inner peace, and to reflect on all of these before taking any action. The key was to be willing to let go of all attachments of what I thought I wanted and go with the flow with the belief all was continually working towards the good.

Let go of outcomes and be in the flow of the present moment.

I realized that by holding on too tightly to an outcome it prevented me from seeing the open doorways of opportunity presenting along the way, including those I said "no" to because it did not look like what I wanted although it may have felt like a better answer than where I was. The more I clung to an "image" of what I wanted in the past, the more it was strangled and withered to dust. Whereas, when I gave my life the freedom to flow, transform, and bloom in Divine timing, not only did it feel better, but life was one miracle after another.

The more I practiced navigating with my heart compass, the greater my inner peace strengthened. I no longer made decisions out of extreme emotion at either end of the spectrum, whether sadness or anger or even overly happy, all came from a centered place of acceptance regardless of the potential outcome. I trusted that I was making the best decision at the time. Even if it meant holding off deciding until more understanding emerged. I was living life fully via my inner compass, the truth in my gut, like the word that was coined as "truthiness:" truth claimed as the truth, not for evidence or supporting facts, but because of a feeling that it was true from inside.

I shifted from the mindset of having to do everything to make something happen to "being open to receiving" what came. This was the same universal principle that worked in the same manner when I used to pray to God in the name of Jesus, but the difference was the freedom I now had to live life to the fullest and to pursue joy without any restrictions of beliefs.

Sometimes the doorways which presented did not resonate with my heart; as I said no to them, new doorways opened. This was as simple as sensing dissonance or misalignment within. Learning to say "No" and to continue onward meant trusting another door would open. Years ago, I clung to the one doorway that did not resonate, believing it was my only chance to get what I thought I wanted even though it did not make me happy inside.

All is One, and each one is of the All

My belief was judgments were both good and bad and as such, they were perceived in varying degrees by different people. For example, someone who did not have a home may believe a cot in a shelter was a good place to rest. While at the same time, another person who lives in a luxurious mansion may believe differently, both were judgments based on their experience and beliefs. I recognized how we made judgments all the time based on what we think and believe, and this separated us from the truth that in the Oneness and the All, good and bad do not exist because All is One without separation.

I began to use my senses to perceive how a person, situation, place, or experience resonated within my heart without judging in my mind. Was it in alignment with my inner world? Was it in dissonance with my inner world? Did it feel "light" and in flow or did it feel "heavy, burdensome" or constricted somehow. This was a new way of living. I stopped labeling or naming things for what I thought they were. Instead, I simply felt them and proceeded onward.

Instead of looking outside to religion, books, or anyone else for answers, I drew upon the deep well of wisdom I found within. It was a wellspring of the water of life, for it was in sync with the Universe and Nature. The tree of life within the heart.

In all this, it became clear that without wisdom and understanding, I could not have known love. It was not enough to hear a story about love or to be taught by someone else what love was, or what it should feel like, or look like. I needed to experience love from within to truly know what it was. Love without images. Love in the silence of a clear mind and an open heart.

Wisdom and love as One, united together without separation where infinity and eternity exist beyond time and space. In the silence of the All, before creation and after the end of time in the new beginning, and they were One within me, the sacred cosmic alchemical marriage.

ALL THINGS NEW

...LETTING GO TO RECEIVE DREAMS AND PROMISES COME TRUE.

A Prescription for my Soul
Be Good = keep my conscience clean
Love myself = body, heart, mind, and spirit
Spiritual Practices = what makes my heart sing and brings inner peace
Create joy = what brings forth creativity, happiness, expansion,
and where I feel free.
(August 26, 2020, age 43)

❊ ❊ ❊

Autumn 2013

Life was stagnant. It had felt that way for what seemed a long while. On one hand, my practice of living fully in the moment, navigating with my heart as a compass, was miraculous. So, what was missing? Any dreams and hopes about the future, even any discussion about the future at all.

I guess that's why it was not surprising when out of the ordinary one morning I heard Erick's alarm and noticed with curiosity he'd changed it to a new song. The rhythms of Led Zeppelin's Ramble On started... *"It's time I was on my way...ramble on..."*

Erick had lived with me for about eight months. Things were content and comfortable and as the summer drew on, he began spending more time out hiking or in Pennsylvania playing hockey. Although I enjoyed his companionship and company when he was around, on the quiet days, I became aware that I was equally, if not, happier inside when he was gone. This was around the timing when I noticed the "Ramble On" song, and an example of the types of foreshadowing that I recognized in symbols everywhere in my life, the little everyday miracle light posts along the way in reflection.

Erick came home later than expected one night and told me he needed a change of scenery. Immediately, I recalled the song on his morning alarm and realized my intuition was right again. I listened to Erick saying he felt too comfortable living with me and believed his life was not getting anywhere because he felt settled in. He emphasized that he needed to find his purpose in life and figure out what it was he was supposed to do next.

He paused and then said he was moving out. My first word to Erick was, "Go!" but not in an upset or mean way. I explained if he felt like he needed to find his path then he needed to follow his heart and go. It was the only way forward if he felt any sort of questioning inside. I believed in the importance of Erick following what he felt was right to do, no matter how much I enjoyed his companionship; I supported his decision to leave.

Then I asked Erick for clarity on his decision and whether this meant we were breaking up as a couple or still together in a relationship. Erick admitted he did not know what the future held and did not know where he would end up, or what he wanted down the road, but he said he did not want our relationship to end. It was a good enough answer to know where we stood for the time being and even after he'd packed up his belongings and moved back to his parents' house in Pennsylvania, we still texted and called each other often.

By the end of the week though, something was not sitting right within me. It was quiet in the house as it had been since Erick left. I'd finished working for the day, and evening had fallen into darkness. It was back to me, Lily, and the cats at home on a Friday night, but something kept nagging at me.

My mind kept flashing back to the day when I discovered Craeg had moved on with a profile on a dating website while he was still telling me that he did not want to lose me from his life. My thoughts kept shining a spotlight on the memory in the past. I'd learned by now, when a thought like that appeared out of nowhere, it was a symbol and had meaning. Sometimes it took a while to interpret and other times the significance presented itself right away. Either way, though, I knew the fact this memory was popping up in my head was important.

And then I stopped in understanding, it couldn't be happening again. No, it couldn't. Not again. The knowing was already in my gut as I sat down at my computer, needing to see it to fully believe it. And there it was, on one of the free dating websites, as clear as a bright and sunny day. "Erick. Single male from Pennsylvania, a hockey player who enjoys hiking and a good beer." Seeking... A relationship.

My insides hardened to steel. A relationship? Seeking a relationship? As far as I knew, he was still technically in one of those with me. Deep breath, I felt anger rising. But there was no heartbreak. No tears flowed.

"Seriously?" Glaring at the computer screen, I realized my anger was not so much directed at Erick as it was with myself. I'd been here before, in the same karmic cycle and now I was going around again. Again!

What happened two years ago with Craeg? The same thing. How could I have let it happen again? I shook my head and sighed. Lily must have sensed my frustration because she lifted her head from the floor near my chair and gazed up at me with eyes filled with concern.

"It's okay, girl," I sighed again and reached over to pat her head, scratching below her ear where she loved most. "It's okay."

Suddenly the answer clicked. If I'm recognizing that I'm somehow stuck in the same karmic pattern—and I don't want this to keep happening over and over (and over) again—I must change my response to transmute the energy in this experience to get me out of this cycle and into a new beginning. So simple right? That must be the solution.

I paced out the door of my home office and Lily padded faithfully behind. Heading downstairs, I was in deep concentration. I must come up with a different way to respond to this than I did in the past. Scrunching my face, I pondered. On one hand, if I used to wait for love to come back, arms outstretched with unconditional love every time a man left for greener pastures, awaiting the return. It was not that again.

The last time I tried a middle way, when Erick shared with me he was not sure what he wanted, I'd offered him an open door, but told him that I wouldn't necessarily wait for him to come back. I questioned, "So, what was at the far opposite end of the spectrum that would elevate me out of this cycle?" There was one thing I could think of to do.

"Lily, we're going for a ride," I said as she gazed up at me, cocking her big St. Bernard head to the side with expectation.

Since I did not know how long it would take, there was no leaving her at home. After Lily jumped up into the Jeep, we were off. I mean, when this idea sprung into my head, I did not think through exactly why I felt the imminent need to do what I was going to do. All I knew was that I was not going to go through this again. This was just the first idea I'd thought of in the moment. I wanted out of this cycle, and I wanted out now.

My hands gripped the steering wheel as the exit signs on the interstate sped past the sides of my vision. The mile markers ticked downward as I drove west to Pennsylvania. Lily and I were on the way to the one place where Erick would likeliest be on a Friday night, the Steel Ice Center hockey rink in

Bethlehem.

As I slowly pulled into the parking lot in the darkness, I noticed how crowded it was with players and fans. Turning the wheel, I drove around to the side of the building. Yep, there was Erick's car. I inhaled and exhaled, but it did not matter how much I focused on my breathing. I reached for my phone and called his number.

"What's up? I'm in the locker room, the game just ended," Erick answered. He did not sound surprised to hear from me until he heard my voice. I told him I was parked outside the rink, and I wanted to talk with him. I emphasized the word, "Now."

A few minutes later, Erick walked out towards our cars. I was already leaning against the back of the Jeep, allowing myself to feel sentimental for a split second as I saw him. But then the unrest in my soul woke me from my reverie, the part inside screaming, "Not again!"

"What are you doing here?" He looked at me.

The storm of emotions raged inside; I was aware they were there, but I did not let them overtake me. Starting calmly and with a matter-of-facteness that could not be questioned or persuaded, I said, "I came to tell you it's over."

Erick looked confused.

My eyes flashed, so much for controlling my emotions, "Seeking a relationship?" I growled at him, "Seeking a relationship? Really? I thought we were still in a relationship?"

His eyes dropped to the ground as he realized what I knew.

"I will not sit here and pretend everything is okay and that we're still in a relationship. You've already moved on to find someone else. I'm done. It's over!"

It was then when he tried to explain how he was not really seeking a new relationship. Nice try, Erick. I knew there was an option to choose "looking for a friend" on that dating website and I'd already known that because that's what he'd set it to when I first met him over two years ago.

My voice rose in a loud declaration in the darkness of the parking lot, "I deserve better than this!"

"Yes, you do," Erick responded.

Unexpectedly, I felt complete, as if what I needed to say transmitted to the Universe and I could go back home. It was done. Turning away from him, I went to get back into the Jeep. Suddenly, Lily popped her head out the open back window and panted in Erick's direction with her silly happy St. Bernard grin.

"Lily!" he exclaimed in a voice so familiar that my heart felt for a moment as if nothing had changed between us.

In mid-step up, I spun back around, "Don't even say hi to Lily! It's over with her too!"

He stood motionless as I backed out of the parking space and drove away. I did not look at him, I couldn't. There was a split second after I turned out of the rink's driveway when my insides turned to remorseful mush. What did I do? Oh, what did I do?

I felt so bad, I wanted to apologize for yelling. I wanted to go back and re-open the door of future possibility I'd just slammed shut. One half of me was trying to get the other part to turn around, but I did not turn back. I deserved better; I really did.

In the deepest of my heart, I believed I was worthy of more than indecisive men who for one reason or another were not ready or willing to commit with their entire heart. I'd rather be on my own.

❋ ❋ ❋

Let go of constructed beliefs and old ways of the past.
Surrender yesterday's expectations, desires, and visions.
From a balanced center of open creative space,
Build the dream,
believe in the dream,
open the mind to all possible paths,
take focused supporting actions,
be grateful for unexpected opening doors,
always thankful for unanticipated joys,
blessed in all life experiences,
while enjoying the journey of fulfillment,
and allow the flow of the Divine to create the highest
and greatest possible outcome of the dream,
and then start from the beginning again.
(2012, age 35)

Autumn 2013 (Continued)

A week or so went by without any word from Erick. Not that I was surprised, I expected it after the way things were left at the hockey rink. But at the same time, I was not pining or holding open the possibility for us to be together in the future. The cycle was not going to catch me again.

I was suddenly in a new space. Yes, I knew I'd been alone before—even as confident and content in "on my own-ness" and open to whatever came next. This time though, I'd slammed the door so tight on the past there was not even a sliver of a chance it would reopen.

One morning I became aware while still immersed in a dream. In the dream: *I noticed I was lying in a bed and started to rise out of it as if it were time to wake up on a new day. Light filled the expanse of my vision as the dream continued. From the light, I then saw the impression of a man standing in front of me. I sensed an immense feeling of love emanating from him and surrounding us together. It was the most love I could recall I'd ever felt. Yet, I did not know who this was. All I could see in symbols in the dream was the man's name was, "David." Then I sensed a child or children around him* and awoke out of the dream. I lay in bed under the covers committing it to memory in wonderment of what I'd experienced while waking up from sleep.

My reverie of the man in the dream persisted throughout the day. I considered what I knew to be true, other dreams of mine had come true in the past. Why wouldn't this one? I believed it could be true, that there was this man named David out there somewhere, the man of my dreams. I was in awe of the love that radiated from the light in the dream. It was greater than anything I'd ever experienced before in my life.

I went on with my day almost giddy with excitement because I knew without a doubt one day in the future, I would meet a man and he would be the love I wanted in my life. No settling, no semi-happy, all the way happy, and his name would be David. I knew it would happen; I just did not know when.

Autumn 2013 (Continued)

> The compass within my heart will guide me,
> it will not let me get too far astray
> from the experience in life that I am seeking,
> such happiness and joy light the way.
>
> As I approach the signs and forks in the road
> I remember my compass and take a pausing view,
> using all my senses in reflection to determine
> in which direction my compass within is leading me.
> (2013, age 36)

✽ ✽ ✽

A few days after the dream, I decided to restart a profile on a dating website. Although, to be honest, I was conflicted in taking any sort of action at all towards an outcome. I did not want to go on dates anymore because I fully believed one day when I least expected it, the man named David would arrive in my life. With faith in the workings of the Universe, I knew no action was necessarily needed. But at the same time, I also felt I should somehow concrete the intention that I was open to receive. I mean, rather than sitting here and doing nothing but... waiting.

Ha! Check off the box, I'd learned that lesson already. Regardless of my faith in the wondrous, miracle-working power of the Universe, I would rather stick needles in my eyes than enter a waiting cycle pattern again. With my decision made, I signed up. It did not matter when the man named David walked into my life—today or years from now, or whether it was through the dating website or outside of the site. It felt all so different this time. I was at peace, and so very, very free because the future was open to all possibilities.

Driving along the freeway one day when I was heading back home after visiting family in Virginia, it all came together as I questioned the sky, wondering why I felt so content and at oneness when I was on the open road. Was it because I was heading where I wanted to go? On the road that I chose?

The wind in was in my hair, and where I'd end up, Heaven only knew. Singing to the beat of the music in my heart, lifting my sights high above. I was free to question, free to choose, and free to let anything go in the moment I decided to do so. Inhaling the crisp fall air streaming in from the open windows of the Jeep, I felt alive. Exhaling, I felt embraced with the deepest of contentment. I realized I could not call this happiness, for it was beyond where words could reach.

This indescribable feeling inside was my heart connected with Oneness in the moment. It was complete and perfect in every way. I felt so fulfilled and peaceful. While in the rhapsody, I noticed it was different than the times when I'd elevated in consciousness in mindful meditation. In silent meditation, I'd experienced my mind expand beyond my physical body and become One with all around me, birds chirping seemed to be in Oneness with my consciousness and every sound a part of the whole.

Gazing up at the sunshine, at the perfect blue sky, and around me at the multitude of autumn-colored leaves decorating the landscape as I drove along, passing trucks and other cars passing me by. Yet, all I saw was the entire open stretch of road before me, beckoning beautifully. This Oneness of the heart felt like I was in Heaven on Earth. I shook my head out of my reverie as the realization of what I'd thought flowed through me, Heaven was on Earth? And I found it along I-81 in Virginia?

There I was, driving on the open road of the interstate with Lily and singing along to the music with one hand tapping the rhythm on my leg and I felt more at peace than I had ever before. It embraced me and held me, and I knew it was Heaven.

As it dawned on me, I burst out laughing. Jesus was right after all. Heaven was not somewhere out there. It was not in a relationship, or a hobby, or a career, or anything external. Blissful Heaven was inside of me, and it was here all the time.

Autumn 2013 (Continued)

I was ready to stop dating completely. Really, what was the point? Each first date was going nowhere. If someone asked me why I was going on first dates, I would not have had a good answer anyway. It was not like I was sitting at home bored or lonely. Additionally, because I believed one day the man of my dreams would enter my life, there was no reason to date. There was more than enough in life to keep me busy, happy in my on-my-ownness.

Why then did I happen to notice the matches email from the dating website I'd joined two months ago on my phone? Why did I not delete it immediately without opening it, as I did every other single day? Rolling my eyes at the situation, while scrolling through the photos of matches, I disdainfully barked at myself, "No more dating!"

My eyes glanced to the very last match at the bottom of the email. A man wearing sunglasses with a beaming smile. Hmm, there was something about him. I could not put my finger on it. His smile stuck with me as I put the phone down and headed home in the evening.

After arriving home, the man's smile still lingered in my thoughts. Fine. Okay, I'll look. I logged into the dating website on my computer and clicked on the man's photo to read more about him. He wrote in his profile he was ready for a long-term and true love commitment. He wanted to experience the pains and joys of life together side-by-side with a best friend and soulmate. He mentioned he had limited time for dating because he was a full-time parent for his 8-year-old son. Anyone interested in getting to know him would have to be patient, as he would not be able to go out on the town like couples usually do. He seemed to be very particular about the relationship that he was seeking, and I was in a bit of awe when I finished reading through it.

I shook my head and said to Lily, "He's too good to be true." She lifted her big head off the floor and gazed up at me. What he said he was looking for felt like the exact commitment and love I wanted with the man of my dreams.

I clicked through his photos. He was too good looking, out of my league for sure. I did not want to start a conversation with him or see where it may lead, but his smile caught me in a moment again. He was too good to be true, and I was done with dating. So, I could not explain why my finger clicked to send him a message.

My fingers typed the stream of thought running through my mind, "Hi there, I just wanted to let you know that out of all the profiles I have ever seen on here, yours seems the most genuine and honest. You seem like you are amazing. Best of luck in your search." Send. Even though I was done with dating, he deserved to know how awesome he seemed. I shrugged. Hopefully, it would at least make him smile.

Clicking the internet window closed, I stretched and stood up from my chair. Lily instinctively knew it was time for sleep. She got up to her feet, took a step forward, and then stretched out her big paws in front of me. Then she padded along faithfully behind me as I walked up the stairs to bed.

There was absolutely nothing I expected back from sending the message. And yet, there was this unexplainable, inexplicable feeling inside my heart that knew exactly what was on the horizon. Something was about to happen. I could not shake the feeling no matter how hard I tried. As I dozed off to sleep, in my head I was still done with dating.

Autumn 2013 (Continued)

In the morning, my alarm went off and I fumbled to hit snooze on my phone. Lily waited patiently with her big head next to my face until she knew for sure I was faking being asleep, and she nudged at me. Time to get up! I opened my tired eyes and pet her good morning.

Lily hopped off the bed, and I followed her down the stairs as she led the way to the back door to go out. Sleepily, I leaned against the kitchen counter while my coffee brewed, and the cats meowed at me for their morning treats. With a yawn, I shook out the treats onto the floor, looked at the back door as Lily whacked at it a few times with her paw, and I went over to let her back in. Life was as it was yesterday.

Except, I still had this unexplainable feeling something was about to happen. After my coffee was ready, I sipped it as I walked back upstairs to get ready for work. Ding! Glancing down at my phone, a message appeared from the dating site app, flashing across as a notification on the screen.

It was from the smiling man in sunglasses. "Huh?" I scratched my head. I did not even say anything in my message about getting to know each other or going on a date. What could he be writing back about? In his one-sentence response, he asked if I knew how far apart in distance we were. I did not. I laughed to myself, why would I have looked at his location when I had no intention of going on a date with him?

But here was his question in my inbox, so I figured the least I could do was answer it. Going over to my computer, I pulled up an online map. Hmm, furrowing my brow in concentration, I calculated the town he lived in was in an area of Pennsylvania more than 80 miles from my home.

"How did that happen?" I wondered, "Didn't I have it set so matches would only be within 50 miles of my zip code? How did he even pop up as a match?" Then my eyes landed on his name at the bottom of the message, I'd missed seeing it when I first read it on my phone: David. The world turned over on itself and felt surreal. Is he the one? Is David the man from my dream?

Suddenly my mind was transported back to a snapshot in time. I remembered Jeremie, the man I was so wrong about, but it wasn't about him specifically, I recalled he had primary custody of his child when I met him. And here was David, who was in a similar situation. Like a blast from the past and flash forward to some sort of symbolic karmic pattern aligning from shadow past to future in the light revealing the way, from a false image in shadow to possibly my actual soulmate in the light of reality? I grinned at the open doorway that appeared to be revealing itself in front of me.

Shaking my head out of the realization in amazement, my fingers clicked at the keyboard in response to his message. The knowing that I could not shake or quite describe in words. It was there—and it was stronger now than before. "No, I didn't realize we live that far apart and that you are all the way in Pennsylvania. But…" I continued typing, "If there was a true connection, the distance wouldn't matter. It would be worth the drive at least once." I clicked send and went back to getting ready for work.

David must have agreed because throughout the entire day we exchanged emails as often as possible. In the evening after he put his son to bed, we talked on the phone for the first time. It felt so right, like perfectly right. The very first instant the video chat popped up on my phone, and I virtually looked into his eyes, I knew without a doubt from the deepest of my soul: he was the David from my dream.

❋ ❋ ❋

True love happens once in a lifetime
and when our eyes met for the first time,
I knew ours was always meant to be.
(December 2013, age 36)

Autumn 2013 (Continued)

Today was the day for some housekeeping. I texted Erick and asked him to meet me halfway to return all the rest of his belongings he'd left in my house. It was not that we hadn't talked at all since the night I ended everything outside the hockey rink in the parking lot, but at the same time, even with those rare occurrences, I could not say we were even close friends anymore. Besides all that, I wanted to clean house. It was less than a week since meeting David in person, and I knew he was my dream come true and we would be married in the future.

I pulled into the gas station where we agreed on meeting, and a few minutes later Erick pulled in next to the Jeep. Hopping out, I opened the back as he got out of his car, and he came around the back to where I was standing. We both said "Hi" and he wrapped me in a hug. It felt like a long hug, but I did not know how long it was. Maybe I was only counting because no matter how sentimental the moment could have been with Erick; my heart was overflowing with love like I'd never experienced before in my life with David.

While we were hugging, I heard Erick sniffle. I pulled away and looked up at him about to question what was wrong. But I did not have to say anything; his eyes were wet. He caught my gaze and looked silently towards the ground and then finally spoke, "It feels so final."

Nodding slowly, I replied, "That's because it is." My tone was gentle even though the words may have sounded firm, it was the truth. "I met someone..." I continued, "not just anyone, but a dream I had come true."

Erick looked at me questioningly. He did not know anything about what had happened or the dream. He leaned against the back of his car while I explained everything about the name of the man who was in my dream. The man named David, who'd I'd met serendipitously from the dating website. I looked at Erick plainly and told him David and I would be married in the future.

He responded, "We'll see," and went back to transferring his belongings to his car.

Motionless, I observed the moment. Realizing how crazy all this sounded, especially since I'd been down this road of believing a man was "the one" more times than I'd like to remember, but at the same time, it was different now. I believed because somewhere in my heart—where I'd found a wisdom beyond words to the very core of my being—I knew it was true. Beyond all rational explanation, it did not matter how illogical it may have appeared to Erick or anyone else, the faith in my heart was unshakeable.

Here I was now feeling a bit surreal. Watching the final ending of my two-year-long on-again and off-again relationship with Erick play out as he pulled out another box to put in his car. I recognized the crossroads. Déjà vu set across my countenance as somehow it suddenly felt like I'd been here before.

Yet not a single question arose in my thoughts, not one tremor of doubt whether I was making the right decision. All I felt was the peace that passes all understanding, fully rooted in the Truth within my heart compass. Trusting that as I continued each day to step out onto the way, as the Persian poet and Sufi master, Rumi, once said, *"the way appears."*

As we said the last goodbye, I hopped back up in the Jeep to drive back home. My heart alighted with joy in the closure. It meant opening more space towards the new beginning ahead. I grinned in recognition of the inner feeling of a shift in the cycle from closing to the closed door to a new beginning and smiled all the way home on a yet untraveled part of my path, almost giddy with the thought. Because at the crossroads, in the mystery of the unknown, everything was possible, even my dreams coming true.

Summer 2014

"I promise to take you as my only love, from this day forward.
To stand by your side, to hold you close,
to be a safe haven in your life,
to listen when you speak, to comfort you when you cry,
to join your laughter with mine,
to warm your body and soul, to never take you for granted,
through good times and bad, all the days of my life.
As our lives unfold together, whatever we may
encounter, let us encounter it together.
I promise to be faithful and to love you always.
Today, I give you my love, from this day forward, now and forever."

It was the 26th of June when I stood in the Colonial Park perennial garden gazebo with David just north of the rose gardens, with a handful of family present including both of our moms. My heart overflowed with love. Everything I'd ever hoped and dreamed for came true in real life, fitting into place like puzzle pieces from two worlds that completed each other as one. As the ceremony continued, we symbolized becoming a family in a sand ceremony with three vivid colors poured into one jar, one by each of the two of us, and one by David's son.

It was just after the pronouncement and the kiss, as I turned from David towards our family, the bright eyes of his young son beamed directly at me.

His smile was bursting with all the happiness in his heart, arms wide open as he called out emphatically with joy, "Mom!" He came into my arms for a hug and I kissed the top of his head. I was in awe.

We left it up to him on what he would decide to call me after we were married, so it would feel comfortable in his mind and heart as we made the life transition into one home. The moment was spontaneous and unexpected, and I suddenly found myself embarking on an entirely new life adventure as a mom.

Later on, as I was reflecting on the joy of our wedding day, my mind recalled back to a vision in 2012, when in my mind's eye I saw a child around what felt to be the age of 9 playing on the front walkway of my house. At the time, I could not fathom how it would come to fruition, that was until I met David over a year later. Now the vision became reality as they moved into my home.

There may have been a moment in there somewhere—in between the first time we met in person and gazed into each other's eyes and after the wedding —when I recognized in some way I'd received the husband God promised years ago.

As I contemplated that God's promise did come true, I felt grateful in the deepest of my heart. It was as if the entire broken road I'd traveled on truly did have blessings along the way that led me straight to my husband.

David was more than I could ever have asked God for if I were to have imagined the perfect companion and partner in all things. We balanced each other effortlessly and finished each other's thoughts and championed each other's dreams. It was an all-new experience in happily ever after, not a life for two, but an instant trinity, which is what we named our new rescued calico kitten who joined our family with Lily dog and two other cats.

Autumn 2015

Today started as an ordinary day with a laundry list of things to do. One item on my list was searching for some old mortgage documentation from way back in 2009, when I first applied for a refinance right after the divorce from Paul, and after being rejected, I applied for a forbearance after another and then another, as I tried to get finances straightened out to avoid foreclosure on my home.

It took a couple of years when all was said and done, and during that time

I'd found ways to keep focused on forward progression, even in baby steps, and worked to make ends meet by starting a little business by selling on eBay. I designed jewelry, key chains, and other inspirational crafts to sell. Eventually, I was promoted in my pharma career and more easily navigated the cost of living.

My mind echoed back to when I was in the middle of those stressful months when I questioned whether or not I'd have to move on from where I lived after the divorce. I recalled God impressed in my heart I would indeed remain in my house because it would be a good home for my husband and family in the future. It was a gift of hope back then, and I realized now in this moment of reflection it was yet another promise God in the name of Jesus Christ spoke into my life had come true. Not that it mattered though, because my faith was securely fastened within the shores of my heart and guided by the light within my soul.

Yet, it was a heart-warming confirmation my life was still filled with the light of holiness even if I was not a Christian anymore. For if I were on a path of shadows and darkness, the miracles of God's promises would not have come to fruition in my life as truth. It may have been over three years since I picked up a Bible, but I still remembered the verse from Isaiah 46, "...what I have said, that I will bring about; what I have planned, that I will do." Further, in John 14, when Jesus said, "I have told you now before it happens, so that when it does happen you will believe." And so it was.

I brought my attention back to the present and the task at hand in our home office, I clicked and scrolled backward into email folders, scrolling the depths: 2015... 2014... 2013... 2012... and my eyes landed on an email with a file attached. Not knowing immediately what it was, I clicked to open the attachment and to my surprise, it was the uncompleted draft manuscript I'd destroyed years ago.

The entire story from when I was broken-hearted and lost, to my testimony that Jesus was like my Prince Charming and saved me, all the way up to when I was practicing the mastery of joy alchemy, until the moment when I surrendered my beliefs and my life as Jesus' disciple into the light of Spirit within my heart.

My inner world shook and rattled as the bones of my past life came alive in my mind. Disbelief filled my consciousness, "How?" I questioned even louder again inside, "How was this here?" The story was destroyed. It was erased from possibility. How was it here now in front of me? It was gone, deleted, shredded, and tossed away years ago.

Yet, all the while my mind questioned the miracle in awe, the knowing in my heart expanded in understanding: this was somehow, in some way, still mine to do. After all, if I looked at my life now, Jesus' promise for me was complete. I received the husband in my life that Jesus said would arrive. Everything came rushing back through me: I'm an apostle, I am announcing the Messianic Age and Jesus' return in a blaze of glory. But none of this fit who I was anymore. Time had moved on, and I was already two years into a new life with David.

Because I never expected the possibility of publishing my journals to ever reappear, I'd not shared anything from the past when I met and married David. It wasn't that they were secrets or ghosts hidden in the closet, it was because my life moved on and none of it mattered to me anymore; so, why bring forward memories that were already accounted for and laid to rest? But now…if this came back for me to complete, and if I was meant to publish the story, this changed everything. It had the potential of devastating my new life.

Don't get me wrong, David was open-minded. He was not raised in a religious home, although once in a blue moon his family attended a local Lutheran Church down the road from where he grew up in the suburbs of Philadelphia, Pennsylvania.

His spiritual philosophies were secular in nature, like the Force in Star Wars, or the light of Christ within American painter and host of the television show, The Joy of Painting, Bob Ross (1942-1995), and the American television host of the preschool television series, Mister Rogers' Neighborhood, Fred Rogers (1928-2003), and the philosophies of actor and martial arts instructor, Bruce Lee (1940-1973), *"Empty your mind, be formless, shapeless – like water. Now you put water in a cup, it becomes the cup. You put water into a bottle, it becomes the bottle. You put it in a teapot, it becomes the teapot. Now water can flow, or it can crash. Be water, my friend."*

Reopening this tomb from the past would be an incredible amount of flexibility to ask of David as it would change the trajectory of our lives. The memories flooded my senses, when Jesus came to me and called me to be his disciple, then when I was appointed as his apostle, God's Word that in the future I may be as well-known as former United States President Bill Clinton after my book was published, the eclipse during the Kumbh Mela on the day of Mauni Amavasya…

Oh, it all came back! Realizations poured through my vision as the neurons were firing in my head. David came into my life just like Jesus said he would. And now, my manuscript had its ending. The promised husband from Jesus came true—this was my testimony about the work of God in my life.

My mind raced in contemplation as I thought about who I was now, an indie-spirit outside of any one single religious pathway. I believed All was God and God was All, flowing peacefully between joy alchemy and oneness with nature in the freedom of following my heart compass. The light within my heart guided with perfect accuracy, unlike my mind did years ago. When I meditated no words came to pray. Life was a flow of navigating for the greatest river of peace inside and joy in our lives and steering away from what created rough or stormy waters. I was not even close to standing near the shores of Christianity anymore.

It wasn't supposed to happen like this, it was gone and done. David did not know anything about this from my past. Not one bit of it. But I realized—I had to tell him.

In the deepest of my heart, I knew this discovery meant I needed to finish writing the book now that it had an ending. Not to mention, figure out how I would explain how Jesus saved me and promised my husband and then I dreamed about the name "David" and met him in real life, and here we were married together. Oh, and somehow explain, by the way, that I didn't believe in Jesus the same way I used to anymore.

I rolled my eyes thinking about how well that would go over, yet it was the truth. I viewed Jesus more like a Guru who was my master and teacher over the course of three years, until the day I destroyed the draft manuscript and let go of the story of my life and all my beliefs about the past and the future (including Jesus) and was reborn so I could learn to trust the light of spirit within my heart instead of the light of spirit in my mind. This was what Jesus led me through before he let me fly on my own.

Ugh! I could not think further into what all this meant or how the ending would be written. I needed to tell David. Making the decision, a few tears crept into the corners of my eyes as I knew I was about to risk everything beautiful in my new life. The truest and most real love I'd ever experienced with an amazing marriage and husband, an equal partner in all things, a companion, and my best friend. By the time I reached the room he was in, I was crying.

"I have something I have to tell you," I confessed to him between sobs. Concerned about what may be so serious, David asked what it was.

As best I could through tears, I shared with him everything I had not told him before. The words sounded strange as they tumbled out of my mouth because I had not spoken about any of it in so long. I told him about how years ago I believed Jesus saved me when I was in a lion's den like Daniel, and then appointed me to be an apostle and publish my life story about the second coming of Christ and the end times.

I admitted to David I'd stopped believing in it years ago when I'd walked away from Christianity and never expected it to come back. I'd found new life after letting go of the cross that Jesus was crucified on. Then I went on to admit if I were to finish the book now, it would not be what Christians wanted to hear because Jesus was bigger than their box of beliefs and all of the denominations.

I acknowledged with seriousness that it would likely upset some people. Then, I went on to describe how it would be welcomed by millions, if not billions, of other people who believe in love, peace, unity, and equality for all. No matter what happened though, I told David that I knew I needed to complete and publish the book to not only share my testimony about Jesus and about how I received my promised husband from God, who was also my literal dream come true.

Beyond the Bible and any single religion of the world, this meant my peace-loving, indie-spirit, joy alchemy crafting, creation of wishes, dreams, and happily ever after, miracles-in-Nature self would have to somehow explain how it was that I was not a Christian anymore, but I was still on the Holy path of God with the blessings of Jesus Christ because the promise he spoke into my life came to fruition.

David didn't say anything. Silence hung in the room. I exhaled; eyes locked on the ground as I waited for his response. I braced myself in the unknown. Curious what he might be thinking, I looked up to find David wearing a grin with a gleam in his eyes. When he saw the pensive look on my face, his amused grin turned into laughter, "That's all it is? You thought I would be upset about that?" I nodded as tears streamed down both cheeks.

With eyes filled with love, David laughed as he said, "Bring it on," and joy filled my heart. I tucked the manuscript into the realm of "sometime in the future," for I intended to meditate on the manner and time of publishing before stepping forward; it was not yet the time.

* * *

I believed in my dreams,
my heart knew the way.
And on a day when I least expected it,
my dream came back into reality.
(May 12, 2018, age 41)

TRANSFIGURATION

...BECOMING THE RIVER OF LIFE.

Summer 2016

There is no single path,
for we have all arrived here from different directions in time and space.
My inner fire burns with burden to know where I am to be led,
or where I am to lead.
(September 2016, age 39)

❋ ❋ ❋

I was perched on a rock along the mountainside at 8,100 feet near the Great St. Bernard Hospice built as a refuge in the 11th Century, at the Great St. Bernard Pass in the Alps. From where I sat with pen and journal in hand, I took in the hospice and gazed at the beauty of it all, including the simplicity of the border crossing where Italy changed into Switzerland on the road across the lake in front of me. I held it within my soul.

There was more for me to do to be of service in the world, but to whose or what glory? The light that flowed within me was neither of Western nor Eastern origin, for it was all as one.

Setting aside this inner exploration, I returned to the nature surrounding me, in awe of how this dream come true came together. After a corporate work meeting that I attended in Rome, I extended my stay in Europe and traveled by train through Milan and up to Geneva, then across Switzerland to the great mountain pass of heroic rescues by St. Bernard dogs and monks who cared for the terrorized and distressed travelers in service to all.

I finally got to see where my beloved St. Bernard dogs originated and met the Saints from the Swiss lineage who answered commands in French. It didn't matter that I could not speak the local language though, I got a big, drooly St. Bernard smooch across my face when I visited with one in the hospice yard.

Summer 2016 (Continued)

Then, I flew onward to Spain, and after quick jaunts in Madrid and the Cinderella-esque castle and Holy cathedral of Segovia, I took a bus on pilgrimage to the Cathedral and Convent of St. Teresa in Avila. I climbed the staircases of the medieval era town walls and looked across the rooftops of Avila and out to the outer lands.

No wonder Saint Teresa's mystical inspirations included depictions of castles and mansions and rooms, for she was from a town with walls and squares that seemed quite befitting for her writings. It was her inner truth, just like every other mystic before or after in time. The expression of how the light came bursting forth from her soul in the delight and joy in the presence of a power and energy of goodness, peace, and love. In unique and beautiful ways, her description and artistry showed through the lens of her faith and understanding, and in the ways of truth of how an experience is felt, none were the only one.

I saw truth as merely an illusion of the mind that was set into the framework and agreements of belief. What made it true or what made it false? It was all in accordance with the belief held by the mind, which was deeper than thought, beyond the symbol that merely pointed to the object that was true.

For example, a tree. Was a tree always a tree? Yes, in its nature, but it was not always a "tree" in the spoken and written word. A tree was also a boom, pu, arbre, fa, crann, albero, medis, copac, árbol, strom, 木, ต้นไม้, पेड़, and δέντρο, among many other names. Which then, was true?

This was also evident in an example of the color of the sky. Was the sky always blue? Not when it was grey and cloudy or brown with smog; further, for someone who was color deficient, the sky may not be any of these colors at all.

The way we described what an object looked like was based on how we observed it with our senses and with our eyes, combined with the knowledge we have from our experiences in life, each just as different as the names that were spoken and written in the many languages of the world. No wonder our truths were all over the place!

I considered how clinging onto these beliefs created struggles that prevented us from moving on from experiences of suffering, even when they were no longer serving our greatest personal and collective good. Humanity became static in the truth and manner of how we ascribed meaning to our story in history. We kept building from the past into the future without going back to resolve the wounds and divisions that cried out for healing.

I noted when I entered the mist and considered that which was in opposition to my truth or my belief, it did not mean I or the truth needed to change. What it did was allow me to bring back into wholeness, understanding received through the wisdom of having considered all sides. Including the entire truth contained in both polar opposites as one.

This sage-worthy understanding in the heart served to create common ground and a platform for harmony and peace in every instance when I encountered opposing ideas in life. I wrote in my journal: the person who holds all together as one in nonjudgment was love and wisdom incarnate.

Many religious and wisdom traditions named and described this inner Divine light differently, but all truths were similar for they were expressions of the same light shining out of the darkness. The golden thread of brilliance connected them as One beyond all names.

I questioned, what was stopping us from ascribing attributes instead of names, such as peace, love, joy, and harmony, and call those Good? If it bore the fruit of anger, jealousy, envy, hatred, fear, or suffering, then it was the absence of Good, no matter what the name or spiritual practices looked like.

Asking whether it harmed or it healed was more important to me than any title or name that came with a teacher or spiritual tradition. For it was through the open-hearted exploration I discovered in understanding: there existed no one truth, just as much as one truth existed in All, and herein lay the inner work preparing the soul to receive gifts from the light.

✻ ✻ ✻

Breathe.
I become aware of my heartbeat, of the energy flowing through and around me.
I become aware of where I lose the sensations of the edges in my energy
into the oneness of Nature, where the line of separation ceases to be.
Between the edges of space and time.
I allow myself to be here.
Thoughts may appear.
Emotions may surface.
Beliefs may emerge from the deep.
I hold these in mindful contemplation.
I consider what reason they have for entering my awareness.
I ponder whether they are serving my greatest good and the good of the world
around me.
Slowly and as I am ready
—I let them go—

one by one;
until the quiet surface of the deep radiates in silence from within.
(Date Unknown, 2020)

Autumn 2016

I was in Japan for work for the second time in six months, this time to Yokohama for a clinical study data presentation at a scientific congress.

The memories of my first trip to Japan earlier in the year filled my heart...I'd flown directly into Tokyo to the corporate worldwide offices for meetings when the sakura (cherry) blossoms were in bloom within Shinjuku Gyoen National Garden; it was breathtaking. I strolled under the boughs of the trees in all their glorious beauty. After I was free of work obligations, I found my way to the Shinkansen, more well-known as the bullet train, and headed south in pilgrimage to the shrines and temples in Kyoto.

In the Kansai region of Japan, Kyoto is steeped in sacred history with 17 UNESCO World Heritage Sites. With more than 1600 Shinto and Buddhist sacred spaces on the map, I knew ahead of arrival that I would not have nearly enough time to visit all of them in only two days of vacation time, but I had more than a dozen on my list for exploration and meditation.

One of these was Shunkoin, a Zen Buddhist Temple that housed the oldest Christian bell in Japan. The High Priest taught a Zen meditation class in English I was excited to attend. My first foray into an Eastern tradition meditation, although I'd already been reading books on Buddhism and Taoism, trained in Reiki, and practiced meditation on my own at home.

All this time, from when I let go of the story of Christianity and Jesus as my savior and teacher to turn wholly within to the light in my heart with a silent mind, I hadn't realized I embarked on a path similar to the religions of the East. The paths that the sages, saints, bodhisattvas, and gurus walked upon long before the timepoint in history when Jesus was said to be born. By the time I found the sacred texts and practices of Buddhism, Taoism, Hinduism (yoga), and Sikhism, I immediately connected with the truth and the light within because it felt similar to the path I'd already traveled on my own. This was what brought me to the Zen meditation lesson in Kyoto at Shunkoin Temple.

As we began, the High Priest explained in a teaching that spiritual practices needed to work in modern daily life, or they were obsolete. He explained how everything changes and continues to change in the present, and this also included what we hold as our traditions...

And as I turned the pages of my journal to the next blank page to write,

I looked at Yokohama through the bus window and hoped where I was heading this time would expand the teachings within me. The entire concept of mindfulness in the present moment in flow and allowing tradition the freedom to evolve with life was in opposition to the static traditions of the Abrahamic religions that were set in stone—even to the degree the Ten Commandments were said to be inscribed by God on tablets and brought down the mountain by Moses, and of the most Holy books. The descriptions were terra firma, like the "rock of Christ" Christians stood upon, not in the ever-changing, evolving, emerging, and expanding flow of life.

Yet, these things were of this world and a symbol of the truth of what they represented, not the living Force of Life whose creative power and energy was the flow itself. The ever-present moment between the past and the future where all was alive and in motion, just as the Eastern traditions taught, "*Life is a series of natural and spontaneous changes. Don't resist them – that only creates sorrow. Let reality be reality. Let things flow naturally forward in whatever way they like*," attributed to Lao-Tzu, an ancient Chinese philosopher, and reputed author of the Tao Te Ching.

Upon arriving at Daihonzan Sojiji, the Soto Zen Buddhism Sojiji Head Monastery, I left my shoes in the foyer and headed down the main corridor to find a quiet space to meditate. I ventured down a hallway that opened up into nature as I'd noticed many Zen temples did, incorporating the inner and outer world together in the creation of a peaceful energy I'd grown accustomed to feeling inside myself during meditation.

Interrupting my reverie, I realized I must have gone farther than the public was allowed to go because two monks came out of a room and walked towards me. I smiled and bowed in respect. Their faces and words were questioning, and I apologized in English and said, "I'm looking for somewhere to sit in meditation." But I knew they could not understand me as much as I did not know what they said.

The elder of the two monks waved at me to follow them down another corridor, and I bowed my head and followed through two different rooms, a hallway, and beyond to an elevator, which he then motioned me to get into with them. Downward to the next floor, the doors opened, and I was standing in what must have been work areas for some of the monks.

The elder monk called out to another monk in the back of the room and I stood silently and humbly, hoping I hadn't caused much trouble. They spoke back and forth a moment, and then he motioned towards me, and the young man who was called to come to speak with me approached and with a bow of his head, said, "Hello."

I bowed again and smiled at him, "I'm so sorry if I was where I shouldn't have been, I did not see any signs. I am looking for a place to sit in meditation."

He said it was okay and offered that if I waited for him to finish his work, he could take me to the zendo to meditate as he was the English guide for the day. My heart alit with joy and I emphatically nodded yes with gratitude. About 20 minutes later, he showed me the monk's quarters across the other side of the building, and we made our way to the meditation hall. Not knowing what to expect, I was in awe to see it was the zendo the monks meditated in, and, oh my gosh, I felt so incredibly honored to have the opportunity to practice in the space.

The guide set a zafu on a zabuton cushion in one of the spaces of the hall and motioned for me to settle into place. He asked if I wanted him to hold the keisaku, but I did not know what it was, after all, I had only taken one Zen meditation class in Kyoto six months ago. He explained as he showed me a flat wooden stick that was used if needed during meditation to tap the shoulders as a remedy for sleepiness or lapses of concentration. My eyes widened. I grinned and in honor and respect of the Zen lineage tradition, immediately said, "Yes!"

Inhaling deeply, and exhaling, I settled on the zafu cushion into a comfortable half-lotus position with my hands centered in cosmic mudra position, eyes with soft-focus partially open and gazing downward at an angle.

As we began, I focused on my breath, and released all thoughts and walls in my consciousness to "no thing." I opened to the one-pointedness of samadhi without any image or object in view except for expansion into the essence of the present moment. Aware and observant that my mind was as empty as a blank slate, I then expanded freely into the dimensions of meditative grace.

The singing of birds nearby peeked in my inner reality as the oneness of mind, expanded as if on clouds of nature in spirit. My level of awareness levitated above my body, and through the soft gaze of my eyes, I noticed the bag I had placed in front of me appeared to be miles away from my level of observance. I simply noticed this and let it go in the flow, and my awareness expanded back into oneness with the skies.

At the end of 20 minutes or so, the kindly guide rang a chime and allowed me a moment to fully re-enter the space of my body. I grinned widely with joy. All of the dimensions I'd traveled in when meditating at home, I was able to replicate in consciousness in Japan with the pressure of the keisaku behind me in the Soto Zen Buddhism Sojiji Head Monastery. I was so happy!

❧ ❧ ❧

To be united with the Lord of Love
is to be freed from all conditioning.
This is the state of Self-realization,
far beyond the reach of words and thoughts.
To be united with the Lord of Love,
imperishable, changeless, beyond cause
And effect, is to find infinite joy.
Brahman is beyond all duality,
beyond the reach of thinker and of thought.

Let us meditate on the shining Self, the ultimate reality,
who is realized by the sages in samadhi.
(The Upanishads)

Spring 2018

What use are the scriptures to anyone Who knows not
the one source from whom they come,
In whom all gods and worlds abide?
Only those who realize him as ever present
Within the heart attain abiding joy.
(The Upanishads)

❋ ❋ ❋

The expansive peace and freedom in my heart were nearly indescribable as I was about to become an ordained interfaith/interspiritual minister after a part-time 2-year seminary program. Somehow, and in some way, even though I knew achieving the title of "Reverend" was not my final destination, it felt essential along the way.

The training affirmed the aspects about the Spirit and Nature of God that I'd discovered throughout my own soul explorations of the Light and felt like home in my heart because it allowed me to be true to the Light I'd found within myself.

The term "Interfaith" originally appeared in the 1800s as an adjective referring to a coming together of people from different faith traditions to complete a particular task, such as in interfaith dialogues. Likewise, if one person from the Jewish tradition married someone from the Christian or Buddhist tradition, it was said to be an interfaith marriage.

More currently though, interfaith was more often used as a noun, referring to a spiritual path that integrated beliefs and practices from a few or more traditional and nontraditional religions, belief systems, and ethical systems. Interfaith was the honoring of the light across all faith traditions, believing there may be different names and spiritual practices and paths to God, but they all pointed to a similar righteous and Good light.

Interspirituality was a more recent concept, first coined by a Catholic monk, Brother Wayne Teasdale, in his 1999 book, The Mystic Heart: Discovering a Universal Spirituality in the World's Religions, and further elucidated in the 2013 book, The Coming Interspiritual Age, by lead author, Dr. Kurt Johnson.

Brother Teasdale asserted the only viable religion for the future was spirituality itself. He believed beneath the diversity of theological beliefs in the world's wisdom traditions lay a deeper unity of experience that was our shared spiritual heritage, that was, a mystical spirituality. A universal unity consciousness in the heart of all inner exploration, a spirituality so deeply rooted in the heart-experience of oneness (a "felt-sense") any creed, belief, background, history, or anything that may cause separation became secondary.

As I trained in and practiced within the traditions of Interspirituality and Integral Theory, Buddhism, Hinduism and Yoga Philosophy, Judaism, Christianity, Islam and Sufism, A Course in Miracles, Transpersonal Psychology, Bahai, New Thought, Taoism, Wicca, Jainism, Sikhism, Quakerism, indigenous religions including Native American Spirituality, and 12-Step Spirituality (such as Alcoholics Anonymous [AA]), I recognized the common values of peace, compassionate service, and love for all creation.

The mystic heart with an awakened inner life transcended ideas, beliefs, concepts, and any individual images associated with religions. It naturally expresses through engaged spirituality similar in ethical and behavioral standards these traditions hold as true, and I discovered one thread connecting all of them together—most widely and well known as The Golden Rule:

Lay not on any soul a load that you would not wish to be laid upon you,
and desire not for anyone the things that you would not desire for yourself.
(Baha'u'llah, Gleanings, Baha'i)

Treat not others in ways that you yourself would find hurtful.
(Udana-Varga 5.18, Buddhism)

In everything, do to others as you would have them do to you;
for this is the law and the prophets.
(Jesus, Matthew 7:12, Christianity)

One word which sums up the basis of all good conduct... loving kindness.
Do not do to others what you do not want done to yourself.
(Confucius, Analects 15.23, Confucianism)

This is the sum of duty: do not do to others
what would cause pain if done to you.
(Mahabharata 5:1517, Hinduism)

Not one of you truly believes until you wish for others
what you wish for yourself.
(The Prophet Muhammad, Hadith, Islam)

One should treat all creatures in the world
as one would like to be treated.
(Mahavira, Sutrakritanga, Jainism)

What is hateful to you, do not do to your neighbor.
This is the whole Torah; all the rest is commentary.
(Hillel, Talmud, Shabbat 31a, Judaism)

We are as much alive as we keep the earth alive.
(Chief Dan George, Indigenous Spirituality)

I am a stranger to no one; and no one is a stranger to me.
Indeed, I am a friend to all.
(Guru Granth Sahib, pg. 1299, Sikhism)

Regard your neighbor's gain as your own gain,
your neighbor's loss as your own loss.
(T'ai Shang Kan Ying P'ien, 213-218, Taoism)

We affirm and promote respect
for the interdependent web of all existence of which we are a part.
(Unitarian Principle, Unitarianism)

> *Do not do unto others whatever is injurious to yourself.*
> (Shayast-na-Shayast 13.29, Zoroastrianism)

(Credit to The Golden Rule poster and interfaith dialogue resources from Scarboro Missions)

For thousands of years, these moral codes for behavior found in The Golden Rule have run throughout the nations across all of the lands and oceans of the Earth.

"And people still can't get along with each other?" I questioned in my journal, "What does that say about us?"

I wondered what would happen if instead of focusing on divisions and differences, we built instead starting on shared ground. Do not do unto others what we would not want to have done to ourselves. It was as simple as that. Do we want to be oppressed? No? Good, then do not oppress others. Do we want to be treated equally? Yes? Wonderful, then treat others equal to ourselves. Do we want to be free to live our lives and pursue happiness? Yes? Awesome! Then allow others that freedom, too.

With a greater understanding of the shared harmonies between the world's religions, I could not view one as higher or any more right or more true than another. There was light within them all.

Not to mention when I read some of the teachings of Krishna, believed to be written down between 400 BCE and 200 AD/CE, they felt so similar to those of Jesus, *"Be fearless and pure; never waver in your determination or your dedication to the spiritual life. Give freely. Be self-controlled, sincere, truthful, loving, and full of the desire to serve. Realize the truth of the scriptures; learn to be detached and to take joy in renunciation"* (Bhagavad Gita 16:1).

I sought and found the Light within each of the traditions I came across and compared my experience of "God." Each time my heart and soul overflowed with peace and joy, and I knew I'd found the Light within the way.

Spring 2018 (Continued)

On the day of ordination, I pulled out the vow I'd printed ahead of time to have ready for the ceremony, my adapted rendition of a prayer known by two names, the "Dalai Lama's Morning Prayer" and the "Bodhisattva Prayer for Humanity."

When it was my turn in the evening, I arose from my seat and without hesitation, walked across to the front of the room. Peace filled my heart as I stood in front of about 80 seminarians, deans, teachers, and supporting clergy. I smiled softly, taking in the moment before speaking my vow of ministry.

I knew not one person in the room had any idea about my testimony of Jesus or that the words I chose as my vow were also setting into motion my life's ministry outside of the unity we had in the circles of sanctuary in interfaith and interspirituality. I knew at some point I would have to go back to tell the Christian churches everything I discovered in the name of Jesus, The Golden Rule, and the mystic yogic heart and meditative mind of Christ. The East and the West were as one within me, and the light no longer separated by constructions and images of the world but returned to the fullness within my heart.

And with this in my soul, I spoke:

> "I vow to illuminate the light of wisdom as a lamp in the darkness,
> the light of compassion as a bridge crossing the flood,
> and the light of lovingkindness as a healing medicine.
> I vow to inspire the light of peace as a resting place for the weary,
> the light of sustenance as a guide on the path,
> and the light of joy as a tree of miracles.
> I vow to continually serve in the awakening of humanity from suffering
> to the infinite and eternal Truth of the light within us all."

It was complete and I was Reverend Shannon.

Autumn 2018

> *My intention for this day is Divine,*
> *I hold no judgments or expectations.*
> *This day I live my soul's greatest joy,*
> *my intention is to fulfill the work that is my highest purpose.*
> *I allow Holy flow to transform within and around me*
> *for the fulfillment of my greatest Divine potential.*
> (September 2017, age 40)

❊ ❊ ❊

Now that seminary was completed, the unfinished draft manuscript alighted in my thoughts during the months of summer, and my heart's response remained unchanged. It was not yet time.

Then I discovered I would be traveling to France for work meetings. This was my first international trip in a couple of years after a job transition to a new pharma company in less of a worldwide global role. My mind lit up with possibilities for a long-overdue pilgrimage and two destinations resounded in my heart for most significant reasons.

With David's blessing, and while he managed everything at home, after my meetings in Paris, I headed south on the train to Marseille. By taxi, I traveled to Saint-Maximin-la-Sainte-Baume, to the place on my sacred pilgrimage wish list ever since I first learned about Gnosticism back in 2010. I planned to visit the Basilique Sainte-Marie-Madeleine and to hike up the mountainside to the sacred grotto of Mary Magdalene.

The town of Saint-Maximin-la-Sainte-Baume was even more remote than I'd realized from online travel guides. Taxis and Ubers were pretty much nonexistent, and although I was within a short walking distance from the Basilique Sainte-Marie-Madeleine, the mountainside where the grotto was located was about a 45-minute drive away.

I first tried to reserve a local taxi to take me to the grotto and was told by each company I called that they did not have a driver to take me all the way there. My next idea was to rent a car, but that meant I'd have to juggle finding time to drop it back off before flying to my next destination tomorrow, definitely not ideal.

Admittedly, I was starting to wonder if I'd even make it out to see the grotto. I kept searching for travel tips online from my room in a 13th Century convent converted to a hotel. I noticed one person mentioned in a forum there was a school bus route that could take travelers part of the way but did not include clear locations for getting on and getting off and where to go from there.

Laughing in a moment of exasperation, I decided as I normally did, if it was not coming together easily, then it was my sign to let go and allow the way to be revealed if it was meant to happen.

Instead of working through it any longer, I grabbed my backpack and made my way over to the Basilique Sainte-Marie-Madeleine to meditate for a while. The Gothic architecture cathedral was founded in the 13th Century and included a crypt that contained the Holy relics of Mary Magdalene. I made my way to the pews inside and sat comfortably, with my backpack down between my shoes, and pen and journal in hand. I inhaled in the beauty of the moment within the sacred space honoring Saint Mary Magdalene and began to meditate on the Holy light.

In the focus of my thoughts, I inwardly sang, "Spirits of the Light, please reveal yourselves in this cathedral. Show me who you are and reveal to me the beauty of your Light! What is the way to the grotto?"

I soaked in peaceful reverie for a bit longer, and in stillness, felt complete. No words came to write, and that was just as fulfilling as when words came forth to write. I gathered my belongings and with my backpack securely on my shoulders, I walked over to the little gift shop to look at all the sacred souvenirs. As I was browsing, conversational sounds drifted in from my periphery where the attendant was speaking with someone who had just come in. My ears perked at the word, "Cave."

"We are going to the cave!" I heard again, distinctly in a British English accent.

Quickly I turned to see where the voices were coming from, and I saw two ladies who were bubbling with happiness because they were about to go to the grotto.

"Wait! Hi!" I called to them and hurried over to where they were. I explained I was unable to find transportation to the grotto, and with a smile, asked, "How are you getting there?"

One of the ladies beamed with excitement and advised that they had a rental car. She said if I wanted to go with them there was enough room for one more, and I was welcomed to join. She mentioned they had snacks and water and plenty of everything to share.

Without hesitation, I agreed, and we rejoiced together and hurried out of the cathedral to meet their traveling companions who were ready to go and waiting at the rental car: a Priest from the United Kingdom and a seminary priest still in training from Ireland. All of them devout Catholics and on an honest-to-goodness pilgrimage to the sacred cave of Mary Magdalene. And here I was, an ordained interfaith/interspiritual minister. The irony of the situation was not lost on me as I squeezed into the tiny backseat of the compact car with the two ladies and we started off to the grotto.

The Priest drove up the winding and curving narrow mountainside road, and as the ladies looked over the cliff edges, their eyes got wide and they started praying the Rosary in unison together,

"I believe in God, the Father Almighty, Creator of Heaven and Earth, and in Jesus Christ, his only Son, our Lord…"

As we railed around another curve in the little rental car their fervent praying continued, "Hail Mary, full of grace, the Lord is with you; blessed are you among women, and blessed is the fruit of your womb, Jesus…"

Finally, the road opened up to a destination and we parked and walked through the open field to the trail markers and stepped into the forest of Sainte-Baume. The holiness of the rocky mountain dated back to ancient times, even before Christians attributed the cave to Mary Magdalene. The Ligurians, Greeks, and Romans believed this sacred place was inhabited by the energy of their goddesses of fertility Cybele or Artemis.

In researching other sacred pilgrimage sites for Catholics, I noted it seemed to be more often than not they were reappropriated from pagan sacred sites and trails (such as Camino de Santiago "the way of Saint James" in northwestern Spain which followed a Roman trade route from pre-Christian times and included grottos and pools originally dedicated to Venus and other fertility goddesses).

It was said in legend after arriving in France after Jesus' crucifixion and evangelizing Provence, Mary Magdalene withdrew to the solitude of these woods and to the cave to finish out the rest of her days. In the Middle Ages, it became an honored site of worship and received visitors such as popes, kings, crusaders, and of course, pilgrims.

As I stepped fully forward and into the woods, I felt the energy shift into an almost supernatural magical flow in a Holy embrace that uplifted my soul. Shadows and rays of light through the branches and the leaves danced together on the forest floor with grace and ease. Worn stone and rocky outcroppings lined the trail upward as we continued, beneath the bowed trees.

In reverence and silence as the cave grew close after a steep incline, I smiled and bowed my head in respect when seeing the Dominicans who have cared for the sanctuary over the years since 1295. Although it was not required, I removed my shoes at the entrance to the grotto, similar to when I entered the sacred spaces in the Buddhist temples and shrines in Japan. My mind was in awe of the deep spiritual energy that I drew inward with each breath as I stepped foot into the cavernous grotto of the mountain.

Drip… drip… drip… came from deep within the cave, the only sound within the silence. No matter where I stepped within the grotto, the sound of the water from the deep into unseen pools emitted in a slow rhythm, the walls moving as shadows and light from the reflections of candles lining the space with flickering illuminations in the darkness.

I remembered reading about caves as sacred places similar to the womb of Mother Earth, and water itself was considered the memory of the world, the connecting element between the cells in our body and our connection in the cosmos. The deep spiritual power I sensed in the cave felt like an endless ocean without waves. Not even a ripple marred the distant echoes of drip… drip… drip, reminding me the grotto was just as alive and in flow as the mystical forest outside.

Not knowing how long my travel companions planned to pray in the silence, I found my way over to a quiet corner, where I alone stood facing Mary Magdalene. I gazed at the statue sculpted as if she were being carried up to Heaven by angels. Then, I brought out my journal and opened to the marked page where I'd written an introduction ahead of time, which I planned to speak and then request a blessing in this sacred space. While remaining respectful of the silence, and in reverence, I whispered as quietly as I could,

"I am Shannon,
child of the most High,
with crown of Divinity,
third eye of inspiration,
voice of wisdom…

As I whispered the words, "voice of wisdom," a warm sensation and energy centered around my throat area at the chakra location. I paused and felt the gentle tingling expand with warmth as if a light was pouring through, and I continued,

"Heart of compassion,
spirit of Holy fire,
gut of truth,
rooted in the Earth,
with hands of miraculous healing
and feet of loving service."

Upon bowing my head in completion, I noticed the sensation at my throat felt like it was blossoming like a lotus flower. I felt as if somehow it was an attunement with the energy presence and flow of the Divine Spirit within the cave. In awe, not having expected to experience any sort of activation of my throat chakra, I did not even continue to get to the part where I planned to ask for a blessing. In reverence, the moment felt complete, and I stood in wonderment and silent appreciation of this miraculous pilgrimage to the grotto of Mary Magdalene.

I put my journal away and slowly made my way around the statue and to the back of the cave where I placed both palms on the cavern wall, feeling the strength of the stone and the energy vibration of the earth. Soon after, it was time to leave the sanctuary, and as my Catholic companions dropped me back off at the convent hotel, and I was still in awe of the miracles as I waved goodbye and they went on their way in pilgrimage to another site, knowing in the deepest of my heart that my request in the cathedral was answered through these beautiful spirits of the Light.

Autumn 2018 (Continued)

The next morning I caught a flight out of Marseille to Ireland to begin the second leg of my pilgrimage. This time I'd planned on renting a car to explore as many sacred and ancient sites as I could a few days. I was grateful I knew how to drive a manual so well since it was the type of transmission I usually drove back at home, especially because it was on the opposite side of the driver's seat, and I was driving on the opposite side of the road for the first time in my life. What a surreal feeling! Actually, truth be told, I settled into it quickly, and headed west on the highway out of Dublin and directly to the banks of the River Shannon.

Almost two hours later, I pulled into the parking lot at the 6th Century monastic site, Clonmacnoise. Founded by Saint Ciarán in 548-9, the monastery flourished for 600 years as a center of learning and religious instruction at a crossroads between the major east-west land route through the bogs of central Ireland. Clonmacnoise was also well known for manuscripts written there, including the Book of the Dun Cow (12th Century) that contained the oldest versions of some famous Irish legends, and the Annals of Tighernach (11th Century).

But these weren't the reasons why Clonmacnoise was on my list. Although to be able to walk the sacred site with its three high crosses, cathedral, two towers, and seven churches was an experience to behold, I chose the location because of its proximity to the ancient river sharing my name.

Until arriving, I did not know for certain how Divinely perfect the location would be for what I had in mind. I immediately saw from the parking lot a path diverged in two directions, one to the entrance of the visitor's area for Clonmacnoise and another down a hillside to the river herself. Giddy with excitement of finally being so close to the actual River Shannon, I grabbed my backpack off the passenger seat of the rental car and headed out onto the grassy meadow cascading down to the river bank.

Ancient ruins of a building to my left and the towers of Clonmacnoise to my right lined the path as I trekked down to the bank of the Shannon. I stood next to her and breathed in the cloudy grey of the sky that glinted every-so-often with sunshine peeking out in the late afternoon. I breathed out as I gazed at the ripples of the water stirred by the cool gentle breeze.

Content and centered in both inner and outer nature, it was time for what I came here to do. A ceremony to honor the River Shannon and to bind my name to the glory of the river's nature and her spirit of life. I had prepared an invocation redesigned from a chant for Brigid I'd found online years ago; my own variation created for this very moment.

Reaching into my backpack, I pulled out a ripped page from one of my journals and stood on the soft bank, facing the river as I spoke with reverence and intention:

> "You are Shannon,
> proudly gliding through the land,
> north to south your healing waters flow.

> You are Shannon,
> east and west bridge your span,
> making God's Earth one and whole.
>
> Soul of Shannon,
> Brigid's well,
> to our land give life."

Pausing a moment, I took in the view of the river from horizon to horizon and all of her flow, and resumed:

> "I am Shannon,
> humbly standing on this land,
> north to south my healing waters flow.
>
> I am Shannon,
> east and west bridge my span,
> making God's Earth one and whole.
>
> Soul of Shannon,
> Brigid's well,
> to our land give life."

Then I kneeled and placed both of my palms down into the cool ripples of the water, and spoke from memory this time:

> "We are Shannon,
> proudly gliding through the land,
> north to south our healing waters flow.
>
> We are Shannon,
> east and west bridge our span,
> making God's Earth one and whole.
>
> Soul of Shannon,
> Brigid's well,
> to our land give life.
>
> May it be so, and so it is,
> for the glory of the Holy kingdom,
> now and forevermore,
> Amen."

I removed my hands from the river, with no expectation of any outcome, and only an abundance of fulfillment within my heart that I'd completed what I had set out to do. And in some way, somehow, in a dimension somewhere in time and space, I became one with the ancient River Shannon.

Since it was done, I crumbled up the page and set it adrift on the river. Like a lotus flower rippling along the top of the waves, I watched it ride along the edge of where the water met the air of the sky. To my surprise, it did not get saturated and sink for as long as I could see down along the stretch of river near Clonmacnoise as it faded from sight.

As the light turned to dusk behind the clouds, I walked back up through the meadow and headed off to find the nearby Bed & Breakfast where I had made a reservation for the night.

The next morning, I awoke to sunshine and blue skies, and I knew I wanted to go back to the Shannon before leaving to explore more of Ireland. I parked in the same area and ventured back down the path through the meadow to the river's edge, taking a quiet moment in reverie with the river again. I stood on the farthest ends of the dock and breathed in and out, filling my soul with peace. As I took one last look before heading back up the hill, I wondered if I'd ever know whether the River Shannon received my invocation.

On the way back to the entrance of the dock all-of-a-sudden I saw a large, long goose feather floating along the top of the ripples of the water just out of reach. I was in awe. Whenever I saw a feather, it signified for me the presence of the Divine, and especially with a wild goose feather, the presence of the Holy Spirit.

About 20 minutes or so later, after I'd merged onto a highway outside of Clonmacnoise heading towards Kildare, I was in a moment of contemplation as I scanned the road ahead. When suddenly in my mind's eye, the presence of a glorious, magnificently beautiful feminine goddess appeared in living Spirit form.

Her long hair flowed in waves around her and onto her robes that flowed like the river. I felt the most immense sense of calm and peacefulness emanating from her, and it was at the moment just as I saw her as a vision in my mind, it was as if she recognized me noticing her and the Spirit with amusement said, "**You can see me now**," as if she were a reflection from within, like a mirror of Divinity from my soul.

As she faded from my inner vision, I gasped in awe and steadied my hands on the wheel in wonderment of what I had just experienced. The goddess of the river was alive within me? It felt so much as if she were a mirror reflection of my Divine self. It was like my own beingness, she felt like me! I could not imagine what would come next on this pilgrimage.

When I parked and found my way to the Cathedral Church of St. Brigid and Round Tower in Kildare, I did not have any specific intention set in mind. In fact, Kildare was not even on my original itinerary. But as my travels normally go, after I arrived in Ireland I went with the flow. I discovered there was a fire temple foundation still on the grounds there that must have at one point in history, been to honor the Goddess Brigid, and felt there may be something for me. But, what? I wasn't sure.

I walked past the cathedral on my right and the round tower on the left and then came to the remains of the fire temple. The stones set its foundation in all four directions with an opening on the side opposite of the cathedral to step down inside. Those who kept Brigid's light still brought offerings of incense and flowers that I saw in a corner of the temple.

Slowly, I turned in a circle, feeling the sunshine overhead and the ground beneath my feet, and came back to center. Since this was spontaneous, I did not pre-write an invocation or ceremony for Kildare, I decided to repeat what I had said in the grotto of Mary Magdalene, an introduction about me and open to what may be received. As I stood in the sunshine, I spoke from memory this time:

> "I am Shannon,
> child of the most High,
> with crown of Divinity,
> third eye of inspiration,
> voice of wisdom,
> heart of compassion,
> spirit of Holy fire…"

In a flash of flame as I said the words, "Holy fire," my solar plexus chakra, at the area of my diaphragm, felt as if it was ablaze in warmth and power, filling to expansion beyond the walls of my body with immense empowerment and courageous strength of Holy light.

It felt as if I'd expect a superhero like Wonder Woman would feel like inside. I basked in the warmth of the sensation—in awe because this was the first time in my life I'd ever felt power emitting from my soul as strongly as I felt it this day.

I inhaled and noticed the fragrance of a hearth fire on the wind, but no fire was seen coming from the earth anywhere around me. I heard the sounds of geese wings flapping above me, but it was a clear blue sky without a bird in sight.

I finished as before, saying:

> "Gut of truth,
> rooted in the Earth,
> with hands of miraculous healing
> and feet of loving service."

The feeling of the power of fire within my soul persisted, and I stood in reverence as the realizations poured over me. Why I needed to come to

171

Kildare specifically, to the place where the veil was thin in history, myth, and legend, where the worlds of God and gods and goddesses and God's children collided with humanity in the heritage of the pagans and Christians. Where Brigid was still honored in her image of a goddess and saint.

This was where the power of the Holy Spirit was delivered into my soul—as if it were the day of Pentecost bestowed by Mother Goddess—attuned with none other but Saint Brigid, "Mary of the Gael," the eternal flame of the Holy Mother.

In awe I raised my gaze to the skies as close to the sun as my eyes could bear it, holding the inner truth in my heart with joy. Remembering the moment years ago when I stood on the red rocks in the middle of the river in Sedona, when a gentle voice guided me to reclaim my goddess power. I could not have ever known the beauty of fullness it would look like in completion, as it was written on my soul: I am a daughter of the Light, river of life, and bestowed with the power of Mary of the Gael.

❊ ❊ ❊

As the light fills my soul,
and pulses through my heart space,
filling my being with radiance and warmth.
I am inspired.
I draw upon the timeless ineffable force, the light of the Ages.
The mystery, the One, that which filled the sages and the buddhas,
and the masters.
All of this fills my awareness
just as it has for millennia before me.
(April 2018, age 40)

Spring 2019

Upon arriving home from Ireland, I knew in my heart this book's time was drawing closer, but it was not quite time. We were already barreling into the grand opening of our little "mom and pop" gift shop in town and life over the winter was a whirlwind getting into a new routine, hockey practices and games for both David and son, and of course, caring for all of our rescued pets. It was when I had another work trip come up in late March I asked David if he could manage everything at home and the shop for me to take a few extra days to finish the draft manuscript with the intention to then submit it to a publisher. He agreed and so here I was now in Key West, Florida, after a two-day stop on Sanibel Island. The book draft was nearly complete.

Nothing was included in the draft manuscript about Japan, or Interfaith/ Interspirituality, or becoming an ordained Reverend, or the grotto of Mary Magdalene in France, or the Shannon River or Brigid's Fire Temple and Cathedral in Kildare, Ireland. I kept those treasures in my heart at the time.

The draft was ready for submission to a publisher, only venturing part of the way into joy alchemy but no further into the path of Divinity within Nature. And it was done, my book finally had an ending for the first time in nearly 10 years.

I stretched from where I sat in half lotus position on the hotel bed in Key West, windows open wide with the salt and sea breezes whirling through the room. Now that the draft manuscript was as complete as it was going to be until the next step of submitting to a publisher, it was time to do a bit of sightseeing. Being a bit of a crazy cat lady, as my husband would attest, the first destination on my Key West pilgrimage was to visit the cats at the Hemingway House.

Since I was already there to enjoy some time with the cats, I decided to find a quiet corner inside the house and spoke quietly, just in case the spirit of Hemingway happened to be listening: "Mr. Hemingway, Sir, I may not agree with everything I have read concerning the life you led, but I know one truth —you mastered your craft of writing. Because of that, and all other critiques I've read about you in history aside, I see the good. I've come, if I may, to receive a blessing for my book."

After enjoying close-up views of old typewriters and the cats in their various lounging locations in the main house, I ventured across the grounds and climbed the stairs to Hemingway's writing room. At the top of the stairs, I peered in to see the furniture set into place. My ears opened wide in silent inquiry just in case a blessing would appear within the space. Silence remained. I waited a little longer until I heard other visitors begin their ascent up the stairs to the writing room, and not wanting to be in the way, I took one last glance around the room and then closed the door on the possibility.

I shrugged, "I guess there is no blessing for me here."

Just then as if on a sharp wind, I heard the spirit of Hemingway speak, "You already have the blessing my sweet, do what you were meant to do."

Slightly stunned and awestruck, I grinned widely. Wondering about what I'd heard, I then stepped down the stairs and over to the garden's benches to sit in contemplation.

"But why my sweet? Why would he call me that?" I questioned.

Admittedly, I'd not ever read an entire Hemingway novel from cover to cover, just bits and pieces here and there. One of the Hemingway cats sauntered into the circle among the trees and padded over to the bench where I sat. It leaned into my leg and I felt purring, and then the cat relaxed a few feet from me where it could observe the house and writing room and gazed back at me with content eyes.

I pulled out my phone and searched online for "Hemingway my sweet," never expecting what I would find. The protagonist male character in Hemingway's first bestseller *Farewell to Arms* used "my sweet" as a term of endearment for his love. Still not entirely convinced this was truly spiritual and Divine; my questioning scientific mind wanted another confirmation to prove this was not just a coincidence in disguise.

Just then a whisper of movement drifted in from above my gaze and into my field of vision. As I sat on the bench my eyes caught it and followed the floating wonder down until it lofted onto the ground in front of me. Bending forward, I reached down to pick up the little white feather that had fallen right in front of my eyes and held it between my fingers. A perfect little feather sent from Heaven above. Joy filled my heart with the confirmation, and I beamed over toward the Hemingway cat to see if it noticed, too. The cat closed its eyes and purred.

When I felt complete in the moment, I put my journal back into my backpack and trekked onward through the streets of Key West to the buoy that marks the southernmost point in the continental United States and breathed in the salty air of the sea in silent meditation. But soon into the repose, my heart chimed in, reminding me it was time to submit the draft manuscript to a publisher.

❃ ❃ ❃

*In all things in and out
and throughout dimensions high and low
from now and beyond the edges of time and space
and to the best of my Spirit and Nature-given abilities
I solemnly promise to intend in all that I am and all that I do
be for the greatest Good in Heaven and on Earth.*
(July 6, 2020, age 42)

Thursday, March 19, 2020

Nature has struck humanity to our knees. Most of the world was on lockdown due to the COVID-19 virus pandemic and nations were either preparing for its arrival or already in the middle of a battle for survival. We stood together at a crossroads with so many questions in the unknown. Even the knowledge we gained from pandemics in previous years such as social distancing and use of protective equipment was no match for the speed and ferocity that COVID-19 hit our world because in our day and age, we were crisscrossing the globe in international travel. Would there be enough personal protective gear to protect front-line healthcare heroes from exposure? Without available medical treatments or vaccinations, how quickly could researchers develop and conduct studies? Where was "God" in all this?

News headlines, videos, and memes served to elevate our fears in the unknown. The United States President even declared today he was a "wartime president," likening the battle against COVID-19 to the historical great world wars. But, this time was different, we were not at war against other nations; this was an entirely new enemy.

Regardless of how this novel coronavirus originated—whether a viral mutation from animals transmitted to humans or in a secret biowarfare research lab—COVID-19 was among us. No matter how many conspiracy theories people could concoct and inject with symbolism and truth, this virus did not choose sides. It was neither one political party versus another nor against any particular race or religion.

My thoughts wandered, and I wondered if our reaction to the coronavirus outbreak in 2020 was similar to what was experienced in the Flu Pandemic that caused at least 50 million deaths worldwide in 1918. The fear that some people must be feeling to cause them to fill their shopping carts in the stores to overflowing with food and essential cleaning and paper products filled my heart with compassion. The courage of each nurse, doctor, and healthcare worker to remain steadfast in service to sick patients filled my mind with admiration and gratitude. But it led to an unexpected question: "What was mine to do?" How could I best help in the world at this time?

I sat back and inhaled a centering breath into the moment to clear my mind and bring my heart to balance in stillness. From the open space of silence within, a vision of the fully published book sprung forth into my mind's eye. I thought back to what had happened since I was in Key West, Florida when the draft of the manuscript was done. I shared it with a few important people in my life to get their input and then submitted it to a publisher for consideration. That was back about 5 months ago in October of 2019, and the manuscript was rejected.

My heart alighted in the rejection because it was clear guidance from the Light, and I put the manuscript away again for a season, until right now in this moment, which just so happened to also be the first day of spring.

Since this was coming up now in my mind, I knew I needed to go back to remember how I felt during the submission process. I remembered feeling slightly uncomfortable during the entire experience. From submitting the proposal (inner resistance throughout the process), discussing potential royalties (inner sense of wrongness because it was an intention about profit and money), and creation of a branded marketing, publicity plan, and platform (inner misalignment: it felt false as I did not desire to be anything else in the world than just me as I was).

The symbols were indicators it was not the right way, which was why I was happy to have the manuscript rejected so I could move on. With the inner knowledge, I could start over on the foundation of the rock of experience and wisdom in my heart.

I went back to holding the vision in mind and I spoke, "Yes, I agree, but through what pathway?"

Possibilities leapt into motion as I meditated on alternate potential roads into the future. As quickly as they appeared, some immediately fell to dust, such as submitting to another publisher. The way of truth emerged, it was the only path that felt right inside, I would self-publish and only David would know. Then, we'd cultivate "active nonaction," with an expectation of miracles, but the fruit would be left up to the forces of life in Heaven and Earth to the greatest glory for the One who called my name and established this work in our lives in the name of Jesus Christ.

Joy amplified in my energy as the vision continued to reveal itself. I knew I needed to go back to the draft manuscript and complete the writings in full: describing the stages of transfiguration and the Mother Goddess/feminine pathway in Nature. It was time for another season and more writing to come.

❋ ❋ ❋

Now the Lord is the Spirit, and where the Spirit of the Lord is, there is freedom.
And we all, who with unveiled faces contemplate the Lord's glory,
are being transformed into his image with ever-increasing glory,
which comes from the Lord, who is the Spirit.
(2 Corinthians 3:17-18)

Sunday, July 26, 2020

Each moment of every day I have a minimum of three choices,
not just "Yes" or "No":

two choices are in complete opposition of each other:
To go in one direction
and not in its opposite direction,
and the third choice is neutral:
remaining silent and still where I am in nonaction.

The wisdom within me knows the difference between
sorrow, despair, depression, frustration, sickness, pain,
or
bliss, happiness, and positive vibes,
or
going with the flow in peace.

These have revealed the way of the light in my heart.
The choice to leap in faith for more of what is Good,
and choosing a path of life that leads to greater happiness,
is up to me.

This is the wisdom of joy.
(August 24, 2020, age 43)

❋ ❋ ❋

As spring flowed into midsummer, the world was more than six months into the COVID-19 pandemic. In many countries, including in the United States, lockdown quarantines transitioned to re-opened businesses and schools—for better or worse—ladened with restrictions and required wearing of facial coverings. The year 2020 continued to tick onward, and the total number of COVID-19 deaths and cases climbed higher and higher each time I looked at the data online.

At least here in the United States, there was no sign of life returning to pre-pandemic normal, with only hazy predictions of future timelines. It was semi-guidance at best, although I imagined how each governor and federal government leader may have felt constantly stuck between a rock and a hard place over decisions that spurred protests and arguing, no matter what decision was made with the best of intentions in mind.

Our little gift shop remained closed and our schedules were in near-constant flux. In the unknown of what the magical date would be in the future when celebrations, get-togethers, vacations, sporting events, and travel could start to be replanned. No one had concrete answers to the question, "Until when?"

We were plucked from the world of "The Way It Was" and were on the road of transition to a New Earth post-pandemic. Every prediction or projection forwarded by leaders, news media, and among social media networks contributed to the creation of the world "The Way It Will Be," but many Americans were tired and impatient of waiting in between, and some became disgruntled and noncooperative because they felt as though they were being forced to change their lives for a reason they did not believe in, and that their freedoms were being denied.

Meanwhile, in the middle of the transition between the old and the new, every one of us participated in life on Earth in the present time, in the flow of Spirit and Nature in the universe. Maybe that was why when I sat out in the garden in contemplation today, a blessing of wisdom came raining down as if onto a parched desert from Mother Nature for us to create more joyful lives while on Earth.

Instead of the feeling of being in an upside-down snow globe and shaken vigorously with no control over where each piece falls, we must not forget the power within us to create a different experience within our lives at any moment in time.

For example, I can swim against the current in resistance, tread along with the flow, surf the curl of the wave, or walk on the water in balance and peace in any storm that rages in the seas. Not just keeping the faith and believing Good will prevail in the end, but also adjusting how I react and respond to what's happening by listening to the wisdom in my heart to experience greater inner peace.

Right now, life was different than it was before the pandemic. If I reflected on how my life felt now compared with my former life before it was disrupted or changed, I received knowledge in the understanding received through the wisdom of which lifetime felt better to be "me" in:

> What changed for the better?
> What changed for the worse?
> What did I enjoy more now than I used to enjoy less?
> What did I enjoy less now that I used to enjoy more?
> Where was my suffering?
> Where was my peace?
> Where was my joy?

As I contemplated these within my heart in the present moment, it was then up to me to choose if I wanted to change everyday life for more or less of what it is that I was experiencing. This was a universal blessing based on the principles of how we organize time—from our memories (the past) compared with the time of "now" that extends into the ever-present future.

Any major life-change can be used as a milestone or a guidepost to stake in the ground like at a crossroads and thereby provides the opportunity to continue going straight or turn to the right or the left. If the middle way is peace and inner stillness in balance, one way leads to the extreme of suffering and the other way leads to joy, with 360 degrees of emotions and infinite possibilities of experience in the spectrum in between.

As an illustration from my perspective of life back in 2012, I was mature enough to know the difference between what suffering and joy felt like inside in the reality of my life experience of the world outside of me; and also, remained unbound from the entire range of emotions. I could clearly distinguish inner suffering, inner peace, and inner joy, and all the infinite shades in between.

Thereby, I applied that inner knowledge received in wisdom back out into my outer world, reflecting on relationships with others or in time spent at work or in hobbies and past times, and instead of trying to change the outer world based on what I wanted or a belief of what was "true," I made changes from the inside to increase the peace and joy in my life experience—even if what I saw outside of my inner world did not look like what I wanted or expected it to be.

Sure enough, when I held onto peace in my heart with joy in the vision, it ended up in a life experience filled with less suffering and more inner happiness when I persevered in faith that everything would work out for the best (and every single time it did).

This brought me to the realization that while love may be the greatest power of the universe unless it was in its purest energy/spirit/light form, words and actions of "love" may not actually be loving, and instead, create fruits of unrest and suffering within ourselves and the recipients of our "love." Any "love" based on a judgment of good or bad, rather than love based on nonjudgment and full acceptance of "what is" and "what is not" as One, leads to destinations that do not quite reach Heavenly joy.

Although we often hear about the love of Father God and the love of Jesus who was sent for us because "God so loved the world" (John 3:16), it was important to notice too, that while love may have been Jesus' essence and spirit, it was not his purpose in life and death.

I recalled from Hebrews 12:2: "...Jesus, the pioneer and perfecter of faith. For the joy set before him he endured the cross, scorning its shame, and sat down at the right hand of the throne of God." It turns out that if love is the way, then joy is the purpose of life.

The author of Hebrews did not say that Jesus endured the cross for the love of the world, he did it for his joy and for joy to come into the world. The prophecies before his birth said Jesus would be a joy and delight to his mother (Luke 1:14) and would cause great joy for all the people (not just "some" of the people; Luke 2:10). Jesus was even full of joy through the Holy Spirit in his ministry (Luke 10:21) and he told his disciples to remain in love so that "*my joy may be in you and that your joy may be complete*" (John 15:11).

Love was the method or the practice or state of being to experience joy and the completion of joy was the ultimate goal. It turned out after a little bit of research, I discovered joy was not just an attribute of the Holy Spirit and the supreme destination in Christ, but was actually in other religions, too.

If The Golden Rule was the thread that wove together the moral code of spirituality in the nonsecular world, then joy was the desired essential state of inner life experience of all souls:

> *A great joy came upon us and a peaceful carefreeness like that of our Lord.*
> *We rested ourselves in front of the gate, and we talked with each other*
> *about that which is not a distraction of this world.*
> *Rather we continued in contemplation of the faith.*
> (The Acts of Peter and the Twelve Apostles)

> *And the redeemed of the Lord shall return,*
> *and they shall come to Zion with song,*
> *and [with] everlasting joy on their heads;*
> *gladness and joy shall overtake them;*
> *sorrow and sighing shall flee.*
> (Isaiah 51:11, Ketuvim, Tanakh)

> *But Allah will deliver them from the evil of that Day*
> *and will shed over them a Light of Beauty and (blissful) Joy.*
> (The Qur'an 76:11)

> *But those who realize the Self are always satisfied.*
> *Having found the source of joy and fulfillment,*
> *they no longer seek happiness from the external world.*
> (Bhagavad Gita 3:17)

> *But where there is unity, one without a second,*
> *that is the world of Brahman.*
> *This is the supreme goal of life, the supreme treasure,*
> *the supreme joy. Those who do not seek this supreme goal live on*
> *but a fraction of this joy.*
> (The Upanishads)

> *Full of peace and joy is the bhikshu [monk] who follows the dharma*
> *and reaches the other shore beyond the flux of mortal life.*
> (Dhammapada 25:381)

Give yourself gladness from the true vine of Christ.
Satisfy yourself with the true wine,
in which there is no drunkenness nor error.
For it (the true wine) marks the end of drinking,
since there is usually in it what gives joy to the soul and the mind,
through the Spirit of God. But first,
nurture your reasoning powers before you drink of it (the true wine).
(The Teachings of Silvanus, The Nag Hammadi Scriptures)

Great expectation leads to great sorrow.
Expecting things from others is slavishness.
Give this up and seek the kingdom of experiencing the inner self.
And you shall find true joy.
(Jainism)

He says that the Lord is all-pervading, the embodiment of supreme joy.
(Shri Guru Granth Sahib, Khalsa Consensus Translation)

It is good to live in virtue, good to have faith,
good to attain the highest wisdom,
good to be pure in heart and mind.
Joy will be yours always.
(Dhammapada 23:333)

It is the Infinite that is the source of abiding joy because it is not subject to change.
Therefore seek to know the Infinite."
"I seek to know the Infinite, Venerable One."
(The Upanishads)

Love is my heritage, and with it joy.
These are the gifts my Father gave to me.
I would accept all that is mine in truth.
(Excerpt from Lesson 117, A Course in Miracles)

That in which the Logos set himself, perfect in joy, was an aeon,
having the form of matter, but also having the constitution of the cause,
which is the one who revealed himself.
(The aeon was) an image of those things which are in the Pleroma,
those things which came into being from the abundance of the enjoyment
of the one who exists joyously.
(The Tripartite Tractate, The Nag Hammadi Scriptures)

The Master said, "Admirable indeed was the virtue of Hui!
With a single bamboo dish of rice, a single gourd dish of drink,
and living in his mean narrow lane,
while others could not have endured the distress,
he did not allow his joy to be affected by it.
Admirable indeed was the virtue of Hui!"
(Analects of Confucius)

They find their joy, their rest,
and their light completely within themselves.
United with the Lord, they attain nirvana in Brahman.
(Bhagavad Gita 5:24)

When the consciousness is absorbed in the supreme consciousness,
great joy and bliss are found.
(Shri Guru Granth Sahib, Khalsa Consensus Translation)

You have no idea how much joy and happiness are waiting for you
as a reward for your (righteous) works.
(The Qur'an 32:17)

You shall let me know the way of life,
the fullness of joys in Your presence.
There is pleasantness in Your right hand forever.
(Psalms 16:11, Ketuvim, Tanakh)

Praised be God that you have received the bounty of true joy,
a spiritual condition that belongs to those who,
irrespective of their material and social circumstances,
strive to draw ever nearer to God and to understand and promote His Word;
who are concerned with the prosperity of all people;
who tread selflessly the path of justice and equity;
and who allow no impediment, not even oppression or imprisonment,
to deprive them of this inner joy.

It is this state of true joy that stirs the heart,
makes the spirit soar, increases human powers,
strengthens the mind, creates hope,
and kindles the flame of longing to take purposeful action for the common good.
So it is that, for Bahá'ís, bringing joy to the hearts is
among the most praiseworthy of deeds.
(Universal House of Justice to the Bahá'ís of Iran, Naw Ruz 2015)

The wisdom of joy is found within the present moment where life is alive in the creative field within one's self. Wherein I can use knowledge from past experiences in experimentation and transformation of my beliefs and intentions, and through observation, scientific methods, and alchemy in motion, I create in life, like an artist with paint on a canvas, or stirring a cauldron of healing herbs and fragrances, or following a recipe to bake a joyful treat, adding a dash more of this in my world or a smidgen less of that, or maybe the recipe called for a variation I hadn't tried before, and resulted in greater inner peace and joy.

All of it begins and ends, right now. At the crossroads in the present time with the creative life force and choosing within the moment which way to proceed. The key is to mindfully center in the present moment to establish a connection with the wellspring of peace within.

The idea of a life filled with greater peace and joy may sound appealing, and there are a multitude of self-help books, spiritual and mindfulness educators, classes, retreats, and more, with teachings in all sorts of diverse words and languages, in all the colors of the rainbow.

Even with all of these, so many seekers continue to question whether or not they've actually managed to reach the place or attained what it is they are trying to achieve. Speaking from personal experience, it isn't an elusive mystery; you'll know it when you find it inside.

Seemingly mysterious or not, to effectively navigate more mindfully from the heart into actions that create healing, joy, and miracles, takes an incredible amount of care, patience, and compassion with one's self. Especially for those who have never tried meditation or silent prayer and contemplation of "no thing" before.

Therefore, with the intention to align us in the same present moment in time and space, these writings are briefly about to slow down almost to a pause right here, in this paragraph, for us to be fully present together in the flow of creation.

Just as you are in this moment now and reading these words on this page. Yes, that's right. Right now as you are reading this sentence. You may be realizing I have brought your mind's focus to this very moment in time, and directly to you.

Yes, right now. I see you, hi there!

(Although if I really "see" you right now, that would be a bit eerie, so please allow me to rephrase and say that my heart and mind are here with you in this moment in time and space, and this is me honoring the light within you, bowing in namaste with love.)

As your eyes take in these words, we are here together in the same space in time created by this story. This, right here, right now, is the moment where life is created, and all things are made new: you are alive and breathing.

Go ahead and feel yourself inhaling through your nose on the next breath and slowly exhale it out while allowing yourself to relax and let go of anything that does not feel like peace... into where your breath reaches the shores of the sky like the waves of the ocean rolling upon the sands of the shore.

If it feels as though you could be even more at ease, you are welcomed to repeat inhaling breath through your nose again, and exhaling, until you feel the peaceful stillness and calm from within, like a pond's surface without any ripples from the wind.

Right here, right now where you are, is the present moment. It is the infinite space where all possibilities exist. Right now the past is history (you can let it go, for it is completed), and the future does not exist (you can let that go, for it has not happened yet). Everything is possible here.

From this moment onward everything is brand new. If you notice yourself drifting into the past, gently bring your mind back to your breath. If you notice yourself drifting into the future, gently bring your mind back to where you are in the present.

While you are filled with conscious awareness and observing the stillness within, you may begin to realize that although you are reading this sentence in your present right now, these words were written in the past. Notice how you are living in the past time just as much as you are in the present time. You can also think about an event that you expect to happen in the future, and you are thus co-existing creatively in the present-future time-space world.

Consciousness is not bound by linear time within our minds—we can draw upon the wisdom from the past to create a better present-future just as easily as we can envision the present-future and imagine what new possibilities may exist and try them on to see if they are paths we want to walk upon. This aligns with what Meister Eckhart, a German Monist philosopher, mystic, and theologian born in 1260, wrote, "*God creates the entire universe fully and totally in the present now... there where time never penetrates.*" This means that the power of creation is right here, right now within YOU, too.

Each of us has the Divine power to shape and participate in the creation of what the future of our world looks like and feels like. We are part of the ever-in-motion creation of life with every breath, action, and word that we speak, write, type, or sign, every day we are alive. As conscious beings with the ability to create, why on Earth would anyone want to waste this moment that we were given to not create more joy in our own lives and the lives of others? Just look at how many religions and wisdom traditions agree on the importance of joy.

But wait, there's more. It may be surprising to learn that joy is one of the few areas where the spiritual realm and secular science through Western medicine have merged onto the same road of agreement together. (Yes, really!) Of course, this is my happy place because my feet are planted deeply in both the spiritual and the scientific worlds of Heaven and Earth and anytime they come together as one in beautiful harmony is music to my soul.

Over the last 100 years, since the first iteration of psychiatric classifications were incorporated into the American Medical Association's (AMA) Standard Classified Nomenclature of Disease Manual, the American Psychiatric Association then began publishing a separate manual for mental disorders that is currently in its 5th edition. The Diagnostic and Statistical Manual of Mental Disorders, more well-known as DSM-5™.

The DSM-5 is the principle authority used by clinicians in the United States to diagnose mental health conditions. A host of disorders are included as having symptoms of a lack of or inability to experience joy; or experiencing symptoms that are in opposition to happiness and joy, including depressive disorders; anxiety and panic disorders; posttraumatic stress disorder (PTSD); acute stress disorders; and bipolar and related disorders. It is important to note only licensed mental health professionals should diagnose any of these disorders in accordance with current medical practices.

However, on a philosophical basis, it stands to reason that if the absence of well-being and joy indicates there may be a disorder present, then the state of well-being and joy is the "right" or desired condition. The disorder is a disruption of the optimal working order and functioning of a patient, and not to forget, is associated with a decrease in quality and enjoyment of life. In another way of describing it from both a holistic spiritual and scientific methodology, if a soul is continually suffering from a lack of well-being, joy, satisfaction in life—something in Spirit and/or Nature is likely to be amiss.

Western medicine's approach came to this conclusion from the opposite side of the spectrum from what I saw in the sacred verses. Instead of joy being the desired state, the scientific view came around from the negative, that was, a missing component or "lack thereof." American psychologist Abraham Maslow, best known for his hierarchy of needs, recognized this and discussed the importance of focusing on the positive in a book published in 1954, Motivation and Personality,

"The science of psychology has been far more successful on the negative than on the positive side; it has revealed to us much about man's shortcomings, his illnesses, his sins, but little about his potentialities, his virtues, his achievable aspirations, or his full psychological height. It is as if psychology had voluntarily

restricted itself to only half its rightful jurisdiction, and that the darker, meaner half."

Thankfully, in the last few decades, the field of psychology caught up to what the ancient scriptures taught thousands of years ago, with the advent of the field called Positive Psychology. The term was first coined by Maslow in 1954 but took off in the late 1990s early-2000s. In a quick search of PubMed, which is one of the preeminent databases for scientific papers and research published in peer-review journals, more than 129,000 publications on Positive Psychology were published at the time of writing compared with just over 23,000 for the search terms "joy" or "happiness."

Positive Psychology flipped the switch from "lack of joy" as a symptom of a disorder to a focus on the significance of joy in life itself as an essential component of the overall well-being and pursuit of happiness. A handful of peer-reviewed papers on the subject of joy indicated that it was important to avoid burnout and stress, was a powerful factor in healing, and restored self-confidence, hope, and meaning in life. Now we just need to get the rest of Western medicine to sing the same song.

However, I would be remiss not to mention an ancient Chinese medical text, <u>Huangdi Neijing</u>, which describes joy as a benefit because it allows for more peace and calmness, but also as a potential cause of disease. Based on Daoist theory, the theory and diagnostic methods in this text were more holistic and based on both science and energy/spirit in the forces and principles believed to make up the universe, such as Qi (life force energy), yin and yang, and the elements.

In this particular case, joy was mentioned to have the potential to "injure" the heart and "scatter" it from its residence. Yet, the text seemed to be referring to the desire or craving to experience ecstatic joy in the way that it became like an addiction to feel the "good vibes" and "high" from an excited joy-filled state. Thus, my thinking was this kind of "joy" that potentially causes disease was describing the attachment or clinging to an invoked emotional sensation or overstimulation that was not the wellspring of genuine joy.

So if I were Dr. Shannon and a licensed physician of the soul, I would say that our nation (and the world for that matter) is in dire need of a prescription of joy. It is our birthright, essential for well-being and in the flourishing of life, and is one of the optimal conditions of inner self for everyone regardless of any demographics. Even the sciences and religions agree on the importance of joy! All that we have to do is believe greater joy in our lives is possible, and it is ours to receive.

✳ ✳ ✳

For just a moment, suspend whatever beliefs you are carrying.
Pick them up and place them gently to the side.
From this open space of curiosity and wonder,
*imagine what a life filled with joy would **be** like?*
*What would it **FEEL like?***
What would it look like?

Do you believe it is possible?

*If Your answer is "Yes," please skip to the last line **in bold.***

If your answer is "no," then what would have to change
in your life for it to be possible?
With that in mind, ask yourself again, do you believe THAT change is possible?
If no, ask again and again
and
keep going
until you find the connecting bridge
of possibility that you believe in.

You have the vision—it is Yours! Believe in joy!
(July 11, 2020, age 42)

Sunday, August 23, 2020

If there was ever a time that I was amazed and in awe of how everything continued to come together, today almost caused all of them to pale in comparison. Well, except for the day I met David.

Illumination came so quickly, I did not recall where I initially stumbled over this online, but I discovered there would be a Great Conjunction of the planets Jupiter and Saturn on the winter solstice and first-quarter moon, on December 21, 2020. The conjunctions are a special celestial event that happens once nearly every 20 years. Not only that, but this particular one was also the closest conjunction for these two planets since 1623, at a mere 0.1 degrees apart.

There is more I will share, but just a disclaimer first before I dive in: It took me some noodling on this in contemplation, diagrams, and reliance on calculations and data published from astronomers and astrologers. Even though my bachelor's degree was in general science from Portland State University in Oregon and my master's degree was in biomedical writing from the University of the Sciences in Philadelphia, my classes were mostly in Human Anatomy and Physiology, Animal Behavior, Zoology, Marine Biology, and Geology, and of course, on conducting scientific research and reporting study data in regulatory and peer-review publications; not Physics, Quantum

Mechanics, Astronomy, or any math beyond Calculus. Please bear this in mind and heart as I continue.

The Jupiter and Saturn conjunctions were known as the Great Chronocrators, the "rulers of the ages" and were major markers of the passage of time. From what I researched; in ancient times they were invaluable resources to astrologers to track longer cycles of time. This made sense given Genesis 1:14, "*And God said, 'Let there be lights in the expanse of the heavens to separate the day from the night. And let them be for signs and for seasons, and for days and years*" (ESV).

I read that since the year 1802, the conjunctions have been occurring in Earth signs of the zodiac. December 21, 2020, the Great Conjunction occurs in Aquarius, which is an air sign, and the conjunctions are set in air signs for the next 200 years. It reminded me of The 5th Dimension's song from back in 1969, "Aquarius/Let the Sunshine In." It appeared as though this celestial event may be somehow related to the beginning of the Golden Age.

Delving further into research, an article at astrosophy.com described the conjunctions and their significance in our history, including researchers identifying one that occurred in 6 BC which could have been the actual Star of Bethlehem written about in the gospel of Matthew! The article went on to say:

One can view Saturn and Jupiter as the great keepers of the Divine evolutionary plan for humanity. Saturn is that sphere who is the keeper of the plan from its inception, the great Father Time, who continually reminds us through karma, of the beginnings of our Earth and the great plan laid out for human evolution...

Jupiter on the other hand, is Father Life. In this sphere the expansive living wisdom envisions the future. The beings of this sphere carry the ideals and great cosmic thoughts that live as the creative shaping of life into the future, eventually towards our next evolutionary cycle...

These conjunctions unfold in a Golden Triangle pattern over time as they occur nearly every 20 years at 120 degrees equidistant from each other, rotating forward by 8 to 10 degrees every 60 years when a full "trinity" is completed. The work also explained the conjunctions cycling through the 12 zodiac signs as mentioned above, in that we were entering the first air sign of the next 200 years with the next conjunction.

Further, "*...this corner of the zodiac* [meaning, the Grand Conjunction in December 2020], *carries the "great Annunciation" theme, calling for humanity to awaken to birth of the new in the world, often revealing in history, events of new revelation, new annunciations for humanity.*"

In this viewpoint, both Father Time and Father Life, represented by the planets Saturn and Jupiter, were conjoining for a great annunciation calling to humanity for a new birth.

Amazing in itself, this was not all because I recognized the conjunction in 2020 was occurring on the winter solstice. The solstice occurs twice a year when one of the Earth's poles is at maximum tilt away from the sun and is the day with the shortest length of daylight and the longest night of the entire year in the Northern Hemisphere in December and the Southern Hemisphere in June, both times at opposition from the day with the most daylight at the opposite pole.

In ancient times, the winter solstice was the symbolic death and rebirth of the sun—and thus, also associated with the goddess giving birth to the sun or birth/rebirth of sun gods—and was celebrated as far back as the Neolithic period, although solstice celebrations and rituals continue today around the world among some religious and cultural traditions.

It was not surprising to me at all that the birth of Jesus was established around the winter solstice given its ancient significance, signaling the end of death and birth of life for a new generation, the birth of the Divine Child, the Son of God.

Structures such as Stonehenge and Newgrange were thought to be associated with the solstice. When I visited Newgrange in Ireland in 2018, I learned that when the sun rose on each winter solstice, the rays of sunlight shined through an ancient constructed open roof box of the underground passage tomb, like an open skylight, and through the long passage inward, illuminating the inner chamber for approximately 17 minutes.

The winter solstice was believed to hold powerful energy for rebirth, regeneration, renewal, and new birth, and it represented complete polar opposition between day (light) and night (darkness) on Earth as the longest daylight or night, respectively, in each hemisphere once a year.

Further, from what I could deduce as truth through online lists of the dates of Jupiter Saturn Grand Conjunctions and knowledge that the winter solstice only ever occurs in the Northern Hemisphere between December 20 and December 23; the year 2020 was the first time since 1 AD that a Grand Conjunction has occurred on a December winter solstice!

In my research notes, I marked the conjunction as a symbol representing the Father and the opposition of light and darkness fully divided in the winter solstice as representing the Mother. I knew I needed to find the "child" to complete the trinity and I did not need to look further than the date this was all occurring on, the twenty-first of December in the year of two thousand twenty, otherwise known as 12/21/2020 or 21/12/2020 depending on what date format is used.

As I wrote the numbers on my page, I immediately noticed an opposition in a mirror-like reflection for 12/21 and 21/12, and a repeating pattern, like a conjunction in the year, 2020. More important though was I knew the date itself was based on "1 AD" as point zero being the year Jesus was said to be born on Earth (1 AD/CE) and we were now in 2020 AD/CE. Here in plain sight was the Son of God in the form of the date in recorded time from the Gregorian calendar.

As currently the most used calendar system in the world, the Gregorian calendar was named after Pope Gregory XIII who introduced it in 1582. Stories from history state the reason for the reform was to correct drift away from the spring equinox for consistent and accurate scheduling of Easter. The Gregorian calendar was actually a revision of a previously used Roman calendar system, the Julian calendar, which was enacted in 46 BC/BCE by Julius Caesar. And the Julian calendar was a reform of the original Roman calendar, which was believed to be an observational lunar calendar: the months beginning from the first sign of a new crescent moon.

Undeniable evidence of the direct lineage of the pagan Roman calendar in the Gregorian calendar is evident in the months themselves: January was named to honor the Roman god Janus, and March for Mars; May and June may have been named to honor Maia and Juno; and July and August were in honor of emperors Julius Caesar and Augustus, respectively.

In 1582 when the transition from the Julian to the Gregorian calendar occurred, 10 days were skipped completely. The calendar jumped forward in our timeline in history. The day, October 4, 1582, was immediately followed by the next day, October 15. But that was not all. AD stands for anno Domini, that is, "in the year of our Lord Jesus Christ," as I mentioned earlier, binding 1 AD to the being the year Jesus was conceived and born. This was not implemented with the Gregorian calendar in 1582, but back in 525 by Dionysius Exiguus. His dating system was based on a previous one, thereby Diocletian Anno Martyrium 247 was immediately followed by 532 AD, a difference of 285 years.

The Diocletian year dating system was said to have been first used by the Church of Alexandria in the 4th Century AD and may have been based on an even earlier Anno Mundi calendar, which was said to be based on biblical accounts of the creation of the world and Old Testament era history, and Byzantine and Hebrew calendars.

My head whirled around in circles trying to match up where one calendar ended, what the new date and year were on the ensuing calendar, and back and forth, and forth and back, trying to order them somehow together along multiple parallel timelines. I was no longer even sure what today's date was anymore, or where we were exactly in linear time. For sanity's sake, I decided this was as far as I needed to research.

In reflection, I realized that the date and year we use most widely in the world was based on the pagan Romans, the birth of Jesus of Nazareth, and the changes made by the Catholic Church in 1582. These three were bound together marching forward in linear time; and today's date and year were an illusion and symbols representing what was real in Nature, flowing in the cycles of the sun, moon, planets, and stars. The earliest Roman calendar was based on these cycles, but then the set dates and months prevailed in misalignment with the cycles of nature. Time as we know it was an illusion and symbol conceived, written, and enforced through the minds and hands of man.

The more we enslaved ourselves to this timeline of symbols, the further we marched away from a connection to what was true—the origin of the calendar we used was based on Nature and the phases of the moon cycle; the months and numbers were not what was real, they were created symbols and images of the original truth that they were based upon: the sun, the moon, and the stars; and the seasons as the Earth rotates around the sun and the sunlight of days and the dark of the nights.

The flow of Nature's time was embedded in the biological clocks of living organisms too, which coincided with the cycles in nature, that is, the innate rhythms of life tied to seasonal cues, such as the time in the year when birds migrate south or return north and the migrations of marine animals in the seas. A sunflower that opens up towards the direction of the rays of sunlight and closes again at dusk is an example of circadian rhythm, another internal clock that runs autonomously to carry out essential processes, such as the sleep-wake cycle.

24-hour cycle circadian rhythms are said to be synchronized with a master clock in the brain influenced by the cycles in nature, such as daylight for being awake and nighttime for sleeping. When functioning optimally, a circadian rhythm provides restorative sleep, and when out of whack or thrown off balance significant sleeping problems may occur, including insomnia.

Multiple factors in life and location of residence can affect the circadian rhythm, including jet lag, night-shift work, and exposure to artificial light at night, or living close to the poles where half the year there was darkness, or it was nearly always light. If the inner flow and rhythms of Nature's time are ignored or pushed to the extreme, life suffers.

Similarly, if we pushed to speed life up, hit the hyperdrive button to get through to a special event as rapidly as possible, or manufacture double the products to make more profit, and so on, life also suffers if the inner master clock of a living organism and/or Nature's clock is disrespected, overpowered, or ignored. An example of this is the number of days it takes for a seed to sprout after it is planted in soil.

We can apply variables to the seed such as extra fertilizer in the soil, we can ensure the optimal amount of water and sunlight, and then through observations and scientific recording of results, determine the fastest amount of time for a sprout to develop. That's great if the goal is to grow as much of a vegetable as possible for people who do not have enough food and are malnourished.

What it does not tell us though was whether or not the length of time from seed to harvest changed the quality of the end result. If speed was the only goal to produce more and more, it was on the timeline of mankind and not of Mother Nature. This concept can be applied to everywhere there is deforestation and forest degradation and other environmental issues both on Earth and within our inner worlds.

Life was supposed to be on Mother Nature's timing (aka, Mother Goddess) not on ours. Kind of like how Father God had His own timing too, "*Wait for the Lord; be strong and take heart and wait for the Lord*" (Psalm 27:14).

Jesus the Son of God was literally embedded in our beliefs—whether Christian or not—because our timeline was established according to the year that the church designated as his birth. Even with the shift to change "AD" to a more secular Common Era (CE), when a curious student asks, "Why did CE start the year that it did?" The answer goes back to Jesus every time. Herein lies a portion of the mystery and truth about Jesus of Nazareth, the Son of God and Christ. With respect to the date and year on most of the world's calendars, we all agree.

So much so that the entire Earth was divided into 24 time zones in 1884 at the International Meridian Conference in Washington, DC, in the United States of America. More divisions between time zones have occurred since then, but 136 years ago there was an international agreement by all participating nations for the establishment of time zones according to the Greenwich Meridian, beginning at Prime Meridian at longitude zero degrees (covering the West and the East).

We, the people, and the authorities, and nations, all around the world, AGREED. Not only did we follow the time in the zone(s) that we live, work, or go to school in, but we agreed to respect the time for our family, friends, colleagues, or travel destinations in other nations wherever they were located. Because it was deemed as so critically important for the development and prosperity of nations and all people within them, somehow humanity found it within themselves to work out the differences between variations of zones and then honored those differences with decisions, choices, and actions.

This was proof that even in a world of extreme opposition it is entirely possible to have harmony and accord among all people, no matter what nation they are from. Indeed, humanity can agree on at least one thing on Earth!

In full transparency, I'd spent most of this summer contemplating whether or not I believed humanity could agree on anything. Yes, even though I believe that everything is possible, this one was elusive. I sought at least one starting point of common ground that we could point to as evidence that it was truly possible. And there it was, in the Gregorian calendar and time of day in the many time zones around the world. We agreed!

Yet, although it is great that we managed to agree to time zones, days, and years, we do not live in a world of healthy and flourishing balance in 2020. Many people were not even willing to take responsibility for their participation in the collective mess we've made. This message was not for just those people though, it was for us all.

Right now we are at a pivotal moment in human history with the opportunity as the first of a new generation to pave the rest of the way to worldwide peace; with equal rights, respect for all diversity, and to restore the healthy balance and flourishing for all of life on Earth, the eradication of suffering for all; and with sights set for joy.

Alternatively, if we do not do what is right, those in power in the nations and industries who deny climate change and perpetuate the suffering of life will continue leading the charge deeper into the devastating lake of fire until we all drown together.

In the discovery of the cosmic conjunction of the planets on the winter solstice, December 21, 2020, that seemed to indicate the arrival of the Age of Aquarius/Messianic Age/New Millennium shift, I knew the date when (God/Universe willing) I would self-publish the first edition of this book.

But I also observed other patterns that indicated we were in a karmic cycle "do-over," so as amazing as all these findings were, they were merely confirmations of Father God/Sky/Spirit and Mother Goddess/Earth/Nature ushering in a new epoch of Heaven and Earth. It did not mean that we, the children, would necessarily step up to the plate and do the work that is ours to do.

Synchronicities and symbols in the events of this year hearkened back to the past, revealing where the energy was flowing forward or backward into the shadows or out of the light, out of the shadows or into the light in karmic cycles and patterns. My case was made in one evidentiary example, our current global health pandemic, and how here, in the United States of America, we were literally repeating the past.

The worldwide 1918 Flu Pandemic was just over 100 years ago. When the 2019/2020 pandemic first started, the timespan felt significant and I noted it just in case another symbol came into view in confirmation, and it did. It turned out that during the 1918 pandemic there were reports of people in the United States arguing and fighting over whether or not to follow the facial covering/mask requirements over their mouth and nose.

Guess what happened again in 2020: the very same conflicts and arguments. We were re-creating the past in the present time because people were once again spewing out the same oppositional and argumentative energy instead of wearing a face-covering like we were asked to do for the good of the whole. This was not a good sign for our future.

If we cannot find it within ourselves to change the world we are creating, we will continue to experience the same suffering we know from the past. In other words, we will continue to carry our karmic crosses until we finally break the cycles of suffering that we keep repeating because as a whole we are unwilling to change what we are creating in the world.

Humanity has spent thousands of years engaged in conflicts and wars. At what point will we decide that it is time to try a new way and undo all of the sufferings we have caused?

Truly, with no time to waste, let's acknowledge we can all choose to agree if it is important enough to us—just like we did with time! Next up on the list is to agree on the very basics of how to treat each other. If we agreed on time, we could certainly agree on a minimal basis for ethical and moral behavior to reduce suffering and pave the road toward peace around the world. The Golden Rule, as well as, multiple declarations, agreements, principles, and accords are already in place, including the Universal Declaration of Human Rights by the United Nations General Assembly in December 1948.

These are starting points for the real work, embarking through a period of healing to then create a world of joy, and that is where this gospel really kicks in, when individually and collectively we decide it is a worthy effort to bring forth the fruits of the Holy Spirit, Christ, Lord, Buddha, Saint, Guru, or other Name of the Pure-Light and the Good, from within where the soul rests within the root of Divinity into what we create in our lives on Earth.

It only takes one person to choose kindness instead of hatred or oppression for our world to start turning more towards the Good. The tipping point is here!

That's why I knew in my heart to the deepest of my soul there was something so indescribably special about December 21, 2020, with the Great Conjunction of Jupiter and Saturn, the winter solstice in the Northern Hemisphere, and the fact that it was the first time they were occurring together since time began at 1 AD/CE. It may be the end of the end of times, but it was also a new beginning that was opening the New Heavens upon the New Earth.

Sunday, August 23, 2020 (Continued)

Later in the evening, I shared with my son the joy of what I'd discovered in this research. He paused in contemplation and then replied in understanding, "You're saying that it is the end of the world." Not an exclamation, not a question, just a thoughtful statement as he considered the trinity I diagramed—the sun, planets, stars, Earth, and the calendar system that humanity created.

I took note of his words because I did not say, "It is the end of the world." His statement was how he conceived what I was describing in the words that I used. I explained it as a once-in-a-lifetime miraculous cosmic event that had the potential to change life on Earth as we know it because of the existence of possibilities that could happen in a new beginning of an epoch generation initiating on December 21.

I told him ultimately it was up to all of us to choose what we do with this gift that we've been given. For ourselves and our family, there was no question we would continue unfettered forward spreading peace, good vibes, and joy, through our hearts to all, whether it was through our little gift shop or other doorways once this book was published.

Satisfied, my son nodded and said something to the effect of, "Cool. Cool," and went back downstairs to play video games.

It was in the moment as he turned the corner at the bottom of the stairs when a memory alit within my mind: in the year 1992, when I was a sophomore in high school and the exact age as my son. I was in the house that I grew up in Concord and my father had a recently published book in his hand. He heard about it on the Bay Area Christian Family Radio station he listened to every day in the car as he commuted to his corporate job at the telephone company.

As typical, my father started droning on and on about the importance of the Bible and religion. I'd just about completely tuned him out until I heard him start to talk about the book, by talk radio broadcaster, author, and evangelist, Harold Camping, it was entitled 1994?, and it contained a prediction for Judgment Day that Camping believed would occur on or about September 6, 1994.

The prophecy was based on Camping's own method of Biblical interpretation, and having listened to Harold Camping on the radio, my father believed it could be true and proceeded to tell me all about how the world as we knew it would end in 1994. Camping used multiple calendars such as the Jewish feast days, the lunar month calendar, and the Gregorian calendar and tropical year combined with other interpretations from the Bible in his prophecy.

Thoughts spun and whirled around in fear as my inner world was consumed by this news. At the time, it rocked my teenaged world off-balance. If it were true it meant I would never even graduate from high school before the world ended. The fear remained within me over the next two years until the date passed and nothing happened.

What I didn't realize back then was that after Judgment Day did not happen on September 6, Camping revised the date to September 29 and then to October 2, 1994. Then later in 2005, he re-predicted the date to be May 21, 2011, and when that did not happen, he re-set the date to October 21, 2011.

By the time Camping died, all of the evangelicalism he'd done within Christianity was overshadowed by his repeated failed prophecies, and in the hypocrisy evident because he was a proselytizer that the Bible alone was the word of God in its entirety, and then went against the very beliefs he taught by setting a date for Judgment Day.

For it was written in Matthew 24:26, "*But about that day or hour no one knows, not even the angels in heaven, nor the Son, but only the Father.*" Further, in Luke 25, "*There will be signs in sun and moon and stars, and on the earth dismay among nations, in perplexity at the roaring of the sea and the waves, men fainting from fear and the expectation of the things which are coming upon the world; for the powers of the heavens will be shaken.*"

And now, as I considered all this after my son left the room, awe filled my countenance in the realization that the spontaneous conversation with my son was a karmic mirror of when I was 15, and this time around, instead of me being the child talking with my dad, I was Mom and sharing what I believed to be true for our future with my son. The pattern was set in place since my childhood, and I did not realize it until now as I reflected over time.

It was another internal confirmation that life experiences and memories serve a higher purpose, whether as opportunities for healing, confirmation of best paths, release, and rebirth into the new, or other significance which becomes clear in ways no one could predict or know in advance until it comes back around in the wheel of life.

Sunday, August 30, 2020

Around one o'clock in the afternoon, I was cross-legged on the stone bench in our sanctuary in the backyard, a meditation and prayer garden circle filled with the sacred and whimsical, Tibetan flags waving in the breeze, birds perching on the oak's branches overhead, rainbows dancing along the ground from dangling prisms on the trellises as the jasmine, roses, wisteria, and hibiscus climbed their way up to the sun from the soil. A hanging gong and wind spinners, a few gnomes, and an altar facing west on the eastern side completed the view.

It was not long after I began to meditate when my son ventured out to sit in the circle with me. I listened to his rants and ravings about video games and friends and school restarting and somehow we got on the topic of the future again.

We talked about how the plan was to publish this book, and in that, I confided to him for preparation's sake, the possibilities that may arise. I first explained the two polar extremes that were valid potentials: the first was no one reads it, and we continue about our everyday life. In this scenario, maybe the book would be discovered in a later generation, and then the glory of Jesus Christ in the return will cover the Earth after we are gone from our lives.

I also explained the possibility of the book being outright rejected by our generation—even though the seed is of pure light and Holy origin with the same teachings as Jesus for peace, love, miracles, healing, and joy—because it would be a surprise and unexpected for many people and would undoubtedly challenge tightly held beliefs. Especially in a time like 2020, where we can easily observe around us each day how much division exists on nearly every single topic of discussion on social media.

The world was so polar, I admitted to my son, that I could not imagine a possible scenario wherein at least one person did not get upset over the writings, even with the cautions and advanced warnings I planned to include in the introduction. I relayed to him there would be those who do not believe in the peace and joy that is offered from God and that was their freedom and choice.

Then I went on to envision the likelier outcome after publishing, somewhere between those two extreme pillars of possibilities. I explained to my son that by holding open these broad avenues—without believing any particular way as the "one-and-only-one way" of how the future will happen—we would not become attached to any one particular outcome or desire for an end goal.

This alleviated any fear, doubt, and mental suffering because we were not building any castles in the clouds that did not have a staircase reaching them from the real world. There would be no missed expectations, no disappointments, and we were free to change our minds at any time because we were leaving it all open in flow.

This way, we could remain steadfast in excitement about all the good we are already doing in our lives, knowing in our hearts that whatever happens in the future had no bearing on who we know we were and the good we intended to continue doing.

"Most importantly though," I paused, with soul-felt emotion filling my voice as I turned towards my son, "No matter what happens today or in the future, always be true to yourself and what is in your heart."

There is nothing greater in life than achieving the joy that comes with living a life devoted to good works in love, service, and charity to all, with an inner wellspring of peace that remains steadfast no matter what life brings.

"Don't ever try to 'be' anything in particular, especially not for anyone else." Just like me, I am who I am, without attaching to sides or labels or names, transcending the binding nature of duality. No longer limit choices to this or that, or right or wrong, or good or bad, but stepping beyond the point of separation to behold the whole world together as one, in this way wisdom develops more rapidly into understanding.

I thought about how I examine the dances of light and the dark together, how they interact, where they agree and disagree, where there are accord and common ground. I look through the lens of love and my radar of inner peace. From this space within, I seek restoration, resolution, renewal, reformation, resurrection, or rebirth, whatever it is that will make the rest of today and the future better than it ever was before in life.

"And in this way," I turned back to my son, "You can learn from what I already went through, avoid all the suffering, and leap ahead to create your own happily ever after too."

Tuesday, October 6, 2020

> *Therefore if you have any encouragement from being united with Christ,*
> *if any comfort from his love, if any common sharing in the Spirit,*
> *if any tenderness and compassion, then make my*
> *joy complete by being like-minded,*
> *having the same love, being one in spirit and of one mind.*
> *Do nothing out of selfish ambition or vain conceit.*
> *Rather, in humility value others above yourselves,*
> *not looking to your own interests but each of you to the interests of the others.*
> (Philippians 2:1-4)

❉ ❉ ❉

In contemplation this evening, I thought back to one of the happy places of treasure I'd discovered along the way when I first found the light of my soul, and from then onward in the visioning of being anything I wanted to be. I was not restricted or confined because I'd gained the freedom to change what I believed and to change my mind at any time. When I had no second thoughts or regrets about what I should have or could have done. It did not matter because even with normal bumps along the road, life continued forward paved with peace inside. With an inner trusting and faith that one way or another, things would always end up being okay.

Life opened up the moment I accepted fully what was with gratitude and opened to the possibilities that there was a happier path than the one I'd imagined. I learned that even undesirable circumstances of physical or emotional suffering were guides and helped to define what it was I wanted instead (that was, the opposite of what I was experiencing that I knew did not want)!

I learned what it felt like to do something I judged as good in my mind, but it felt bad inside my body as I was doing it (and realized this feeling was a premonition indicator of what would be born in the fruit). The ability to detach from thoughts and emotions to observe and recognize emotion and recognize this misalignment between the mind and the heart opened space to change the trajectory and align my head and heart before I proceeded each time.

Ultimately, it was up to me to persist in the choice to change my beliefs and perspective each time I sensed a misalignment, and it took discipline and practice. When "not good" thoughts entered my mind, instead of allowing them to grow and stew in a pot, I stepped forward into the thought potential and removed whatever I perceived as negative by flipping a switch to turn on the light to give it a joyful completion instead... a happily ever after ending. That, right there was setting the course for joy.

The key to this practice was to not become attached to any particular outcome though. To keep the faith of the good and to hope is the strongest hold permitted on a projection without it becoming detrimental with the potential to tumble into suffering. To elevate it even higher in joy, I released the "best-possible dream come true imaginable" to Spirit and Nature to conceive of and bring about an even greater miracle from Heaven into my life on Earth. The more and more I looked to the good, the more of the good appeared within and all around me.

This did not mean I would sprint zealously toward the direction of what felt good when I was ecstatic about a particular idea. I learned to sow it into my inner possibility garden, I could pray or meditate or choose other spiritual practices and rituals for support from spiritual allies and guides in the light. The principles of creation and alchemy were set into motion with my intention, focus, and actions, and all I had to do was keep the faith, believe in the good, and follow the joy in my heart. The Life Force of creation met me right where I was in time and space and helped me attain my dreams and visions, whether I called it God in the name of Jesus, Father Sky/Mother Earth, Great Holy One, in the sound of Om, or silence and expansion.

I kept in mind that the forces of Spirit and Nature continually opened the way in their timing, I encountered coincidences, synchronicities, meaningful symbols, and signs. I took this knowledge into my heart and weighed it like a feather with my vision inside my mind's eye. I questioned, "How does this pathway into the ever-present future feel compared to what I believed it would feel like before I got here?" The next step was to choose my own adventure: Do I continue on this course? Or do I scratch this path because it was not exactly what I thought it would feel like and start anew?

Once I entered the flow between multiple dimensions of possibilities, that was, the opening of two simultaneous worlds—reality and the world of dreams—I achieved holding these open without creating or building anything that would bind my future within them. In mastery, I transformed and shapeshifted through these dimensions gracefully into new worlds there and back again, because I believed they were all ultimately GOOD, and therefore, kept wide open spaces for a future that was even better than I could have dreamed of on my own.

As I remained in contemplation, I thought about how these practices manifested in our little "mom and pop" gift shop over the last 5 years. My mind alit on the memory from 2010: when I was trying to hold onto my house and mortgage financially on my own and someone introduced me to selling on eBay. I'd casually sold used personal items online in the past but had never considered reselling products until then.

It turned into a little side business and I expanded into jewelry designing and other handmade crafts, and then officially opened, "Shannon's Little Shoppe." By the time I met David in late 2013, I'd already expanded to selling at craft fairs, local festivals, and pop-up shows in addition to selling online.

When we got married, it could not just be my shop anymore, so we came up with a new name. David designed the logo, and our little gift shop was born online on the International Day of Happiness in 2015. No longer just a destination for spiritual and inspiration-filled gifts and handcrafted jewelry, it was now a blend including David's influence of all things pop culture, toys & games, and fun, including doses of witty and light sarcasm; pretty much all kinds of gifts you would find on the sunny side of life.

We continued to do local fairs and festivals and decided to take the plunge and try out a brick and mortar shop location. Of course, a trail of miracles brought it all together, and we opened the doors on the autumn equinox in 2018, right after I returned from Mary Magdalene's Grotto, the River Shannon, and St Brigid's Cathedral and Fire Temple.

As I held these memories in my heart, the flow of wisdom carried me deeper in inspiration, I saw the inner space of our little shop in my mind, the shelves and cases of gifts, and our spiritual nook with a lending library of more than 1000 religious and wisdom books across a symphony of traditions, an altar, and chairs for me and other spiritual teachers/practitioners from our community to lead classes and sessions. I contemplated how so many diverse people would walk into our shop and say that it "felt" different, or like "Zen," or peaceful, or it reminded them of the such-and-such metaphysical store in a destination location, and they could not believe there was a store like that nearby. Some people would come in regularly to just relax in the nook and listen to the waterfall or open a book to read.

I realized the energy we created in our shop transmuted the flow within the space itself, and thus, those who were open in mind and heart when they entered were transported to other places in time in their minds. This was evident by how many would step in and their eyes would widen, and they would get big smiles on their faces and say, "This reminds me of..." name of a special place they remembered.

The metaphysical and interfaith gifts were not really even within view from the front of the store; it was the energy in the experience (and likely the fragrances of the incense from the back wall). I'm sure big chain stores pay lots of money for specialists and merchandisers to create specific experiences, but this was all just us in experimentation; David and I wearing all hats.

Everyone coming through the door was welcomed and treated equally just as they were—no matter what. We had some surprises like a duet of husband and wife born-again Christians who were enjoying conversation with me and asked if I would like to hear them sing "Amazing Grace." Of course, I nodded enthusiastically, and they sang out their hearts at the top of their voices in our little shop. At the end, I cheered and applauded and asked, "That's the Michael W. Smith version, right?" To which they lit up with joy.

Even online, we did little things, like offering free gifts and random acts of kindness, and I sent love with a heart and gratitude from both of us handwritten on every packing slip for gifts we shipped out around the world.

The ideas we had for the future were not linear or defined, just possibilities in motion that we could consider further if we decided on a change. I noticed just as with our shop, that I no longer allowed myself to ascribe any concrete defined meaning of truth onto anything in life because the world was in constant creation. Whether it was in the past, future, or present time, all was in a complete flow and, when needed, I would focus where prompted, but fully willing to let go of the details just in the case my inner truth changed based on new information to make a new decision...

Then I stopped writing for a moment. Paused, and the words flowed onto the lines of a page of my spiral notebook,

"This constant balance of co-creation in the heart-mind and future-past completed the trinity so the soul could fully align with Heaven; as I realized that I was in the 9th dimension of Heaven and did not even know it."

My mind rolled like the waves of the ocean reaching the shore ever so gently as the realization poured over me like a river of luminous wisdom, and I was in awe, as I said softly, "The shop..."

Without realizing it, we tested the fruit of our creation in our shop. Gifts from the sunny side of life! I realized that with my husband and co-creator, David, we created a space in the world that was genuinely a unique brand and blending of our true selves in a perfectly balanced yin yang. We did it! Our fruit was good!

A sensation of joy flowed from my heart and I put down my notebook and pen and settled back into meditation form. I breathed in and expanded my field into oneness and the sensation of ascending upward with light rays streaming down filled my mind's eye.

I saw the impression of an oak tree of life alight across my third eye chakra with both the upper branches and lower roots before I noticed that I was rising higher and an impression of a dove opened across my crown and its wings parted across my third eye chakra as I ascended again.

From the stillness and silence in closed-eye meditation, the light rays arrived upward to what felt like a palace upon the clouds. I relished in the sensation of comfy-cozy and on my forehead, I felt breath. Through the skin inward through my third eye chakra, it felt like someone was breathing into me, flowing into my third eye and as it curved downward through my nasal passages, the breath opened outward and down as it emptied from my nostrils. It was a constant stream of flow, and I observed it was not in the rhythm of my own breathing.

Then the flow shifted to going down and through the skin of my neck at the throat chakra location. The energy grew and gathered around my throat getting tighter and more difficult to hold in the inside of me until I opened, and it burst forth out of my mouth, and the breath exhaled into the space around me.

My beingness felt the impression of a chorus of cheering, "Welcome to the 10th from the 9th" in celebration. I realized that if it were true, if I'd just achieved consciousness in the 10th Heavenly dimension while still in my body on Earth, it opened in an ordinary moment of reflection and realization that the fruit of my indie-spirituality, Golden Rule abiding, good works, and miracles, with peace and joy in my heart way-of-truth and love for everyone to create a happier and kinder world, was Good.

Not only that, but David's was also. We created it within our little shop in town and bore good fruit in our community and all across the United States of America together. With our free gifts and smiles and surprise gifts. It was good!

As I recorded these observations in my journal, I noted as soon as the realization connected in my mind—when I saw the expansive landscape of the significance of opening our shop across our lives and perceived our good fruit, it somehow invoked me in the bestowing of what felt like it was called the "breath of life," which already flowed with ease from my third eye and out my nostrils, but in this sacred experience, also now flowed out of my mouth like a river of the breath of life.

From previous studies, I recalled the wording "breath of life" appeared in multiple verses in the Shri Guru Granth Sahib: Khalsa Consensus Translation, from the Sikhism tradition, including the following: *May I never forget God; He is my heart, my soul, my breath of life; the Divine Light of the Infinite Lord, who owns the soul and the breath of life, is deep within the inner being; and He is the Giver of the soul, the heart, the breath of life. Being with Him, we are embellished with joy.* But before I considered the meaning of this experience any further, I needed to first go back to what I'd learned over the years about the dimensions in the heavens.

I'd explored the concept of dimensions of the heavens back in 2010 when I first experienced the sensation of consciousness out of my body in visions through multiple levels while in elevated consciousness. Although later on with practice I replicated the experience of astral travel in meditation without the aid of "herbs," the first time was the most distinctive, wherein I envisioned a multitude of levels and dimensions at one time. The Apostle Paul provided a basis for this concept in 2 Corinthians 12:2, as he described he knew a *"man in Christ who fourteen years ago was caught up to the third heaven—whether in the body or out of the body I do not know, God knows."*

Looking into the Nag Hammadi Scriptures, I noted other texts described dimensions of Heaven, including The Apocalypse of Paul, which described his journey to the throne of God, *"And I saw the twelve apostles. They greeted me, and we went up to the ninth heaven. I greeted all those who were in the ninth heaven, and we went up to the tenth heaven. And I greeted my fellow spirits."* Similarly, also in the Gnostic tradition, the story of Pistis Sophia described her fall from grace and how Christ was sent from the Godhead to bring her back into the fullness, and she ascended through levels of Heaven towards the light.

Another Apocrypha text, the Second Book of Enoch, written in the 1st Century AD/CE, described the mystical ascent of the patriarch Enoch through 10 heavens, including the Garden of Eden in the Third Heaven to meeting God face-to-face in the Tenth. Enoch was mentioned favorably in The Bible: in the genealogy of Jesus (Luke 3:37); the Epistle of Jude (1:14-15) as the *"seventh from Adam"*; and most importantly, in Hebrews 11:5, which confirmed Genesis 5:21-24, *"Enoch walked faithfully with God; then he was no more, because God took him away."* Enoch, at the age of 365, was said to have been taken by two angels through the 10 heavens, one by one, depicting a multidimensional reality of the heavens and one dimension of time.

However, at the time of this writing, it was too early for me to personally ascribe any concrete meaning to the experience and the bestowing of the breath of life through my third eye and out my nose and then through my throat chakra and mouth. After all, I was on a publishing deadline! But I did write a couple of thoughts in the margins of my notebook. I recalled in John 20, beginning with verse 21, " *Again Jesus said, "Peace be with you! As the Father has sent me, I am sending you." And with that he breathed on them and said, "Receive the Holy Spirit. If you forgive anyone's sins, their sins are forgiven; if you do not forgive them, they are not forgiven."*

And then, in keeping with my practices of allowing Spirit and Nature to bring forth greater wisdom and understanding in time, I held off further contemplation until the day the concepts may present again in retrospection, in the ever-present future to come.

❊ ❊ ❊

The goal of this command is love,
which comes from a pure heart and a good conscience
and a sincere faith.
(1 Timothy 1:5)

RIVER OF LIFE

Tuesday, October 20, 2020

I am the rivers and the waves of the seas,
where the sands and rocks of the shores rest upon each other in sanctuary.
I breathe in day and night in balance as I walk upon
the deep waters and the edge of the sky
in the Holy Light as a cup filled with the living waters of Christ.
(June 20, 2020, age 42)

✻ ✻ ✻

Talk of the "End Times" was in the online news headlines today. On his show, 700 Club, longtime Christian televangelist Pat Robertson shared a story that over the weekend he asked God to tell him "how it is going to happen." That was, what was going to be the outcome of the United States 2020 presidential election. Reverend Robertson proclaimed on his show that God told him the current President would defeat the former Vice President, and it would usher in an apocalyptic era of assassination attempts, civil unrest, world war, and ultimately the full-on end times.

As if the irony was not already inherent in what I read, I laughed out loud at the opposition from where I stand in Christ. One of the prominent household-name Christians in the United States of America was prophesying that the end times were about to happen, and here was unknown, humble, little me who nobody knows from Adam; not from wealth or fortune or royal family; not attached to celebrity or people of power in the world; and I'm the one who was about to announce that technically speaking, the end times are done as of December 21, 2020, and Christ's return is imminent in our minds and hearts with the New Heavens merging with the New Earth.

Inconceivable!

Scrolling down the page, I saw a multimedia section of Twitter posts about the article. One of them immediately caught my eye. It was written by someone who went by the name of "Shannon is in FIGHT MODE" who tweeted, *"Well the Goddess told me that he was going to lose, and women are going to take over."* I laughed out loud again and shook my head. No way. Yes, way. Of course, her name is Shannon, and of course, she is speaking about the goddess and a restored connection with Nature and the Mother Goddess/ Divine Holy Mother.

In keeping with my practice of ascribing no meaning until wisdom brings forth understanding after a period of contemplation, I held them together in my heart. Then as I opened to thoughts, the first one that came into my mind for both of these predictions was Isaiah 44:26: *"But when my servant makes a prediction, when I send a messenger to reveal my plans, I make those plans and predictions come true. I tell Jerusalem that people will live there again, and the cities of Judah that they will be rebuilt. Those cities will rise from the ruins"* (Good News Translation).

Even after all these years, I still believed the truth within the words of this verse. Not just for Christians but for anyone who prophesies or makes predictions. If words are spoken in projection into the future and do not come to pass, it means God in Spirit and Nature did not agree with what was said and did not make the plans and predictions come true, and therefore, it was not of God. This applied to anyone within or outside of the church in equal measure regardless of where the prophet(s) stood.

In truth, I could have published this book within either of those two worlds as both are within my Divine heritage and spirituality, just like they are within everyone else. The Gospel of Joy could have been published as a promise of Father God coming true: Jesus promised me a husband and just like the Israelites entering the Promised Land, just like Abraham had a son through Sarah, there he was! Praise Jesus! Praise Father God! The only way of truth! But it would not have been the whole glory of the story of what the living spirit of Jesus and Christ in us can do.

Alternatively, I could have published this book as an indie-spiritual mystic joy alchemist and priestess of Nature singing praises of only the Goddess Mother, who brings forth life in co-creation with us and from whom I received David in reality from the Earth, after receiving his name in a dream that came true. In this case, I would have only written about joy alchemy and the universal principles of creating miracles in real life.

Both sides were equally true but left the message in two separate worlds. If I expanded the two halves of my story out to polar extremes, it may look similar to Reverend Pat Robertson, a messenger of the Christian Father God versus a messenger of the Mother Goddess. These were like two sides of a coin I could observe as a whole and also undivided, because they were both within me, and were at the same time, expressing in the world outside of me.

I turned it over in gentle contemplation until the fire of insight illuminated in understanding. Neither of those outcomes between Christianity and the Goddess was written with love nor did they contain words of peace and tidings of joy for all that would bring all things into a return to balance in the world. This meant, they were not the true ending. They were the pillars of opposition in our world of which this gospel walks between, just to the left or the right from the narrow way of love that is Christ.

The restoration of paradise on Earth in Revelation 21 was depicted as the river of the water of life flowing from the throne of God down the middle of the great street of the city and on each side of the river stood the tree of life. And the leaves of the tree were for the healing of the nations. Let me repeat, for the healing of the nations: not for fighting or further perpetuating unloving divisions among all people.

Any "end times" prophets and apostles coming in the name of Jesus Christ should have the attributes of unity, peace, and love, charity, humility, nonjudgment, mercy, fairness, generosity, and be equal to all. If they did not have these qualities, and if how they conducted their lives and the fruit of their words and actions were filled with judgment and in opposition to the Spirit of Christ, why would I believe they were sent by the Holy Spirit and Holy Light? Was it Christ-like or the antichrist? If it looked like a duck and quacked like a duck, chances were likely, it was a duck.

Reverend Pat Robertson's end times prophecy and the backlash opposition it manifested on social media among atheists reminded me that there was one avenue of wisdom and understanding that I had not explored fully. One belief about Jesus I never so much as tipped-toed across or touched with a 10-foot pole, especially not on a tight rope in the air like the one I suddenly had in mind.

The path I envisioned spanned ocean waves with circling teeth-snapping, ravenous sharks below for I needed to put on the mindset of an unbeliever to understand what Jesus looked like from the opposite perspective. Somehow I needed to find a crack in my beliefs that I could use as the diving platform into imagination to disbelieve.

I cringed at the mere thought of it. I'd never given any credibility or merit to where this was going ever (EVER!) in my life. So much so, it was difficult for me to even get my head around it. I knew to start the ball rolling I just had to come out and say the words even if I did not believe them, so here it went:

"Jesus was a fabricated HOAX!"

It almost felt like a blow to my gut when I typed it. "Hoax" was such an emotionally-charged word over the last four years in the United States of America, and it brought forth the energy that was now imprinted on the word when it was used in vernacular. Some people may have had no internal reaction to the word, but if there was any sort of upsetness in mind or heart or indigestion when reading "hoax," now would be a good time to take a centering breath before continuing to read on.

After getting settled in again, it may be advisable to hold onto a safety rail because I was about to head back down into the energy realms where I started at the beginning of this book. I had to dig through the muck of an obstinate one-way-as-the-only-truth closed mindset to thoroughly convince myself that someone has merit in believing Jesus was or is a hoax, and, spoiler alert, I found it. But don't worry, I did not have to bring much of it back with me for the purposes of illustration, and we'll keep a light on to illuminate the way the entire time, for I found the crack that I was looking for in the canonized Bible.

If it starts to feel like we're about to go off the rails, that's the moment to spread your wings in faith of your beliefs and fly on your own. Soar like an eagle, wild goose, or dove in the sky, and if by chance your faith-wings fail you, know that Jesus is alive and standing by to swoop in and catch you if you start to fall. (See? I couldn't help myself by adding that in here to give you something tangible to hold onto in faith.)

And here we go, for the completion of joy!

❋ ❋ ❋

Then Jesus appeared, saying to them, "Peace be with all of you
and everyone who believes in my name.
When you go, you will have joy and grace and power.
Do not be afraid.
Look, I am with you forever.
(The Letter of Peter to Philip, Nag Hammadi Scriptures)

Wednesday, October 21 ~ Friday, October 30, 2020

Imagine that it's an ordinary day and you're on the way
and someone approaches you and calls out, "Judgment
day! What is in your heart?
Are you good or are you bad?"

How would you respond?

If you responded good and believe that you are good,
you will know the truth.

If you responded good and believe that you are bad,
you will know the truth.

If you responded bad and believe that you are good,
you will know the truth.

If you responded bad and believe that you are bad,
you will know the truth.

If you responded both, or either, or neither, or all, or none,
the truth is the feeling inside before you answered the question.
(June 7, 2020, age 42)

✳ ✳ ✳

Here I was back with Jesus, after all this time. Even though I knew I needed to do this in fair balance for opposition's sake, and because it was bringing me full circle. The truth was, I had zero opposition within my heart about the man and Son of God, Jesus. Not because of who he was or was not in history, none of that even mattered anymore. It boiled down to this: I agreed with the life that Jesus led.

It did not make a difference whether he was a real man or a storybook legend, Jesus was all about peace, love, healing, and miracles; nonjudgment and equality and acceptance for all; and went around doing good works and praying on top of mountains in nature. Those were all things I was all about too.

How was I possibly going to get my mind into a mindset like those who believe Jesus was a made-up lie or a myth to deceive humanity for power and control? For the creation of an army of mindless drones who would fill cathedral coffers, confess all their sins to the church, and follow the church in whatever they directed them to do? It was just so inconceivable for me to even consider that was the original intention behind the stories of Jesus—such evil-mindedness!

Certainly, if it were true, the church would not have included the teachings about freedom in Christ, the treasure found within the heart, that anything was possible, or Jesus' teaching that we could do what he did on Earth and even more. The conspiracy theories just did not make sense without more evidence. How on Earth was I going to find a way to believe that Jesus was a hoax? To disbelieve everything I know in Truth about Jesus because I experienced his living Spirit and knew he's all the gospels say that he is.

It was not easy. It took me a while... But then, I found it! The thorn I pricked my finger on was sticking out from Jesus' character (and seriously, it took me all of the summer moons to find one), and there it was in plain sight. An event was discussed in two (yes, two) of the canonized gospels, so I discerned it must have been important. The time when Jesus cleared the temple courts.

Matthew 21:12-13 and John 2:13-17 depicted a scene in the Jerusalem temple courtyards where people were selling cattle, sheep, and doves, and other people were sitting at tables and exchanging money. Seeing all of this, Jesus was said to have made a whip out of cords, and he drove all from the temple courts. The sheep and cattle! Drove them out with the whip! Go, go, go! Get out! And then he grabbed and overturned the money changers' tables. He scattered their coins and yelled out to the merchants who were selling doves, "Get these out of here! Stop turning my Father's house into a market!"

It sounded like Jesus was frustrated and angry and in the moment his adrenaline may have been pumping as he cracked the whip near the animals, and they stampeded out of the temple court. In Jesus' perspective, what they were doing in the temple courts was so horrendous he needed to cause a huge ruckus with chaos and confusion of the cracking of whips and scattering of coins as tables toppled over on the ground in loud thuds.

For the Son of the God of love, whose top two greatest commandments for his disciples were: to love God with all your heart and soul and mind and love your neighbor as yourself (Matthew 22:37-39), this was not an act of love. In the light of my heart, there was enough of a division in what I knew love to be and multiple other ways Jesus could have handled this situation that would have been more loving alternatives.

I could not think of any scenario or convince myself that chasing animals —especially those that did not belong to me—out of anywhere and away from their keepers was the right or loving thing to do. What if they created a stampede? What if one or two or more were harmed? What if the caretakers could not find them and they got lost?

Overturning tables and scattering coins was also not such a loving action either. Perhaps a list of 95 theses nailed to the temple door would have been more peaceful, and more loving, than creating chaos, not to mention, destruction of someone else's property. We did not hear in the story about him asking forgiveness for his outburst or stopping to help clean up or search for the scattered animals. This moment was the closest act of violence we see of Jesus in the gospels.

Some people may defend Jesus and say that because he was the perfect human and Son of God—because of who HE was—and as the King of Kings and Lord of Lords, this was acceptable behavior. These believers so tightly closed in their boxes of belief are unwilling to concede that maybe, just maybe this was out of character, and perhaps not the best choice of loving action in the moment for a man whose life consisted of demonstrating the path of peace, healing, good works, and miracles.

Staunch believers may call this a direct testimony of Jesus following his own greatest commandment, to love God with all his heart and soul. In this vein, the unloving outburst with a whip in the temple courts was a demonstration of his love for God to show what was Holy and Righteous because what they were doing was wrong! This was for the love of God! That would make it a Holy Outburst with a Holy Whip, and therefore, would make it the righteous hand of God against what was wrong in the world!

Yet, if we put someone else in Jesus' place and read it on social media about the "Left" or the "Right" in the United States of America protesting and creating chaos at a religious site, would we say they were acting in love? Would we say it was an okay thing to do? Or would the answer be different depending on who was the one having the angry outburst in public and causing chaos in the courtyard at the sacred temple where people were praying? Was it okay for Jesus to do, but not acceptable for anyone else? After all, the animals he drove out of the temple courts were not his, nor was it his money or tables that he scattered and overturned, even if it was his Father's house.

There was no difference in who did it. Either the person who cleared the courtyards with a whip behaved correctly or not. If we apply The Golden Rule, it applies to all. It does not depend on who he was or was not. This then was further evidence of how love is a stumbling block to judge right or wrong. Someone can always argue it was for the love of God or the right thing to do as a "Christian," and thus attempt to justify a multitude of sins.

The bottom line was this story did not sound like love or the Jesus I knew. Especially because of an event depicted in all four of the canonized gospels (Matthew 26, Mark 14, Luke 22, and John 18), when Simon Peter, one of Jesus' disciples, struck and cut off the ear of Malchus, one of the men who came to arrest Jesus before he was judged and crucified. Jesus said, "No more of this! Put your sword away! All those who draw the sword will die by the sword!" He then touched Malchus' ear and healed him. This was the love that Jesus demonstrated even under duress right before he was seized and arrested.

With my inner experience as the truth, from what I knew from the canonized and apocryphal scriptures, and his living presence in Spirit, this did not fit Jesus' loving character of "going around doing good works," healing, and miracles. I did not think Jesus would have created chaos like this, especially not with the animals because of the harm it could have caused them, and the animals had done no wrong. I believed he would have found another nonviolent way to make his statement.

The connections were rewiring in my mind, and I felt the opening on the horizon. I saw in my mind's eye the moment I began to believe that this story about Jesus may be a fraud. This was the crack I was looking for because it then begged the question... if this story may have been a fraud, how many other stories may have been included in the canonized gospels that weren't the whole truth or maybe did not happen in real life the way it was written?

This time it was not a can of worms I knew I'd opened, but it contained the very subject matter I'd specifically not included in any other version of my manuscript because of the sensitivity. And now, here it was again, so here we go.

I started with a handful of possibilities in one storyline that were so clear they should not be a big surprise to anyone, the Jewish-to-Jesus lineage connection. Not only were there multiple points of archetype patterns and foreshadowing, or masterfully written fulfillment of the prophecy, as the case may or may not be, the message was crystal clear in the canonized gospels. Jesus was meant to be believed as the prophesied Messiah of the Jews.

Additionally, Jesus referred back to the Hebrew Scriptures numerous times, connecting him to the religious tradition. He was also directly connected in the manner of his birth and ancestry of parentage through the house of David. He was set up to take on the mantle of the Jewish people. Any or all of this may have been written with creative connections and not literal real-life truth.

But this was not all. In comparative mythology, there were numerous similarities in scriptures and events between the stories of Jesus and other ancient religions that existed pre-Jesus. In this vein, here is a selection of examples that have parallel connections with at least one aspect of Jesus' life, and these were likely just the tip of the iceberg. In every example, the myth, story, archetype, or god/goddess was already well-known in the world pre-Jesus' time.

First, there was a story in Greek mythology about when Apollo appeared to Perictione's husband Ariston and told him not to consummate his marriage with his wife. This was a close parallel to the annunciation to Joseph as depicted in the gospel of Matthew. Other gods in mythology were also said to have been born of virgin mothers, including Attis (Phrygia), Tammuz-Adonis (Sumeria; also mentioned in the Old Testament), and Perseus (Greek). Further, there was a striking similarity between the artwork of Isis and the child-god Horus and the later Madonna with the Christ child.

Other parallels include Hermes, the Greek messenger of the Logos/Word as a trinity with similar symbolism used such as the lamb and caduceus. Healing and medicine were similar to Asclepius from the Greek tradition, and he also had a snake wrapped on a pole, which paralleled John 3:14-15: *"Just as Moses lifted up the snake in the wilderness, so the Son of Man must be lifted up, that everyone who believes may have eternal life in him."*

Some similar scenes and events are seen when comparing the stories of Pythagoras (Greek) and Jesus with fishermen. Both Pythagoras and Jesus performed miraculous signs. Pythagoras' sign was telling the fishermen how many fish were in their net and later; the number that Simon Peter brought ashore in the net in the story with Jesus was 153, which was the Pythagorean "measure of the fish."

Jesus was not the first to die and resurrect; other death-rebirth deities spanned across ancient beliefs, including Tammuz-Adonis, Attis, Osiris from Egypt, Dionysus from Greece (also known by a laundry list of epithets and similar to Jesus with wine symbolism). In Norse and Viking Mythology, Balder was doomed after death in the Underworld but was reborn after passing through the End of the World and Ragnarok.

Other belief systems had judgment by a king or a god after each person died, such as Anubis who weighed each person's heart on a scale against the feather of Ma'at; or Osiris who sat in the Hall of Judgment with the scales of justice before him. If a person was unable to pass, they encountered the "second death" to destruction in the lake of fire. (Yes, that's right, the lake of fire. Similar words were used in the book of Revelation). Ancient Greeks believed at the time of death a person would enter the realm of Hades in the underworld and be judged by King Minos, Aescus, and Radamanthus. In Hinduism judgment was done by the God of Death in accordance with karma.

Additionally, I also noted similarities in the Eastern traditions, such as in the Tao Te Ching written around 400 BC/BCE included a verse, "the sage puts himself last and becomes first," which was similar to one of Jesus' sayings. In consideration with Buddhism, multiple life and teaching similarities exist, both Buddha (who lived approximately 500 years before Jesus) underwent and overcame temptation, had disciples, performed miracles, rebelled against the religious elite; and taught The Golden Rule, love (*"Let your thoughts of boundless love pervade the whole world"* from the Sutta Nipata), turn the other cheek, help others, do not judge others, disdain wealth and worldly possessions, and do not kill.

A few more to wrap this quick tour up, in the 4th Century AD/CE, Pope Julius formalized Jesus' birthday on December 25, which was the same date as the birthday of the Roman sun god, Sol Invictus, and around the same time as Saturnalia celebrations mentioned in the Jewish Talmud. And the Eucharist (Holy Communion with the bread/wafer and wine) was a spiritual ritual traced back to Neolithic "theophagy" practices of eating the body of a fertility god; especially a god who needed to die and rise again to feed the community.

Finally, when I entered this research my hypothesis was not that the story of Jesus may have been sourced from previous sacred Divine deities, rituals, and celebrations from many other cultures and religions, or that Jesus was a "repeat" or reappropriation to widen the fishing net of conversions.

Rather, I hypothesized the writers of the gospels entwined together with the symbolism, the powers of the gods, the rituals and celebrations, and all devotion/worship to one head of the church: Son of God, by the name of Jesus Christ to give him all of the power that was in the other deities' names in one name. Since Jesus was made head of the entire church (Colossians 1:18) and all nations, and all authority in Heaven and Earth was given to him (Matthew 28:18-19), it seemed to make sense this could have been the primary motivation. In the next example, it appeared as though that hypothesis may be plausibly correct.

Serapis Christus was a Greek-Egyptian deity, a combination of Osiris and Apis from Egypt and with attributes of Zeus, Helios, Dionysus, Hades, and Asklepius. On the orders of Greek Pharaoh Ptolemy I Soter of the Ptolemaic Kingdom in Egypt, the cult of Serapis was pushed forward during the 3rd Century BC/BCE to unify the Greeks and Egyptians in the realm into a new age. Serapis was also a death-rebirth god and was annually sacrificed for the sins of Egypt.

Where this really became intriguing was when I read that during the church Council of Nicaea in 325 where the Holy Trinity was established, "Serapis Christus" became "Iesoys Christos" (Jesus Christ). This example seemed to demonstrate how interweaving may have occurred in the writing of the gospels to bring all deities under One belief system and God.

Then I turned upwards to the grand overarching vantage of a shared lineage of myths, scriptures, and sacred stories built upon a system of celestial metaphor as seen in the stars, planets, moon, and sun in the heavens above. Perhaps the stories of the Bible, similar to other founding myths in history, were not real-life literal events, but were written in the universe by the placement and movement of the planets, sun, moon, and stars, and scribed into human history as stories.

One such scholar who investigated this extensively was David Warner Mathisen, author of Star Myths of the World and How to Interpret Them, Volume 3: Star Myths of the Bible. The grand volume described how celestial and mythological story connections were embedded from the beginning of the Old Testament to the end of the New Testament, and that the scriptures, archetypes, and events were closely related to the myths of ancient China, Japan, Greece, Egypt, Sumer, Babylon, and India, *"or of the Norse of far* northern Europe, or the Aborigines of Australia, or the Maya of Central America or the people of Africa and of the Pacific islands, and the shamanic peoples of the vast plains and steppes and mountain lakes of Asia and Alaska and icy Greenland." Far more than I identified in an evening of research.

Mathisen pointed out a major issue in the baby Jesus storyline regarding the Magi (the 3 wise men). The Magi from the East saw the star in the east after Jesus was born in Bethlehem in Judea; they traveled from the east to Jerusalem to find the king of the Jews (Matthew 2:2). The issue was they should have headed east towards the star in the eastern sky, not west (away from the star in the east). Could this be proof that the story was designed to match constellation positions in the sky and not that it was a record of a real-life timeline from Earth?

As described by Mathisen in volume 3, an English clergyman and radical free thinker, Reverend Robert Taylor (1784-1844), came to similar realizations in his studies of Biblical texts—the scriptures were celestial metaphor from beginning to end. That was, none of it happened; all were symbols in the sky.

His beliefs came with expulsion from the church and imprisonment more than once. But from that point onward, he preached, "As the Psalmist sublimely explains: *"For ever, O Lord, thy word is true in Heaven." And so it is: but it was never true on earth: and none but a fool or a dunce would ever have dreamed that it was so. And they who have represented Christ and his apostles as persons that ever existed upon earth, do turn the truth of God into a lie."*

With these discoveries, I now held within my mind the very real possibility that all of the stories of Jesus, and the four canonized gospels, were entirely made up stories based on the constellations in the skies. I traveled from one event of Jesus clearing the temple courtyard that did not quite fit the Jesus I knew to a slew of shared symbols, signs, events, miracles, teachings, and stories.

This was heretical ground for sure. Almost 2000 years have gone by and this was still such a sensitive subject in our world. People argued, fought, and harmed each other over their beliefs about whether or not Jesus of Nazareth, the Son of God, was a real man who walked on the Earth.

I stepped back and held an intention of love in my heart. Out of the silence in my mind, I wondered if the writers of the gospels designed in their creation of the Son of the One, Holy, Almighty God of love, with the intention of a perfect, universal man to repay the karmic debt for the entire lineage of humans back to the split of the 12 tribes of Abraham (remember, Jesus mentioned that he was the seed of Abraham). This karmic atonement also then went further because he was also noted as the "New Adam," therefore repaying the karmic debt for the first Adam who sinned.

Through his atonement for the sins of man back to Adam, Jesus cleared the road for salvation for all sinners by closing the cycle of the story in humanity, so that we would be free from judgment because the original sin and judgment in the founding mythological story in the Garden of Eden that started this whole cycle were wiped clean. An entirely fresh, new start for humanity.

In this manner, he showed us the way (The Golden Rule, love, healing, miracles) and the destination ("*who for the joy set before him...*" Hebrews 12:2) and it appeared in design to include all people, not just the 12 tribes in Judaism, as a funnel of the ancient religions into the name and under the head of Jesus, and therefore, with the expectation then, that the one church in the name of Jesus would be the last church upon the Earth all people would be a part of the one body of Christ. It sounded like a forward-thinking all-encompassing interfaith movement to love, freedom, justice, and equality for all universal-minded organization of religion. A valiant endeavor from where my heart rests.

Alternatively, I acknowledged it was also entirely possible it was a universal attempt to convert masses of people and have all power and control possible in the world, as much as my heart pained me to say it. Here is the reason it was a valid possibility: If the Light and the Spirit within the church remained pure without the blood, torture, and deaths of the Crusades, inquisitions, and other atrocities done in the name of Jesus Christ, this would not even be a consideration.

Yet, unfortunately, it must be considered because horrible events took place, and thus, in all fairness, the possibility cannot be ruled out. If the original intention was love—something somewhere went wrong.

The bottom line was this: the church founders and early church leaders were using the same instruction manual and directions for the church as clergy are today. The church was to be the "one and only" true body of Christ established fully on the Earth to receive the Holy Spirit and the promised reward of Christ (Luke 6:35, Col 3:24, 2 John 1:9, Phil 3:14, Rev 22:12).

I imagined what a transfigured church within the one body of Christ might hold dear in their minds and hearts:

> We set a joyful destination in our hearts and give up
> control to God of how we get there together.
> We practice what we preach, and we don't forget to love everyone,
> especially those who oppose us.
> We are good to the children and we allow clergy to marry,
> We honor nature and all of life on Earth.
> We always remember that symbols are only images

of the truth that they represent,
and we hold no idols of the world (including our beliefs).
We believe Jesus is ALIVE in Spirit
and we forgive everyone without judgment just like Christ.

We welcome all people without labels or discrimination,
racism and inequality have no home in our church.
Any person with qualifications can become any level of clergy
(even the Pope) regardless of gender.

We seek to unite One Church as the body of the light of Christ,
and when we have done as was originally directed,
The Holy Spirit will come again to our church in the name of Jesus Christ,
On Earth, as it is already in the Heavens, Forevermore,
all glory and power to the Holy One.
Amen

In 2020, this was not what Christianity looked like in the world. It was as if somewhere along the way the light went out in the church. Whether it was when it became more important to be right (in pride or ego) than to be one in the light of Christ, or if the living Spirit fled from the cathedrals when the church first harmed a living being in the name of Jesus Christ—not to mention, harming millions of people—for death was then brought upon the karma of the pure virgin church.

Instead of turning inward to search within their hearts to reconcile with their brothers and sisters inside and outside the church walls, Christian missionaries marched outward across the lands and leaders founded denomination after denomination.

No matter which way I sliced it, there was no doubt in my heart a human error (or two, three, or more) of interpretations, beliefs, and actions were made at some points along the timeline of history, and the original joy of the gospel became part of the mystery that was lost. There was no other explanation for a religion based on peace, love, healing, and miracles not to be a powerful and glorious force on Earth today. What happened to the miracles? And the joy in all hearts?

After crucifixion, death, and burial in the tomb, Jesus returned in the visions of Mary Magdalene, wherein he directed her to tell the rest of his disciples that she had seen him alive. This meant, she felt the familiar presence of Jesus surrounding her and may have smelled his essence or felt his energy or heard his voice in her mind. The joy was in the miracle of the living Spirit of Christ reborn within Mary. That in itself should have been enough for everyone to stop in their tracks and shout, "Hallelujah! Jesus is alive!" End of story! He was who he said he was and now let's move on to miracles and joy for all the world.

Besides, Jesus' discourses with his disciples after he was resurrected in Heaven were not necessarily just the handful of times depicted in the canonized gospels. In <u>Pistis Sophia,</u> it was said that he returned over 11 years to continue advanced teachings with the apostles. Lest I forget, the Bible also described how Jesus appeared as the living spirit of Christ to Saul/Apostle Paul. Thank goodness this story was in the canonized Bible because it proves an apostle can be appointed by Jesus Christ himself even though the apostle did not know an alive Jesus in the flesh as a man on Earth. Apostle Paul believed on the basis of Jesus as a living Spirit speaking to him in vision.

Similar to when Jesus appeared as the living Christ in December 2009 when he entered into my world from the Heavenly realm, as I was on my way back from the cross-country trip. Alone in the early darkness of the morning somewhere in Ohio, Jesus came to me and told me that I ready for my new life. I laughed remembering Jesus said I could tell people I was a born again, but he knew I wouldn't, and that was okay with him.

That memory was still one of my absolute favorites of all-time ever in my life because it was so spontaneous. There was no way I could have strung together those words in my head all on my own. It was not me or a narrative voice in my mind. It was not two different spirits' energies. It was Jesus who knew my heart so well, he knew I would not ever say it about myself because of the connotation and energy the label "born-again Christian" carried with it in the United States of America.

Jesus is everything that the Bible and the Apocrypha say about him and more, If he was not who he said he was in life (or what was written about him), his soul would not have passed through judgment nor would he be alive in Spirit working miracles and healing. Even if he never walked on the Earth and if he was a "celestial metaphor," the living Spirit associated with the name Jesus is very much alive, as demonstrated through the story of my life.

Whoever seeks the living Jesus within will most certainly find him. Not outward in a cathedral or a church or any other sacred place, but in the Holy Temple of the soul as experienced in the trinity of mind, heart, and body. Jesus spoke about his body being a temple in John 2:19-21 and the concept was not limited to just Jesus either, for it was written in 1 Corinthians 3:16, *"Don't you know that you yourselves are God's temple and that God's Spirit dwells in your midst?"*

His teachings beckoned us to become like him, as described by Jesus in The Gospel of Thomas:

> *Jesus said, "He who will drink from my mouth will become like me.*
> *I myself shall become he,*
> *and the things that are hidden will be revealed to him..."*

Jesus said, "The heavens and the earth will be rolled up in your presence.
And the one who lives from the living one will not see death."
Does not Jesus say, "Whoever finds himself is superior to the world?"

Jesus said, "Woe to the flesh that depends on the soul;
woe to the soul that depends on the flesh."

His disciples said to him, "When will the kingdom come?"
<Jesus said,> "It will not come by waiting for it.
It will not be a matter of saying 'here it is' or 'there it is.'
Rather, the kingdom of the father is spread out upon the earth,
and men do not see it."
(The Gospel of Thomas, as translated by Thomas O. Lambdin)

We were now almost 2000 years out from the 33 years in the timeline of human history when Jesus was said to walk on the Earth, and the world was still tangled in conflict about what was right or not to believe. What was the truth? What was fiction? What was the real-life report and what was a metaphorical myth?

Ever since the first person read one of the gospels that depicted the joy of the apostles and early Christians, the truth that the living Jesus returned within their hearts and minds was in plain sight. After a renewal of mind and heart in Jesus, the joy of Christ resided in the inner temple of the soul.

Such as in my life, Jesus was the living Spirit through whom my mind opened into the light and filled with the Holy Spirit (2009). When I was ready to advance, he baptized me in the Spirit, which led to the rebirth of my true self in the death of my ego (false self; 2012).

From there, I navigated with my inner heart compass after I'd left the image of Jesus behind, learning to trust my own wisdom in the same way that I'd learned to trust God to guide me in mind and the world. It was all about faith beyond beliefs. My life was a new creation, just like in 2 Corinthians 5:17, *"Therefore, if anyone is in Christ, he is a new creation. The old has passed away; behold, the new has come,"* and the power of the Holy Spirit filled my soul (2018).

This was confirmed in the following excerpt from November 26, 2014, in St. Peter's Square, when Pope Francis spoke: *"God is preparing a new dwelling place and a new earth where justice will abide, and whose blessedness will answer and surpass all the longings for peace which spring up in the human heart." This is the Church's destination: it is, as the Bible says, the "new Jerusalem", "Paradise." More than a place, it is a "state" of soul in which our deepest hopes are fulfilled in superabundance and our being, as creatures and as children of God, reach their full maturity. We will finally be clothed in the joy, peace and love of God, completely, without any limit, and we will come face to face with Him!"*

The truth my soul discovered was that the nature of Jesus, the Son of the Almighty One God of Love and the most High—whether man or celestial metaphor—does not matter at all once someone experiences the living Spirit of Christ and knows through inner gnosis, what is Holy and of the Good Light within one's self. Once a seeker experiences Christ on the inside, whether it is by the name of Jesus or another name in the Light, the living Spirit of Holiness enters and that's when we are truly alive.

Everything we need for salvation, liberation from the cycles of samsara (rebirth), and eternal life are all found in the light within. As described in The Upanishads, "*I have become one with the tree of life. My glory rises like the mountain peak. I have realized the Self, who is ever pure, all-knowing, radiant, and immortal.*"

Anyone anywhere can call upon the name of Jesus whether they are a Christian or not, for his light was given unto the world and to all the nations. We may follow his example and shine bright like the sun and stars in the skies, with the light and the love of Christ in our hearts and minds, until we once again partake of the tree of life as a child of the living Spirit of God and receive the river of peace from the living waters within.

This is the way of miracles for the completion of joy, and it is given to each and every one of us to do our part in the creation of Heaven on Earth:

> *Let your love flow outward through the universe,*
> *To its height, its depth, its broad extent,*
> *A limitless love, without hatred or enmity.*
> *Then as you stand or walk,*
> *Sit or lie down,*
> *As long as you are awake,*
> *Strive for this with a one-pointed mind;*
> *Your life will bring heaven to earth.*
> (Excerpt of the Sutta Nipata, Pali Text known as,
> Buddha's Discourse on Good Will)

HEAVEN ON EARTH

...THE FUTURE BELONGS TO THOSE WHO
BELIEVE IN THE BEAUTY OF THEIR DREAMS
(ATTRIBUTED TO ELEANOR ROOSEVELT)

Saturday, October 31, 2020

Forty years ago the United States was in another rough patch in our nation's history. Americans were grieving lives lost in the war in Vietnam, dealing with inflation and gas shortages, and the value of the dollar was low. The economy was stagnant and high rates of crime were rampant across cities in the nation. A general malaise was said to have set in from sea to shining sea.

Then on February 22, 1980, a miracle happened that no one expected— a David versus Goliath upset of epic proportions during one particular ice hockey game during the Winter Olympics.

"Great moments are born from great opportunity..." the coach set the course before the miracle, *"One game; if we played them ten times, they might win nine. But not this game, not tonight. Tonight we skate with them. Tonight we stay with them, and we shut them down because we can."*

The United States men's ice hockey team went on to win in the medal round against the heavily favored four-time defending gold medalist champions, the Russian team. The United States team had no reason or chance to win in the circumstances, but with less than a minute before the final buzzer, everyone watching on television heard,

> *"11 seconds, you've got 10 seconds, the countdown going on right now!*
> *...Five seconds left in the game.*
> *Do you believe in miracles? YES!"*

After the 4-3 win, the United States team went on to the gold medal round where they won again and became gold medal champions. After what felt like living through a long national nightmare, the United States was said to be in a patriotic fervor with excitement for the future because of the Miracle on Ice.

Fast forward to 2020 and an article I read today about a family in California

221

who decorated their front yard with skeletons as the hockey players from the once-in-a-lifetime miracle game in an iconic decoration for Halloween quoted the mother as saying, *"I think, this year, we could all stand to believe in miracles."* Yes, it was definitely time for another miracle in our nation.

For skeptics and doubters who do not believe in miracles, especially not miracles big enough for an entire nation or the world to behold, in the words of physicist Albert Einstein (1879-1955), *"There are two ways to live your life. One is as though nothing is a miracle. The other is as though everything is a miracle."* From first-hand experience, believing in miracles is a lot more fun, and it's not impossible to conceive a miracle as big as a nation as America because it had already happened with the Miracle on Ice in 1980.

Besides, the possibility of miracles as big as a nation is actually Biblical, for instance in Malachi chapter 3. Malachi was a prophetic scripture in the Old Testament thought to be written during the period of restoration after the reconstruction and dedication of the second temple in 516 AD/BCE.

People strayed from God's path and needed Heavenly intervention. Although the temple was rebuilt, there was a malaise and apathy in their relationship with God, and this led to rampant corruption. The people struggled to believe that God loved them, and instead focused on their suffering in grief and consternation of everything that was wrong; and at the same time, refused to account for their own sinful attitudes and actions. Through the words of the messenger, Malachi, God pointed directly at the people and told them specifically where they had fallen short on their side of the covenant.

The verses described how if the people turned their hearts and minds back to God, the Heavens would open up and blessings would pour out beyond their wildest dreams; and this sounded much like the American Dream come true for an entire nation. For us in the United States of America, this would mean going back to the words in the Preamble of our Declaration of Independence, *"We hold these truths to be self-evident, that all men are created equal, that they are endowed by their Creator with certain unalienable rights, that among these are Life, Liberty and the Pursuit of Happiness,"* and going back to being a nation under God.

There hasn't ever been anything stopping us from holding true to the words of equality and the right for life, liberty, and joy for all in our nation under God—except for us. We have not stood together in word and action with the courage needed to persevere through the storms, nor put in the work or sacrifice to build a better nation to change the trajectory of our shared future by finding ways to get along.

And now, we were on the precipice of a monumental presidential election set to take place on November 3, 2020, the most contentious and bitter than we'd ever seen in the modern history of the United States. Masses of people standing up for equality, justice, health, and well-being, and in a firm commitment of the words stated in the Preamble—in two utterly divided and polar sides. Both believed their truth was right. Where was the American Spirit the founding fathers wrote about in the Preamble?

First and foremost, history was clear the founding fathers did not live up to the values they set forth in their visionary aspirations for the future of our nation. Rather than going down the slippery slope of their egregious actions towards the peoples and life on the land they commandeered or declaring where they made errors in judgment in their lifetimes, I focused on their intention for our nation. For all intents and purposes, this country was established under God. The American Spirit they held in highest esteem for all was modeled after Jesus Christ, the Son of God, and they afforded religious freedom for all.

In 1765, Patrick Henry, a politician and statesman, who was better known for his famous words, *"Give me liberty, or give me death,"* mentioned this very point in a speech to the Virginia House of Burgesses, *"It cannot be emphasized too strongly or too often that this great nation was founded, not by religionists, but by Christians not on religions, but on the gospel of Jesus Christ! For this very reason, peoples of other faiths have been afforded asylum, prosperity, and freedom of worship here."* Not only did he specifically call out freedom for other faiths beyond Christianity, but he affirmed it was on the values of peace, justice, forgiveness, and love, that the United States should be based—Jesus' way.

This concept was also stated by Benjamin Franklin when he discussed his personal beliefs in 1790: *"Here is my Creed. I believe in one God, the Creator of the Universe. That He governs it by His Providence. That He ought to be worshipped. That the most acceptable service we render to Him is in doing good to His other Children. That the soul of Man is immortal and will be treated with Justice in another Life respecting its conduct in this. These I take to be the fundamental points in all sound Religion, and I regard them as you do in whatever Sect I meet with them. As to Jesus of Nazareth, my Opinion of whom you particularly desire, I think the System of Morals and his Religion, as he left them to us, is the best the World ever saw, or is likely to see."* Thomas Jefferson also echoed in similar belief, *"I am a real Christian, that is to say, a disciple of the doctrines of Jesus."*

Arguments of whether or not America was founded as a Christian nation are irrelevant because it was clear that the wording used in the founding of our nation included the pure essence of Christianity in the manner and way of Jesus Christ. John Quincy Adams said, *"The highest glory of the American Revolution was this: it connected in one indissoluble bond the principles of civil government and the principles of Christianity."* God's hand was inextricably bound in the co-creation between the founding fathers of the United

States and Benjamin Franklin concluded in 1787 during the Constitutional Convention that: "...*the longer I live, the more convincing proofs I see of this truth – that God governs in the affairs of men, and if a sparrow cannot fall to the ground without His notice, is it probable that an empire can rise without His aid?*"

It appears we are seeing the answer to his question in our nation right now. In fact, the father of American geography, Jedediah Morse stated in 1799, "*Whenever the pillars of Christianity should be overthrown, our present republican forms of government and all the blessings which flow from them, must fall with them.*"

My heart hurts to say it, but we are there. It was not even that we've turned away from God. We have turned away from what is Good: instead of common decency and cooperation, there is complaining and negativity on social media and in our communities, and rampant "cancel culture." We've fallen from grace—that is, if our nation ever actually achieved a state of grace to begin with, or at any time during the last 244 years, given all that we have done, both good and not-so-good in the world.

What would happen if for the first time in the history of America the citizens of our country actually committed to conducting themselves in a manner reflective of what our Preamble and the Pledge of Allegiance pronounce as the rock of indivisible, liberty, and justice for all that we stand upon? To forgive, to love, to have mercy and compassion, and to strive for healing instead of causing harm.

Even in the times when it feels difficult or impossible to "love our enemies," to at the minimum, treat each other according to The Golden Rule. It also means a willingness to admit where we'd gone wrong, to forgive, and to atone for the healing and cleansing of our nation's karmic slate, so we can move into a new beginning that is better for all.

Talk about making America awesome in a way that had never been seen before in history. Benjamin Franklin foresaw it in 1778 when he said, "*Whoever shall introduce into public affairs the principles of primitive Christianity will change the face of the world.*" That's what we must do here and now.

It was not about a religion or a specific denomination, but through faith and conducting ourselves like children of God in the ways of Jesus Christ. To step forward in the right direction of equality and justice for all, regardless of gender or sexual orientation, religion, age, color of skin, disability status, country of origin, language spoken, career and work, body size, hairline, tattoos, piercings, or any other self-identifying label by which millions of Americans judge, bully, and assault each other day in and day out. This is the only way we will build a better America one step forward together at a time.

Given where we are now, my common sense and rational nature hold no illusions about this being an easy task. It will take a miracle by the hand of God and the people united for the glory of peace and love to reign across America from sea to shining sea.

❋ ❋ ❋

I know that there is nothing better for people than to be happy
and to do good while they live.
(Ecclesiastes 3:12)

Thursday/Friday, November 5/6, 2020

May we hear only what is good for all.
May we see only what is good for all.
May we serve you, Lord of Love, all our life.
May we be used to spread your peace in earth.
OM shanti shanti
(The Upanishads)

❋ ❋ ❋

On November 5, ballots were still in the tallying process and the presidential race was tight. As the evening drew onward, it was looking as if votes from Clayton County, Georgia, would be enough in former Vice President Joe Biden's favor to flip the state "Blue." That meant, towards the Democrat party instead of the Republicans who'd been victorious in Georgia for every presidential election for nearly the past 30 years.

Thus, the coveted state Electoral College votes, which determined the president-elect over the popular majority vote, would go to Biden. A history-making moment for Georgia; but also a much-needed miracle of hope for those praying for a wave of change in America toward a more equal, inclusive, and just society for all.

With tempered joy—knowing there was still a road of darkness ahead for our nation—I looked in on Twitter to see what I could find out about what was happening in Georgia. Specifically in @ClaytonCountyGA, "Where the world lands and opportunities take off":

...If Clayton Co. flips this thing....Y'all...Clayton County GA - home to Atlanta's

airport, and 87% people of color - is gonna decide this thing and it will be beautiful...Man... I'm at a loss for words right now. Clayton County has literally been looked down upon since I was a kid growing up here. And we're about to make HISTORY...Fun fact: Clayton County, Georgia was the setting for Tara in Gone with the Wind. Now, it could well be the County that turns Georgia blue... For those learning about Clayton County, it's home to ATL airport. Largest employers include logistics & auxiliary services that fuel the world's busiest airport. Ballots delivering GA's electoral votes are from essential workers who've been on the front lines of this pandemic...The hood is really about to save this country. Clayton County, Georgia is about to change the world WOW... This is what the count looks like inside #ClaytonCounty, GA tonight. High-risk volunteers putting their lives on the line to count our votes during a pandemic. They're American heroes...Forensically watching the votes in Clayton County - somewhere I have never been, will never be and previously didn't really know existed but I suddenly have very strong feelings about...Where were you when Clayton County dropped will be a legendary question for anyone who follows elections for a long time to come...Everyone, especially Nevada: "Who the hell counts votes at 3AM?" Clayton County, Georgia...Imagine being one of these women and knowing you're the person counting the ballots that will flip your state, and therefore your country, blue...Queens doing the Lord's work, sending blessings and love...I see our ancestors there beside them urging them on led by Congressman Lewis...Y'ALL. My hometown of Clayton County is about to save America and flip the state blue! Biden is 1,800 votes away from winning GA, and ClayCo will drop their last 5,700 ballots in an hour. The late John Lewis represented this county. He would be so, so proud. #GoodTrouble...

John Lewis (1940-2020) was a civil rights icon and served 17 terms (33 years) in the United States House of Representatives for Georgia's 5th congressional district, which included part of Clayton County where this miracle was potentially about to happen.

In January 1963, he was arrested for the first of what would be more than 40 times for civil rights activities. Later that year, Lewis was the youngest speaker at the March on Washington on August 28th, and the youngest member of the leaders representing six prominent civil rights organizations who were instrumental in the organization of the march, known as the "Big Six."

On March 7, 1965, John Lewis attempted to lead a group of marchers across the Edmund Pettus Bridge in Selma on their way to Montgomery. They were marching to bring attention to the lack of voting rights across the country for black people, and specifically in Alabama. When the estimated 600 peaceful marchers reached the apex of the bridge, they were beaten back by police officers who used clubs, whips, and tear gas. It was known as Bloody Sunday and Lewis spent two days in the hospital after being one of those attacked. The event spurred support throughout the nation and Congress to enact the Voting Rights Act of 1965.

But it was not just Lewis' dedication to securing civil liberties, protecting the rights of humans, or building the Beloved Community in America that garnered respect across the aisles in Congress and across America; he was admired for his high ethical standards and moral principles. Lewis believed in getting into good and necessary trouble to help redeem the soul of America in nonviolent action. He lived his life in accordance with the character and morality of Christ.

This was demonstrated no greater than in 2009 when he accepted the apology of a former Ku Klux Klansman who had beat him and left him bloodied 48 years earlier when Lewis was a part of the Freedom Riders who rode interstate buses against segregation in the south. His attacker recalled that when the police arrived and asked if Lewis wanted to file charges against the men who beat him, Lewis said, *"We're not here to cause trouble. We're here for people to love each other."*

Lewis believed in the light within all of us, just as former United States President Barak Obama spoke during the eulogy at Lewis' funeral earlier this year, *"He believed that in all of us, there exists the capacity for great courage, that in all of us there is a longing to do what's right, that in all of us there is a willingness to love all people, and to extend to them their God-given rights to dignity and respect. So many of us lose that sense. It's taught out of us. We start feeling as if, in fact, that we can't afford to extend kindness or decency to other people. That we're better off if we are above other people and looking down on them, and so often that's encouraged in our culture. But John always saw the best in us. And he never gave up, and never stopped speaking out because he saw the best in us. He believed in us even when we didn't believe in ourselves."*

Ensconced in history is John Lewis' dedication to the work of restoring the soul of our nation in the light of Christ and demonstrating with his own life the way of nonviolence and love like Jesus. His memory reminds us all that we can do just as he did, because the light is within us, too. On July 17, 2020, John Lewis entered Heaven, passing the torch to all of us to continue the work of civil rights, equality, and justice through nonviolent action in peace and with love.

No wonder there was a miracle on the horizon in Clayton County. As the hours drew onward overnight and it turned into November 6th, my focus remained there:

> *...Clayton County expected to put Joe Biden over the top in Georgia later tonight.This county was represented by John Lewis!If you listen quietly you can hear a faint Gabriel's horn...@RKempNews @RKempNewsDaily...Dear World: I am here...Clayton is still counting. I am watching them...4:46am, Friday, Nov. 6, 2020. Still counting in @ClaytonCountyGA...Atlanta TV*

*crews setting up for morning live shots in a tiny echo-y room with observers
also there.I grew up in TV news biz so have no problem moving out of the
way so they can get the job done…Trying to see but kinda crowded…I see
empty tables…They are done…Wakes up at 5:30. Checks phone. Expects to
see Biden wins Pennsylvania.Instead sees Biden ahead in Georgia because
of Clayton County.Feels the spirit and shining force of John Lewis.Good
morning!…John Lewis, we did it. Thank you. And thank you, Stacey Abrams.
O my heart!…Rest in Peace King…Clayton county!!! The world loves you…
Thank you everyone!!!!Sending much love and gratitude to all of you who have
worked so hard to get us to where we stand now!Get some food and rest!!…*

This is what Good looks like, all of these beautiful hearts and minds in the co-
creation of this miracle, from the support in anticipation to the humble pride
of those who call Clayton County home; to the accurate and transparent on-
site local reporting, and the gratitude and love that poured out afterward.
This is how miracles are created, not just through one person, but many
people working together for what is Good, with focus and intention and not
giving up on the goal.

At any moment anything can change for the better, even if it is a signal of
hope on the horizon for another day and time to come. This is what having
faith—the true faith that moves mountains and creates miracles—is all
about. We can live in radical joy because the light within will always lead to
all good things for those of us who believe. Just as Saint John Lewis wrote:

*You are a light. You are the light.
never let anyone—any person or any force—
dampen, dim or diminish your light…
Release the need to hate, to harbor division, and the enticement of revenge.
Release all bitterness.
Hold only love, only peace in your heart,
knowing that the battle of good to overcome evil is already won.*
(John Lewis, Across That Bridge: A Vision for Change and the Future of America)

Saturday, November 7, 2020

*In circumstances as dark as these, it becomes us…
to reflect that whilst every prudent measure should be taken
to ward off the impending judgments,
…at the same time all confidence must be withheld from the means we use;
and reposed only on that God rules in the armies of Heaven,
and without His whole blessing, the best human counsels are but foolishness…
Resolved; …to humble themselves before God
under the heavy judgments felt and feared,
to confess the sins that have deserved them,*

to implore the Forgiveness of all our transgressions,
and a spirit of repentance and reformation ...
for the redress of America's many grievances,
the restoration of all her invaded liberties,
and their security to the latest generations.
(John Hancock, A Day of Fasting, Humiliation and Prayer, with a
total abstinence from labor and recreation, 1775)

✻ ✻ ✻

This morning tumbled into a bit of the sensation I'd experienced on and off during the last week like I was watching scenes of a movie where the director wove events in a flowing timeline as the storyline played out in two parallel universe worlds.

First, the incumbent president tweeted an update on the lawsuits he and his campaign were pursuing in mistrust of the democratic process in his seemingly-soon-to-be loss against Joe Biden. The tweet announced a scheduled press conference later this morning at "Four Seasons" in Philadelphia. But soon after, a clarification was posted. It was to be held at "Four Seasons Total Landscaping," and not the luxury, marble-clad Four Seasons Hotel that soars above Center Cit which everyone apparently thought he meant by the first tweet.

Photos from on the ground at the press conference location at "Four Seasons Total Landscaping" showed an industrial-looking building between its next-door neighbors: a "Fantasy Island" adult sex shop including pornography viewing booths and the Delaware Valley Cremation Center. Meanwhile, other reports were coming in through tweets that the president was golfing in Virginia substantiated by photos and a video posted in real-time.

Then, switching back to the press conference coverage, some accounts stated that as the president's attorney began speaking, reporters suddenly started packing up their equipment to leave... because several major media outlets had just "called" the election for Joe Biden.

11:25 AM EST
Breaking news! The Associated Press declared former Vice President Joe Biden the winner of his native Pennsylvania to become President-Elect of the United States of America with Vice President-Elect Kamala Harris alongside him as the first woman, first Black woman, and first person of South Asian heritage to be elected vice president.

Within moments of the announcement, Twitter lit up. One of the first tweets in the feed acknowledged the heart-felt emotions many people were experiencing upon hearing the news. The tweet said, *"This is very moving. This means a lot to a lot of people. A very raw & authentic moment just now on CNN, Congratulations America."* It linked a video broadcast with Political Commentator, Van Jones, choked up and trying to hold back tears on-air as he discussed what this meant to him,

"It's easier to be a parent this morning. It's easier to be a dad. It's easier to tell your kids, character matters…. telling the truth matters. Being a good person matters. And it's easier for a whole lot of people. If you're Muslim in this country you don't have to worry if the president doesn't want you here. If you're an immigrant you don't have to worry if the president will snatch babies away or send dreamers back for no reason. It is vindication for a lot of people who have really suffered. "I can't breathe." That wasn't just George Floyd; that was a lot of people who felt they couldn't breathe.

Every day you're waking up, and you… just don't know and you're going to the store and people who had been afraid to show their racism are getting nastier and nastier to you and you're worried about your kids and your sister; can she just go to Walmart and get back into her car without someone saying something to her, and you spent so much of your life energy just trying to hold it together. This is a big deal."

And he wasn't alone, emotions poured out all across America and throughout the world:

…I feel every bit of this and felt all of these emotions every. single. day. And I still will for a while with a new hope that things will change. Thank you America for coming through for ALL of us…For four years, America was ruled by its darkest impulses. We had a leader who sought to scare us, divide us, and diminish us. The people have spoken, as only those in a democracy can: By voting. And demanding that America live up to its much loftier promise…It's so hard to find words but some of first coming to mind are relief, joy, & gratitude. Thank you to everyone who worked so hard campaigning, thank you to the tireless poll workers & vote counters, & of course thank you to the voters!!! WE DID IT!!…Senator Bernie Sanders issued a statement of support and congratulations following the election of Joe Biden: "Let us create a government that works for all and not the few. Let us create a nation built on justice, not greed and bigotry"…Today is a great day not just for our American friends (whether they realise it yet or not), but also for the rest of the planet. The healing can soon start…I am so happy for the USA right now!!! We are all in floods of joyful tears here in my little kitchen in Ireland… #PresidentElectJoe I'm here in Germany and crying with joy! And so many millions around the world are celebrating right now. The American people voted for democracy and decency and truth against dictatorship, crime and lies. THANK YOU!!…My wife just got congratulated by a cousin in Italy!!! The world was indeed watching!…I really hope America is feeling the love, joy, support, celebration,

happiness, tears, and smiles radiating from the rest of the world tonight. We might not be with you in the streets, but we're definitely with you...Celebrate America! You took your country back and Canadians couldn't be happier!...The WORLD celebrates...We are living in the ending of Return of the Jedi......Manhattan feels like if we overthrew a dictator. Honestly. Everyone out in the streets. Crying. Cheering...Harlem, NYC blew up after the news. I heard the celebration out my window and knew even before I turned on the news that #PresidentElectJoe won... It's a party in the USA! It's a party in #Atlanta!...A massive crowd of thousands of jubilant people have gathered at the White House — and overwhelmingly, the people celebrating Joe Biden's victory have masks on. It's a beautiful sight to see... Currently at Black Lives Matter Plaza at the White House: the LGBTQ+ community, BIPOC, Muslims & people of all religions & backgrounds are celebrating outside w/ signs & the pride flag & trans flag! This is historical!...DANCING IN THE STREETS! Columbus Circle, NYC...Celebrations in downtown Denver today. A happy mood. We can all finally breathe!...[Video of Native Americans dancing] Hello from Minneapolis right now, in front of the police department's 3rd Precinct, which was burned down following the police killing of George Floyd...Large crowds gathering in Cleveland to celebrate the election of President Joe Biden!...The #BidenHarris2020 celebration is packing Miami's Biscayne Boulevard! Pots and pans...Celebrations all over the DC Metro. I think I saw Ewoks and shiny spirits of John Lewis and John McCain giving Biden a head nod...Scenes from the Boston area: A vehicle flying a Biden-Harris flag drove through Maverick Square in East Boston as the driver beeped the horn. A man carrying a rainbow-colored flag that read "Pace" (the Italian word for peace) walked down Meridian Street...A victory for the soul of our nation...It feels like the USA has won the World Cup, Copa America and the Olympic Soccer Gold all at the same time....Church bells ringing in Paris, cheers erupting in Rome, and fireworks in London. Our allies around the globe are celebrating the victory of Joe Biden and Kamala Harris...Live Blog: Latin American politicians and activists from Argentina to Mexico were celebrating U.S. President-elect Joe Biden's victory on Saturday, Milagros Costabel writes...Mayor of Paris France just tweeted this! "Welcome Back America!" ...a day to remember!...Live on French television. America today seems celebrating their own Berlin Wall fall...Thank you Jesus!!!...What a beautiful day in the history of the United States of America... Love is bigger...This one was for you Ruth Bader Ginsburg and John Lewis... @JoeBiden @KamalaHarris and the American people, you just gave the world one of the greatest acts of kindness and bravery humanity has ever seen...Celebrating today by sitting by a fire in Manhattan with our closest friends. Here's to a future America where the dream is accessible to all people of all types, cultures, and points of origin. Forward together...Joy came to America today!...

In the evening, I tuned in to watch the live stream of President-elect Biden and Vice President-elect Harris' speeches. The joy in my spirit was palpable, but not a type of amped or excited rejoicing, it was an inner illumination as I sensed there may be some inspiration to journal in this moment of history. I centered and cleared my mind and heart into stillness, and then allowed my awareness to open and expand into oneness. Then, in a stream of consciousness, I wrote:

"Tonight, we have in this glorious moment the joy of an entirely new beginning given to us through the grace of God. The beginning of the Heavenly reward after years upon years of endured suffering and hard work in dedication to the cause of liberty, justice, and the pursuit of dreams come true for all Americans. This is what life is all about. If we all truly put into practice through our words and actions what the principles of our nation were founded on, the United States will be a beacon of light for all the world to see. We can do this! Believe in the Good!"

Vice President-elect Kamala Harris took the stage first in Delaware and spoke: "*Congressman John Lewis, before his passing, wrote, "Democracy is not a state. It is an act." What he meant was that America's democracy is not guaranteed. It is only as strong as our willingness to fight for it, to guard it and never take it for granted. Protecting our democracy takes struggle, it takes sacrifice, but there is joy in it and there is progress, because we, the people, have the power to build a better future.*

When our very democracy was on the ballot in this election, with the very soul of America at stake, and the world watching, you ushered in a new day for America… you delivered a clear message. You chose hope and unity, decency, science, and, yes, truth. You chose Joe Biden as the next president of the United States of America. Joe is a healer, a uniter, a tested and steady hand, a person whose own experience of loss gives him a sense of purpose that will help us as a nation reclaim our own sense of purpose, and a man with a big heart who loves with abandon."

As she transitioned to discussing this pivotal moment brought about by the inherent possibilities for dreams to come true in a nation like the United States, I turned to my notebook and wrote, "The American Dream is on the precipice of coming true, miracles and dreams come true for all of us if we keep the faith in what is good and just for all. We are the generation of a new beginning, but unlike the founding fathers, we are standing on the shoulders of those who came before us…"

Just then, I heard Kamala speak, "*…I stand on their shoulders…*"

I exhaled as tears welled in my eyes and awe rushed through my senses in instant recognition of what just happened. I wrote the same words literally a second before she said, "*stand on their shoulders*" and the meaning this had for me was that the spirit within her words was 100% aligned with where my heart is in Christ, to the very exact choice of words. The spirit in leadership they are offering is a renewal of the pure essence of Christ that was in the Declaration of Independence.

Even if the lives and the vision of our founding fathers did not quite create the nation they aspired to become, the vision remains with us and is in our hands to complete the work they started, just like King Solomon completed the temple that his father, King David, prepared but was forbidden to build because the wars he engaged in and the blood that was shed (1 Chronicles 28).

My attention went back to the live stream as Kamala introduced President-elect Joe Biden, and I listened with earnest to his words:

"Tonight, we've seen all over this nation, all cities in all parts of the country, indeed across the world, an outpouring of joy, of hope, renewed faith, and tomorrow brings a better day. I'm humbled by the trust and confidence you've placed in me. I pledge to be a president who seeks not to divide but unify, who doesn't see red states and blue states, only sees the United States, and work with all my heart, with the confidence of the whole people, to win the confidence of all of you. For that is what America, I believe, is about. It's about people. And that's what our administration will be all about.

I sought this office to restore the soul of America, to rebuild the backbone of this nation, the middle class, and to make America respected around the world again and to unite us here at home. It's the honor of my lifetime that so many millions of Americans have voted for that vision. Now the work of making that vision is real. It's a task, the task, of our time… To make progress, we have to stop treating our opponents as our enemies. They are not our enemies. They're Americans. They're Americans.

The Bible tells us to everything, there's a season, a time to build, a time to reap and a time to sow, and a time to heal. This is the time to heal in America."

As President-elect Biden mentioned the verse from Ecclesiastes 3, my mind flashed to the inherent synchronistic symbolism of the word "season" from where the press conference for the incumbent president's attorney was held earlier in the day at "Four Seasons Total Landscaping."

I perceived the two parallel universe worlds again in my mind, split into two but flowing as one in linear time. All of this was of Divine timing and design, down to every minuscule detail. I felt the rush of awe come upon me with the two worlds reflecting each other as two sides in creation, but then I balanced it right back into one flow as my ears were opened to hear Joe Biden's words:

"What is the will of people? What is our mandate? I believe it's this: Americans have called upon us to marshal the forces of decency, the forces of fairness, to marshal the forces of science and the forces of hope in the great battles of our time, the battle to control the virus, the battle to build prosperity, the battle to secure your family's healthcare, the battle to achieve racial justice and root out systemic racism in this country. And the battle to save our planet by getting climate under

control. *The battle to restore decency, defend democracy, and give everybody in this country a fair shot... Folks, I'm a proud Democrat, but I will govern as an American president. I'll work as hard for those who didn't vote for me as those who did. Let this grim era of demonization in America begin to end here and now."*

With his use of the word "demonization" my ears perked, and I listened more intently to the spirit in his choice of words. In his declaration, I sensed a preacher with the sharp-edged sword of the Word of God.

Biden continued, *"The refusal of Democrats and Republicans to cooperate with one another is not some mysterious force beyond our control, it's a decision, a choice we make. If we can decide not to cooperate, then we can decide to cooperate. I believe that this is part of the mandate given to us from the American people. They want us to cooperate in their interests, and that's the choice I'll make. I'll call on Congress, Democrats and Republicans alike, to make that choice with me. The American story is about slow, yet steadily widening the opportunities in America. Make no mistake, too many dreams have been deferred for too long. We must make the promise of the country real for everybody, no matter their race, their ethnicity, their faith, their identity, or their disability...*

I've long talked about the battle for the soul of America. We must restore the soul of America. Our nation is shaped by the constant battle between our better angels and our darkest impulses, and what presidents say in this battle matters. It's time for our better angels to prevail."

As he spoke, I felt the energy of spiritual warfare in the Heavens above, and into my mind's eye leapt a vision of Revelation 19 in motion, with the Heavens standing open in his directive through the authority and light of Christ for better angels to prevail. I envisioned a white horse, whose rider was called Faithful and True; with the armies of Heaven following, dressed in white and clean fine linen. The saints and all the angels taking their places in the skies through the words that he spoke as he placed Satan underneath not just his feet, but under the feet of all Americans.

My eyes widened in realization, "This is it! It is really happening!"

It is judgment day for the soul of our nation.

As in Matthew 24, when Jesus' disciples were said to have asked him what the sign of the second coming would be, and the end of the age, and among other indicators, Jesus told them it would be during a time of wickedness when the love of most people would grow cold. This was evident nearly everywhere in headlines and across social media across our nation today.

Jesus said it would be then when the gospel of the kingdom of God would be preached in the whole world as a testimony and the end would come, for the day of judgment is the day of decision (Joel 3:14) and *"displays to all the seal of truth...for then will everyone bear his own righteousness or unrighteousness"* (2

Esdras 7:104-105).

Biden spoke, *"…Tonight, the whole world is watching America, and I believe, at our best, America is a beacon for the globe. We will lead not only by the example of our power, but by the power of our example. I know I've always believed, and many of you heard me say it, I've always believed we can define America in one word: possibilities. That in America everyone should be given an opportunity to go as far as their dreams and God-given ability will take them.*

You see, I believe in the possibilities of this country. We're always looking ahead, ahead to an America that's freer and more just, ahead to an America that creates jobs with dignity and respect, ahead to an America that cures diseases like cancer and Alzheimer's, ahead to an America that never leaves anyone behind, ahead to an America that never gives up, never gives in. This is a great nation. It's always been a bad bet to bet against America. We're good people. This is the United States of America. There's never been anything, never been anything, we've been not able to do when we've done it together…"

Illumination lit within me and I knew, this next part was mine to do. I was about to check off another box on my Holy Apostle To-Do List. Turning back to my notebook I wrote:

"On the precipice of this new beginning for our nation, breaking ground on the New Earth merged with the New Heavens, God whom we name in our Pledge of Allegiance and Declaration of Independence, has sent me to you as one of your own. In the name of His Son, Jesus Christ, the Light of the Universe, our Great Father Sky and Mother Earth, and of the Almighty Holy God of All, everything that is Good, Righteous, and of Love, this is God's message for the people and leadership of the United States of America at this moment in time:

We in Heaven agree. If you stay true to your words, as promised in Matthew 18:19, in accordance with the joy of Christ, this nation will be blessed with miracles beyond imagination for the rest of your days. Keep the faith and believe, and you will receive all of the joys in life as evidenced through the work of Christ in the light from the river that flows from the throne of God: dreams come true and miracles across America."

As I paused in writing, I realized that unbelievably, I'd written about this in a vision more than a decade ago, in 2010. Until this moment, I couldn't fathom how it would apply or when would be the right time for it to be said, in fact, I omitted it from the version I submitted to the publisher in 2019 because it was not relevant at the time. From my writings on July 4, 2010:

"…Do you realize what this means? God WANTS to bless this country. God is literally holding out prosperity, liberty, and the dream of happiness for us—the honest to goodness opportunity for each one of us to freely pursue a life of joy, to receive blessings and happily ever after for all of us in the United States of America!

This is beginning here. But it is up to each American to decide whether to turn inward in hope and faith to reconnect with the true light and love within, and then to turn back outward unto the world and shine bright with peace, acceptance, and goodwill. It will take more than one or two people to turn our nation around; it will take more than one election or special event like Hands Across America in 1986. Will we shine together to make a brighter future for our families and children and all the world to see?

The One Holy Almighty God of Goodness, Righteousness, and Love through Jesus Christ is giving us this opportunity; Jesus is in the wings ready to come forth in a blaze of glory. His return is imminent if we call upon the true living Spirit of love to work through our lives to create a better world. We have the opportunity for this miracle to be established here in our land.

Imagine how much positive change we could achieve if the 300+ million people in the United States of America came together under one declaration for peace, brotherly love, and liberty, showing the world what it looks like when we actually hold ourselves accountable in words and actions to our Pledge of Allegiance, as the Church of Philadelphia depicted in the book of Revelation.

What do we get if we do this? (That's always the question, right?) Well, besides a wellspring of peace and joy in our every-day lives with all needs met and miracles abounding from on high, God's promise to us is golden. If we do this, scripture states, *"You'll be voted 'Happiest Nation.' You'll experience what it's like to be a country of grace"* (Malachi 3:12, The Message Bible).

God is ready to grace this country more than we could ever imagine. But it will take each of us to go within and do the work to heal the broken pieces and divisions that we carry with us from the past. Ask, seek, knock, and the door will be opened—even a door big enough for the entire nation of the United States of America. Everything is possible for those who believe!"

I turned back to listen to President-elect Joe Biden's speech as he was wrapping up, *"Now together on eagle's wings, we embark on the work that God and history have called upon us to do. With full hearts and steady hands, with faith in America and in each other, with love of country, a thirst for justice, let us be the nation that we know we can be, a nation united, a nation strengthened, a nation healed, the United States of America."*

I perceived where we were in this moment in American history was not only in a karmic re-cycle of the 1918 pandemic, but also reverberated back to the Revolutionary War, and thus, reminded me of Thomas Paine's writings, *The American Crisis*, published in the *Pennsylvania Journal* on December 23, 1776.

When I read these words for the first time over 10 years ago, *"Would that heaven might inspire some Jersey maid to spirit up her countrymen and save her fair fellow sufferers from ravage and ravishment!"* I knew it was somehow calling to me, but it was not yet time.

Here it was now a decade later, and the calling was in motion because we were now standing at this karmic crossroads as a nation—together on the threshold of suffering or joy, of Hell or Heaven—and where we go from here is up to all of us. From *The American Crisis*,

"I call not upon a few, but upon all: not on this state or that state, but on every state: up and help us; lay your shoulders to the wheel; better have too much force than too little, when so great an object is at stake. Let it be told to the future world that in the depth of winter, when nothing but hope and virtue could survive, that the city and the country, alarmed at one common danger, came forth to meet and to repulse it. Say not that thousands are gone, turn out your tens of thousands; throw not the burden of the day upon Providence, but "show your faith by your works," that God may bless you. It matters not where you live, or what rank of life you hold, the evil or the blessing will reach you all. The far and the near, the home counties and the back, the rich and the poor, will suffer or rejoice alike."

Just like Thomas Paine said, I also see no real cause to fear, because I know our situation well for I am one of this nation's own, and I am here in this moment with you, too. The vision of the way, just as President-elect Biden and Vice President-elect Harris spoke of towards a better nation for all of us to feel proud to be citizens and enjoy better lives is the way of Jesus Christ, the Good, and the Light. If we persevere in this work to eradicate our demons for good, the soul of our nation will be fully redeemed.

Our allies in the world knew that we are all in this together and that our great nation was on a slippery slope towards drowning in the lake of fire. That was why so many of them were overjoyed and celebrating that, "America is back" because we demonstrated our commitment to democracy and the greater good for all. The New Heavens merged with the New Earth begins here. With us. In the United States of America!

It is in our hands to show the world how healing, joy, and miracles happen through the light that is within us all. Call it Christ, call it the Tao, call it the Force, or call it scientifically or spiritually whatever you choose to call the energy of life in motion that is God; the Divine light source in our soul which brings forth peace that surpasses all understanding drawing upon the wisdom found within the heart, the light of Goodness within us which will always guide to love.

More patriotic pride was welling up in me than I think I'd ever felt before in my life. Even more than when I used to gaze at the poster of Rosie the

Riveter on my mom's classroom wall where she taught United States History to 8th graders, and I'd dream about the future. It was then, during the 23rd presidency of the United States with Franklin D. Roosevelt as it was now: We are in this together and our nation will be healthier and happier if everyone pitches in and does the work required of us for the good of all. This time around, we have wisdom from lessons learned in the past. We've carried our crosses of missteps and errors along the way, and in this election, millions of Americans chose a new beginning.

We are at the moment in time as spoken by Martin Luther King Jr., *"And when this happens, and when we allow freedom to ring, when we let it ring from every village and hamlet, from every state and every city, we will be able to speed up that day when all of God's children, black men and white men, Jews and Gentiles, Protestants and Catholics, will be able to join hands and sing in the words of the old Negro spiritual, "Free at last! Free at last! Thank God almighty, we're free at last!"*

If we stay true to the course set in front of us, our true American Spirit will shine because the battle of good and evil in duality will be overcome and put to rest in the history books of the past. This is the way! One day we will look back and see we are a nation truly filled with abundance and blessings and grace as promised by God in Malachi. Now it is time to get on to healing and head towards joy.

Keeping in our hearts that it will not always be easy, and patience will be required. Some days may feel like baby steps forward, but if we are mindful to act and speak in accordance with what we want to experience in our lives, day-by-day the world will be a better place to live in.

Create joy; and if you cannot create joy, create peace; and if you cannot create peace, create harmony and accord; and if you cannot find it within yourself to cooperate where you are, then remain silent, lest you cast darkness into the world through your words and actions, and thus, draw more suffering into your own life.

If we should ever slip deeper into the lake of fire, these are the words to hold onto as a reminder of the way to move forward, if we want the favor and grace of God in our lives and our nation. Keeping in mind that the spirit among the people in our nation collectively contributes just as much as our leaders to what the rest of the world sees in America. If we veer off course in the future, for any one of a multitude of reasons, may these words serve as the focus, intention, and Spirit of Goodness to return to the pure essence our founders aspired for this nation to become for us to receive the blessings and grace of God.

As former First Lady, diplomat, and activist, Eleanor Roosevelt said years ago: *"The future belongs to those who believe in the beauty of their dreams;"* a truth

I have believed in since I was young. The light that shines with the joy of possibilities and in hope carries us through the storms and darkness and into better tomorrows.

We have the opportunity to show the rest of the world the American Dream is not a lie or a lofty idealistic fantasy in the sky. Our brightest dreams can continually come true in our nation for all of us to truly live our very best lives. Everything is possible for those who believe!

By the day you read this gospel, there will be no time left to wait, and as John Legend sang, *"the future started yesterday and we're already late."* So without further ado, let's put love into action and complete the Good work that was given to us to do. All together now, may all Heaven and Nature sing unto the Earth. This is the way of joy. Let's go!

Namaste with love!

Always,
Shannon

ShannonofJoy.com

❊ ❊ ❊

Rev 22:10, "And he saith to me:
Seal not the words of the prophecy of this book:
for the time is at hand...
And the spirit and the bride say: Come.
And he that heareth, let him say: Come.
And he that thirsteth, let him come:
and he that will, let him take the water of life, freely.
(Revelation 22:17, Douay-Rheims, 1899)

BLESSINGS

...FOR LIFE AND THE LIGHT OF JOY FOR ALL.

May the God of the light within your soul be with you now and always; where ever you go, may your light be as glorious as the stars in the sky and may you shine brightly like the child of the Good that you are, on Earth as it is in Heaven, and...

May the road rise up to meet you.
May the wind be always at your back.
May the sun shine warm upon your face;
the rains fall soft upon your fields
and until we meet again,
may God hold you in the palm of His hand.
(Gaelic Blessing)

May the Lord bless you and keep you.
May the Lord make his face shine on you and be gracious to you.
May the Lord turn his face toward you and give you peace.
(Numbers 6:24-26)

May the long-time sun shine upon you,
all love surround you,
and the pure light within you,
guide you all the way on.
(Lyrics from A Very Cellular Song, written by Mike Heron
and performed by The Incredible String Band, 1968)

Live long and prosper.
(Leonard Nimoy as Spock, Star Trek, the hand symbol
represents the first letter of the word for God in Hebrew)

Look not too far ahead! But go now with good hearts!
Farewell, and may the blessing of Elves and Men and all Free Folk go with you.
May the stars shine upon your faces!
(Elrond, Lord of Rivendell,
in <u>The Fellowship of the Ring</u>, by J.R.R. Tolkien)

EPILOGUE

*They went forth three by three to the four zones of heaven
and they proclaimed the goodness of the kingdom in the whole world,
the Christ inworking with them through the words of confirmation
and the signs and the wonders which followed them.
And thus was known the kingdom of God on the whole earth
and in the whole world of Israel as a witness for all the nations
which are from the rising unto the setting [of the sun].*

POSTSCRIPT, SIXTH BOOK OF PISTIS SOPHIA